I AM A
KILLER

I AM A
KILLER

WHAT MAKES A MURDERER
THEIR SHOCKING STORIES IN THEIR OWN WORDS

DANNY TIPPING & NED PARKER

Published by Sourcebooks
P.O. Box 4410, Naperville, Illinois 60567–4410
(630) 961-3900
sourcebooks.com

Originally published as *I Am a Killer* in 2022 in Great Britain by Pan Macmillan,
an imprint of Macmillan Publishers International Limited. This edition issued
based on the paperback edition published in 2022 in Great Britain by Pan
Macmillan, an imprint of Macmillan Publishers International Limited.

Cataloging-in-Publication Data is on file with the Library of Congress.

Printed and bound in the United States of America.
VP 10 9 8 7 6 5 4 3 2 1

CONTENTS

INTRODUCTION

When we made the *I Am a Killer* films, we knew we had more fascinating material than we could include in each episode. We had to be selective, and this meant a raft of interesting interviews, details, and background details regarding the killers and their victims had to be left out.

That's why we decided to write this book, choosing ten of the most compelling stories featured in the first two series.

Here we can give an even fuller picture, including more of the research that went into choosing the killers. The book also gives us the opportunity to explain the protocols we set up for making *I Am a Killer*.

From the moment we first talked about making *I Am a Killer*, we knew we did not want to make another typical true crime, drama series. At our initial discussion, we felt strongly that it had to be different. Most true crime films have a formula, involving the investigator, a couple of journalists who followed the case, a reconstruction of the crime, and a forensic psychologist or criminologist who has no direct connection with the case but who can talk generically about the killer.

We realized that the one person who could tell us what really happened, and usually the last person to see the victim alive, is the killer, and we wanted to talk to them. That raised the bar: we needed a face-to-face interview with the killer, not a letter, not a phone call. Was that even possible?

We hoped that through these interviews we could learn more about the causes and consequences of violent crime, and this has always been our main aim.

We ruled out interviewing serial killers and anyone involved in sexual crimes, pedophilia, or mass shootings. We did not want to feature anything that might encourage copycat behavior. We wanted viewers to see the individuals we featured as human beings, but that doesn't necessarily mean they are going to like them.

Finding the right cases was a massive undertaking. America was the natural place to concentrate on. In the United States, the average time from conviction to execution is about seventeen years. This gives us the opportunity to talk to the killers, and it also means they've had time to contemplate their crimes and perhaps to work out exactly what was happening in that one moment that has defined their lives. The United States is also a country where the death penalty is still prevalent, with about 2,800 people on Death Row. The murder rate in the States is high (5.8 per 100,000 people, compared to 1.2 in the United Kingdom), and the incarceration rates are far higher, and with much longer sentences, than in any other developed country.

Crucially, in the United States there is a very strong tradition of free speech and press access, so our film crews were able to get inside the prisons to carry out the interviews.

We started writing to prisoners and the prison services, and we received a flood of replies, several thousand. Many of those who responded insisted that they did not commit the crimes for which they'd been incarcerated, so straight away we were not interested in them. We didn't want: "I wasn't there, I didn't do it." We weren't looking for campaigns to have justice overturned. We had to find people who admitted their guilt, who took responsibility for what had happened.

In order to create a shortlist of the ones we really wanted to feature, several criteria were laid down. All the men and women featured in the series either pleaded guilty or were found guilty at their trials, and they accept their guilt. They are either on Death Row, waiting for their lives to be legally ended, or they are serving very long sentences that will, for most of them, mean they will never again see life outside prison walls.

An admission of guilt entirely removes the whodunnit element. It takes the film away from being purely entertainment. We are asking: Who is this person? Why did this happen? Because we are not trying to prove anything, it becomes a lot more compelling.

The films are not only about the murderers' version of what happened. Every story is looked at through their eyes, but also from the perspective of others involved in their case, and features the anguish of the victims' families, the insights of the police, the lawyers, and the jurors, and the pain of those who care about the prisoner. They, the murderers, also have to confront what others are saying about them, often with surprising results.

Like the films, this book leaves it up to you, the reader, to make up your own mind about the killers. We do not know for certain to what degree they, or anyone else we speak to, are telling the truth. Where there is an obvious untruth, we make it clear, and where there are conflicting versions of events, we are careful to illustrate that fact. Otherwise, we allow everybody the opportunity to say their piece, and we leave it to the reader to decide what to believe.

There is no agenda from us as film makers: we are not campaigning; we are not inviting you to share an opinion. Instead, our aim is to lay out the case in front of you, and then it's over to you.

Most of the cases had never been featured on film before. The killers' are not well-known names. But every one of them has a compelling story to tell.

Another of the key criteria was: Why would we tell this story at all? What's the point? We felt we wanted to shine a light on bigger issues, and all of the stories we selected have a larger purpose; for example: studying the effect of childhood sexual abuse and racial and gender discrimination on offenders, and an examination of the law. We never wanted our coverage to be based in mawkish curiosity. We aren't really interested in the crimes themselves; we only feature them in order to make sense of the stories. We don't sensationalize them or describe anything vicariously.

The stories may have a binary outcome in terms of innocence or guilt, death or life in prison without parole. But that massively oversimplifies what's happened. There are other dimensions and complications, and that's what we wanted to show.

We're introducing the topic, asking the questions. We feel making documentaries is as much about the questions you ask as the ones you answer. Do we believe our subjects are telling the truth? Do we believe the circumstances the killers found themselves in can be mitigated? Do we believe they have been treated fairly by the law? Quite deliberately, we don't answer these questions (although we have discussed them endlessly). We want the audience to make up their own minds, because we hope to encourage debate about the issues.

We decided the films would not have a narrated voice-over, prompting the viewers to follow the story in a particular way. It was a huge challenge for us, because the voice-over is normally the "Get out of jail free" card: if something needs signposting, you just write a line of commentary. But in keeping with the whole ethos we'd established, we couldn't do that. It meant we had to tell the entire story through the interviews.

For the first series, we narrowed our list down to twenty or thirty strong cases, further whittling these down to fourteen, all suitable as far as we could see from contact with the prisoners. Having chosen our list, we negotiated with the prison authorities, a long process. Then our researchers set out to find other people who could be interviewed about the prisoners' stories.

It took over a year to finalize all the plans for shooting those ten films. Only when everything was in place did we contact the victims' families. We felt there was no sense in approaching them earlier, because we did not want to worry them about something that might never happen. But if we couldn't get their participation, sometimes a story had to be abandoned. Even with everything else in place, unless we could get someone to speak for the other side of the equation, it didn't qualify as an *I Am a Killer* film. Although the series gets plaudits for focusing on access to the prisoners, we think its great strength is the other contributors. Without someone to represent the victims, we cannot move forward.

In a couple of cases, an exception was made when, for reasons of personal history, no one could be found to speak on victims behalf. In these cases, we had to decide whether or not we could tell the stories without those voices. In Cavona Flenoy's case, the victim's family and friends did not want to talk, and we understood why, given his cultural background. Although nobody directly spoke up for Hassan, we had the testimony of the police and the prosecutor. We always ask: Is it balanced? Are we genuinely being fair to all the parties involved?

James Robertson, for instance, has spent his whole life from the age of seventeen in prison, and there was a real worry that we would struggle to find anybody to speak about him. The director who interviewed him rang us immediately after filming. He told us that the interview was unbelievable, the character was unbelievable, but he was worried about who else we could talk to.

But we persevered, and in the end we found enough people.

We also knew that once we started filming, one or two of our stories would probably fall by the wayside. We were in the hands of the prison authorities, who regarded visitation as a privilege that could be revoked, even on the day of the interview, if the prisoner in question was involved in an infraction or any sort of misdemeanor. There were any number of reasons why they might not be allowed to see us.

Once we started filming, we found everyone, including the killers, was articulate and happy to talk. There's a social openness in the United States, and this extends to detectives, sheriffs, lawyers, and others in positions of authority. They are less encumbered by process and procedure than their peers in the United Kingdom, for example. You get a very honest take from them.

Sometimes we didn't have any clue what a prisoner would say. In the case of Linda Couch, there was a real problem with getting letters in and out of her prison, so although we felt there was a story there, we didn't really know what it was until the director sat down opposite her.

The structure of the films is such that, after the initial interview inside the prison, the opinions and feelings of others involved are explored, often giving a completely different take on what has happened. Then the prisoner is interviewed a second time, with excerpts from the tapes of the other interviews played to them. They are then asked some challenging questions about the original story they presented.

This format came about almost by accident and was born of what was originally a problem. Filming of inmates in Texas was restricted to one-hour windows, and the crew were not allowed to return for another three months. That's when we quickly realized that this limitation could become our format, giving us time between the two interviews to talk to the others impacted by the crime. It started as a necessity and became an integral part of our process.

Often, the stories we were told by the prisoners in the letters they sent us and during the first interviews were the stories they'd been rehearsing since their trial and through all their years in prison. We sometimes didn't get much more than that in the first interview, which is why going back for a second time was so important.

In a normal TV format, you are told what the story is in the first minute, as well as what's coming up, and then you are reminded at different points of what's happened before. The idea of having someone talk and then not hearing from them again for another half an hour was new. But we felt that we were treating the viewer with respect and crediting them with the intelligence to follow if something they heard in the tenth minute wasn't mentioned again until the thirty-eighth. From all the feedback we get, that's certainly the case.

Netflix gave us the freedom to not patronize the viewer, to

assume that they can take in a complicated, multifaceted story with no conclusion. It's a bit like when you serve on a jury: you hear evidence from one side, and you may make up your mind about the accused; then you hear the other side, and your opinion shifts. Nobody recaps for you. Nobody is telling you what it means along the way. You have to remember what you hear from the beginning and weigh it against what you hear later.

For the crews who went into the prisons, traveling beyond the tangles of razor wire, being escorted along sterile corridors with heavy, clanging metal doors and through endless searches and security checks was a new experience. We were entirely in the hands of the prison authorities, and the facilities made available varied from large empty rooms to visitors' halls in which we had to film through reinforced Perspex screens. It was always a case of making the best of whatever was on offer. It's gratifying for all of us involved that the series has been a global success. We presumed people in the United States and the United Kingdom might be interested, but we also have a large following across Europe, particularly in France and Scandinavia, and a big audience in Latin America. We have twelve new episodes for 2022, again all from the United States.

Danny Tipping and Ned Parker, senior
executives of Transistor Films

1

OVERKILL

DAVID BARNETT

"I agreed to be adopted. I have my own room. I got a summer camp I go to every year. I mean, I was ecstatic. I was overjoyed. I could live, I was doing it right. You always had fun.

"But it came with consequence..."

Things were finally going right for eight-year-old David Barnett, a troubled child whose early years had been dominated by abuse and neglect. He was going to have a stable life, a future, an education, a comfortable home with his own bedroom. He was moving to live in an affluent area, where the detached houses had neatly mown lawns and trimmed hedges. It was a huge contrast with his early years. David's mother had abandoned him after his birth in St. Louis, Missouri. He found out years later that she was walking out of the hospital where he was born without him when a friend went back and fetched him, handing him over to a prostitute the friend knew, who was known as Crazy Jane. David was the second of his mother's six children, and all but one of them would be given away or taken from her. Crazy Jane, in turn, handed the baby boy to another friend, and like an awful game of hot potato, this woman dumped him with her sister, who was living with a man called Rob Biggerstaff. The little boy grew up believing Rob Biggerstaff was his biological father. Rob was an alcoholic and was in and out of prison. David soon learned to fend for himself, often becoming so hungry that he had to get food out of vending machines by using a bent coat hanger. He did not go to daycare or school, and his vocabulary was very limited. His clothes were ragged and falling off him, and he was rarely bathed.

Rob Biggerstaff, David told us, was "the only parental figure I had." But while his self-appointed guardian moved from woman to woman, temporary accommodation to temporary accommodation, and was in and out of jail, David was beaten and sexually molested by at least one of the women who casually took care of him. One of Rob's many girlfriends broke his nose so badly that it was permanently flattened. His overriding memory of these years is of being alone.

"I think I was like a stuffed animal that sat on a shelf and when people wanted me they grabbed me," he said. He has few memories, "but the smells and sounds of St. Louis are things you never forget."

When he was about four or five, the city's Department of Family Services (DFS) became aware of his existence, and one of his few memories of this time is the social worker who told him, "I'm going to take you away from this."

"I still remember that woman to this day," said David, nearly forty years later, talking to us from Potosi Correctional Center, a maximum-security prison in Missouri where he is imprisoned for a brutal double murder, a shocking crime that appeared at first sight to be without motive.

"I don't remember any of her features, and I don't know why my mind clouds that. But it was the first loving hug that I had in a long time." Tears welled in his eyes as he recalled it.

After a few days in a children's home, Rob Biggerstaff had been traced and came to visit (the authorities believed he was David's father). Left alone in a room with David, he seized the little boy, who was clutching a cuddly toy he had become attached to in the home. An old photograph taken in the home shows David with the white, stuffed cat in his hand.

"He just scooped me up and ran away. The last memory I have of that place is dropping that animal in the hallway. He hid me for a couple of weeks in the trunk of his car. I'm cramped in the back of a dark trunk. And this is the only person that I see striving to try and keep me and everyone else not wanting me. So I'm thankful, but at the same time I was scared. I didn't know what was going on. It seemed like there were thunderstorms every day. I wasn't being bathed, I wasn't being fed every day; it was really hard. But a couple of weeks later, the department caught up with him and took me back into their custody, and he was eventually arrested and I never saw him again."

One of the legacies of this terrible time is a lifelong fear of thunderstorms.

David got a lucky break after a few weeks back in a children's home when he went to live with the Reames family. Rita Reames was a foster carer who volunteered because she wanted to share the love and stability of her home. David joined Rita, her husband Ed, and their two children. "It's challenging to be a foster parent because the children are all going to have some degree of problems because of the background, they've had unstable childhoods. David was no exception. He was a challenge in some ways, and in some ways he was wonderful, and I think he would have continued to improve and blossom in a stable family environment, which he never had," Rita told us.

For David it was all a new experience.

"I instantly fell in love with that family. Rita was the first female that I didn't have a bad memory of or didn't make me feel icky. She was the first one I called mother. I just felt that if you had a mother, that's who she would be. Ed was a normal dad who went to work and came home. She caught on that my vocabulary was bad and I would communicate with objects. She got me a stuffed animal that was like my security blanket... I wasn't judged by any of them. They took me for what I was and everything they did was trying to make me better."

David's idyll ended after six months, when Rita was given the opportunity to study in England and the family made a decision to move to the United Kingdom for a time. Without any legal position in David's life, and with the authorities still regarding Rob Biggerstaff as his father and therefore as having parental rights, there was no choice but for the Reames family to hand David back into the care system. He was too young to understand why.

"They broke the news to me that they would be leaving and that they couldn't take me with them, and the only thing I thought was that I did something wrong." David wept quietly at the memory of that day.

"It's just hard. So many doors were closed. I just figured that I got beaten and molested for the first five or six years. It stopped and now it's like they are getting rid of me because I wasn't doing something right."

He had another short foster placement with a family who made him welcome, but unbeknown to the couple fostering him, a female babysitter molested him while they were alone.

"It was the same that I was used to growing up, being touched by other women. I felt I was back into the norm of what I knew."

But once again, life turned around for the better when David was eight, and it looked as if this young boy was going to get his happy-ever-after. He was taken to meet a man called John Barnett, who wanted to foster him. They had a couple of meetings, with John taking him on outings to play miniature golf among other treats, before David moved in with him.

"He looked like a middle-aged man. He was single, and he seemed relatively down to earth. He was a charming man, very caring, and the one thing I liked was that he didn't touch me, like he knew 'This child's damaged, I don't want to push him away.' I was not taken aback by the fact he was single."

The white clapboard house was in Webster Groves, a desirable part of St. Louis. John Barnett taught computer sciences in a local school, and he was involved in coaching local sport for boys, so David soon found himself on different teams, and he was enrolled for a summer camp to keep him busy during the holidays. Although he had never been diagnosed with ADHD, he says he was a "very hyper" kid. David loved the family cat, and he went to school with other kids from the neighborhood and made friends. It was a stark contrast to his early years.

"I felt I was moving into a different lifestyle," David said. "It was clean, the houses were in good condition."

He was soon introduced to John's parents, who lived a couple of houses along on the same street, and Clifford and Leona Barnett slotted into his life as grandparents.

"Clifford was a little stern. But I had a really good relationship with Leona. I loved her. She taught me how to cook. We saw them on Wednesday nights at church and every other Sunday when we'd have a family dinner.

"John was everything to me. He was like a mother and a father all in one. I couldn't have asked for anything better. He took me out to dinner one day and he sat me down and said, 'Would you like to be my son?' I said I *was* his son, but he asked if I wanted to be adopted. I didn't know what it meant and he explained it. I was ecstatic, overjoyed. I wasn't a sex toy anymore. I could live, I was doing it right. "We went to court and that was actually one of my happiest childhood memories—the day I was adopted and I knew I had a parental figure forever."

But only a couple of months later, the vision of a happy future started to dissolve.

"I got worried about who John was. Things started going badly. John expected excellence. He was a very intellectual man. And when it came to sports he pushed me every day. He bought all the equipment and he was out in the yard practicing, and then I started getting hit for not reaching his expectations, which were already higher than for kids of my age. He was forcing me to perform out of my age group.

"He would get physical, leave marks, break skin, bruises, welts. And then his comfort was starting to cradle me and hold me closer and start kissing my ears, and that didn't feel right. That gradually became more and more: every other night, or once or twice a week, to every night. 'Hey, come and sit on my lap for a while. Give me a hug.' I was uncomfortable and there was something going on with his body. I was only eight years old. I knew something was wrong, and that's where the relationship with John started going downhill."

After one beating, the sexual behavior escalated.

"He called me into the living room from my room. It was the usual, 'Come over here,' you know, snuggles, hugs, this and that. And he touched me inappropriately, genitals, like comfort holding. He'd stick his tongue in my ear. That stuff started to happen for a couple of months. I'd start to almost black out when I sat on his lap. Sometimes I wouldn't remember what he did, because I told myself if I didn't want to feel, I had to be numb. I didn't want his sexual advances, but I kept thinking there was something about me, like the women in my early years, that John wanted. That I brought it on myself. I didn't know how to handle that."

John capitalized on David's fear of thunderstorms, bringing the boy into his bed to continue abusing him.

Shortly after his ninth birthday, John asked David if he would like a foster brother, and an eight-year-old boy entered the family and was also adopted by John. David and the new arrival were not close and never discussed life in the family, and his addition to the household did not diminish David's abuse. (This adoptive brother did not want to take part in our film.)

Soon after this boy was adopted, Eric, another eight-year-old, arrived.

"I instantly liked Eric. He was charming. He was real conscious about these two little buckteeth he had in the front. I really loved him. He was a bundle of joy. And anything I wanted to do, he liked. He thought it was the coolest thing and he would follow me. So I wanted him to be there, but I didn't want this to bleed over to him. I figured if the abuse didn't happen to the other one and it was only happening to me, I could bear it. It won't happen to Eric.

"But after Eric was adopted, I started seeing John call Eric out and I felt defenseless. I felt I robbed Eric of his childhood. I'm the oldest and I'm supposed to protect them. But I couldn't. And at the same time I was glad it wasn't me. I was too small to do anything."

(Eric did not take part in our film, only finally deciding

that he was willing to participate when the film had been completed.)

During his teenage years, David had a best friend, Jason Kingdon, and they, along with Jason's brother Mike, spent hours together.

Jason told us: "At first it seemed like they were this really cool family that had this dad that was a soccer coach and really into kids and sports."

But after knowing David for about six months, he began to realize that the Barnett household was far from normal. Jason took us on a tour of all their teenage haunts, driving us through the leafy, sun-dappled streets of Webster Groves, with roadside signs telling motorists to "Watch for Children." He drove us past the two houses, one where John Barnett lived and one where his parents lived, just thirty meters apart.

"It's crazy that the whole backdrop to this is so serene," Jason said, cruising past the immaculate gardens and swept driveways. "It's tough looking at the house just because I know the horrors that went on in there. The things John did to these boys in this house was a nightmare.

"We never went inside that house. David didn't want us meeting his dad, John. He wanted to come to our house, to be away from his place as much as possible."

Jason remembers seeing water pouring from an upstairs window.

"I found out from Eric later that they were so scared to come out of their rooms and be around John that they wouldn't go to the bathroom, they would open the window and urinate. That's how much they wanted to stay away from John, how scared they were, how their lives were spent huddled up in their rooms."

By the time Jason was spending a lot of time with David, he was no longer being sexually abused, but he was still physically abused. He turned up for school with a black eye, and once he had a bloody mouth.

"The sexual abuse was centered on Eric," Jason told us. "So David felt he had to protect him... David would start a fight with John, misbehave to take the attention from Eric. And John would beat David. He chased him down the yard once with a rake."

It was Eric who first spoke outside the home about the abuse, telling a friend, who in turn told his parents, and a social worker from the DFS came to the house. But John, with his polished veneer of middle-class respectability, managed to placate them. By this time David was twelve and Eric and the other boy were both eighteen months younger.

There were other attempts to raise the alarm, more calls to the DFS hotline from concerned parents of other boys. A counselor from David's school called them, and so did the school principal. Nothing happened.

Eric even took two Polaroid pictures to a local police station, one a photograph of himself naked in the shower and the other of two other naked children. John was interviewed by a rookie cop, who later reported that he was uncomfortable with the situation, but his superiors told him not to pursue it.

None of the boys told John's parents, their surrogate grandparents, what their homelife was really like.

"I was nervous of how Clifford would react," David told us. He said Clifford would give them a clip across the back of the head if they were misbehaving.

"He wore the same kind of class ring as John and he'd always catch me with that ring. So every time he hit me it was like John was hitting me again, over and over. So I started seeing Clifford as John, John as Clifford. But Leona would give me a hug. She was the only loving part of that family."

David found it impossible to tell even his best friend, Jason, the full reality of their lives.

"I found it really hard to open up to friends and their parents, unlike my brother Eric. I think Eric knew that what happened to him wasn't his fault [Eric had been taken into care after his mother died, so for the first seven years of his life he had experienced love and normality]. But I thought it was my fault because all my life I had been subjected to physical and sexual abuse."

Jason was aware of what happened in the Barnett household, even if David did not talk openly about it. He knew from Eric about the sexual abuse, and he challenged David once, when they were hanging around the local tennis courts, asking if he had also been sexually molested by John.

"David flipped. He attacked me; he was angry. It was almost like he was possessed. It was just black in his eyes and he was attacking me and not seeing anything. I was pretty beat up. He turned away and could not look at me." The two teenage boys had scuffled before and were pretty evenly matched, but this fight was different. For the next couple of weeks, Jason noticed that David was acting deliberately macho. When Jason tried to talk about the fight later, David seemed to have no memory of it.

When they were both fifteen, David showed Jason a photograph he had taken from a drawer in John's bedroom, showing a naked boy with a man's arm, identifiable as John's, with his hand with its distinctive ring holding the child's penis. They decided to take it to the police. After all the previous failures to raise the alarm and get help, they felt that this was the clincher: the authorities would have to do something.

"We knew it was time to try to take John down any way we could," said Jason. "The arm and the ring were in the picture; we knew it was John. The child was prepubescent, no pubic hair. We thought we had him. Here is the irrefutable evidence. Nobody could argue with this. We were going to end John doing this to little boys. We walked on foot to the police station and we were so happy. They were going to have to look into John, into the abuse."

When Jason drove us to the red-brick police station, we noticed a prominent "Safe Place" sign outside, a more modern addition that runs counter to what the boys found there that day.

They showed the photograph to a female detective who had previously dealt with the two of them for, as Jason put it, "normal stuff teenagers do, smoking a little pot, making too much noise, knocking on doors and running away.

"She just didn't like us. We thought this will maybe explain to her why we were so unruly and angry. As soon as she saw the picture I could tell she was scared to death. She told me to get out of the room. I waited about twenty minutes and David came out and just stormed past me; he still had the photograph in his hand. He said, 'They're not going to help us.' I could tell he'd been crying. It was like he was destroyed, and that taught us never to go to law enforcement for anything. It left us in a really bad way. It was a big turning point. That's when we started getting heavier into drugs. What happened with David could have been prevented right then and there on the spot.

"We didn't try again after this failed. This was the top of the food chain. There was nowhere else to go. It changed David that day."

No follow-up investigation of John was conducted.

Shortly afterward, David attempted suicide. He poured petrol on himself.

"I decided, miraculously, not to do it, which sometimes I wish I would've." Once again, the social workers were informed, and he spent a spell in a psychiatric facility for adolescents. John Barnett's reaction was to say to David's counselor, "David looks like a poster boy for a suicide prevention program," and in therapy sessions he used to taunt David, all of which was noted by his psychiatrist, who recommended that David not be returned to the Barnett household. This recommendation was ignored, and David went back to live with his abuser.

Soon after this, another member was introduced to John Barnett's household, a fifteen-year-old girl called Secil Blount. She was a pupil in John's computer class, and she had a crush on her teacher.

"He was tall, he was nice. His eyes were blue, and he would make little jokes," she said. "When I came to school I'd be excited to say hello or just to see him and have him smile back at me; that would make me feel special. I would just stare at this man in class, with my arms and elbows on the desk, wondering if he could love me back.

"When I was fourteen I was being beaten a lot at home. That's when I started running away. I was sleeping at everyone's houses, sleeping on couches, on the floor. It was scary not knowing where I would end up each night after school. That's how I ended up at the Barnetts' house. John said, 'We'll have you over the summer.' He got me a pool pass, and I guess that was maybe a way of luring me in, and later on he kept buying me things. I was fifteen."

John Barnett was thirty years older than Secil. "Somehow he had caught up with the fact that my heart beats for him. The house had a dog and a few bedrooms. I felt at home. But should I have felt out of place? A little Black girl at the home of a single male and three boys, no relations? I began to stay there a lot. It was becoming a dark little secret in my mind. I enjoyed being loved and sitting on his lap with his arms wrapped around me. I started thinking I was his girlfriend. I wanted to kiss him, I wanted to love him. I was even thinking about what it would be like to be his wife. He started touching me. He started wanting me that way, and in my brain I thought it was OK because I loved him. Now I know it was wrong. I was just a little girl, prey. Now I would say he was a pedophile, a predator."

Secil slept on the couch, and after the boys were in bed, John would join her. Some nights she would go upstairs to share his bed, where she would be molested.

"He would rub on me and kiss on me and put his hands different places and things like that. I was feeling like he loved me, I was feeling special. The funny thing is that we never had intercourse. He was kissing me or my leg or other parts. I just had this love for him. I don't know where I was at, what I was doing, where my mind was. I think I was looking for something."

Secil told us she never saw John touch the boys sexually or be physically abusive. She accepted the family setup.

"I just thought it was this old White guy with three boys, single parent, and that was just our life. Every household is different. I just thought it was their family."

John Barnett lavished money and presents on the young girl.

"At the time, you couldn't tell me anything wrong about him, and I loved him. But now I see that him being sexual with me was wrong. Now I have two daughters and if anyone touched them I probably would kill him. But that's my mindset now I am an adult. It took me a long time to come to grips with the fact I was a victim," said Secil.

Despite her ongoing involvement with John Barnett, Secil and David started seeing one another.

"David and I had some type of connection. We were hanging out, dancing, singing songs, something was brewing." They ended up spending a night together, and a couple of months later Secil found out she was pregnant.

When she told John Barnett, he demanded that she have an abortion and he kicked David out of the house.

"John even offered to pay for the abortion. He's mad that I'm with his son. Now I understand he was probably jealous and upset I was not with him anymore," said Secil. "I just decided that wasn't the road I wanted to take. I chose to keep my baby."

Remarkably, Secil kept up her school and college classes, working as a waitress to support herself and her son, Seth, who was born two weeks after she graduated from high school. She and David tried to make a go of their relationship.

"David was so proud of the baby, he wanted to just hold him, feed him. So we tried to make things work. But he was up late, smoking with friends, playing cards, and I had to go to bed early because I had college classes. I had to pay a lady to look after Seth because David just couldn't do it. He was not as hard a worker as I am, and I expected more from him. He possibly wasn't ready. We were only eighteen. I wanted my son to have a dad. I didn't know how to handle it. I just couldn't be with him anymore. I pushed him away, and I'm sure that hurt him. He's always been pushed away. He was in the system and then he gets John Barnett and then he's hurt and pushed all over again. Then I did the same thing. He had been through so much and I wasn't there for him, but I didn't know. I had no idea. I felt horrible when I found out later he had been through so much."

The couple were living with Secil's mother.

"I threw all his stuff all over the front yard. He started living with different people, staying here and there, it was so unstable. I wouldn't let him look after the baby anymore."

David said that after splitting with Secil, "I didn't care if I lived or not. I went to several locations to try to [kill myself]. I didn't have the nerve to jump from cliffs or set myself on fire again or crash a car or anything. It was this abysmal pit that I could not get out of. I had no driving force to say life was going to get better. I was trapped. I was already in prison... No one could bring me back at that point. There wasn't enough love that could be given to take me out of that state. I knew something was brewing. I had dreamt of different plans for killing myself for a long time. I don't know if I wanted revenge on John. I don't know if I wanted revenge on my mother... I think I wanted revenge on the system. I wanted the world to feel my pain. I didn't want to exist. I wanted to die. No more."

Although he never went back to John's house, he occasionally visited Clifford and Leona, and he could see that Leona was concerned about him.

"I was still holding a job, but I was sleeping everywhere. Leona kind of caught on and she asked me how I was doing. I said, 'Oh, I'm fine,' but she's like, 'No, how are you really doing?' And I wanted so much to tell her about John; I just wanted to look at her and tell her about the abuse, about him basically trying to fuck me when I was nine or ten years old. I wanted to tell her all that, but her solution [to my problems] was to talk to John, 'Talk to your dad and work it out.' But I couldn't go back into that environment. And anything negative about John, she would speak up in a supportive or protective way. I felt that if I pressed too hard I would be rejected instantly."

The day before the murder, Secil took a phone call from a restaurant where she had worked as a waitress and where the staff knew her. They told her David had been sitting there for over twenty-four hours, not sleeping, drinking coffee, and smoking cigarettes. Secil went to try to talk to him.

"He looked at me with the most evil look. His eyes were red and he was very tense. It was the scariest face I ever saw from him. I was trying to talk to him and he freaked out. I didn't know what to do or say, so I left."

Desperate for money to survive, David told friends that he was going to get his grandparents' car and sell it. He went to their house in February 1996 and let himself in while they were at church.

"When they came home I was asleep, and when I came to we started discussing things. The last thing I remember was talking to her [Leona]. I've tried to remember every day since my case what happened. How did the events go down? What was said that triggered it? She was talking about a conversation she had with John, I remember Clifford said something about John and...I don't know where I went...I went somewhere." David struggled to hold back tears as he relived the events.

"I went into a state of overkill, manic rage. I killed two innocent people.

"When I finally realized what was going on, I was standing looking at a wall, and when I looked down, Clifford was at my left. I was scared to death; I don't know what to do. I was like, 'Man, what did you do?' And I'm looking around, like is there anybody else here, and I see Leona down the hallway. And there was nobody there but me. I had killed them both. I had stabbed them to death.

"I grabbed the car keys and some money out of her purse. I locked up the house. I didn't know what to do. I didn't know if I should call the police. The first thing I thought was to drive off a cliff. And I end up going to a friend's house and found some drugs."

When the police surrounded the friend's house after a tip-off, David turned himself in and immediately confessed.

"I said, 'I'm the one that you want. I did it.' I didn't know what else to say."

He was confronted with police reports about the appalling damage done to both victims.

"Broken ribs, jaw completely disaligned, dozens of stab wounds with multiple knives. I don't know where the knives came from; they said they came from the kitchen. I don't remember getting them. I snapped.

"There wasn't a day that I didn't think about Clifford and Leona. About three months after being incarcerated, I needed medication because I was having nightmares. I felt that I would never be able to forgive myself. My mind was punishing me because of what I had done."

The trial, in May 1997, had two phases, the first to determine David's guilt and the second to determine his sentence, whether it should be life in prison or the death sentence. He did not contest his guilt: from the moment of his arrest he had confessed several times to the murders. What was at issue was whether or not the murders were premeditated, and after long deliberation, the jury decided they were.

David didn't give evidence at his own trial, a decision taken by his lawyers, who felt that he was too emotional.

"I was very angry at the world. I thought every child molester or rapist deserved to die. They did not want me to say anything incriminating on the stand. If I had known the state was going to present my case as premeditation instead of something that just escalated out of control, there is no way I would not have testified at my own trial."

One of the witnesses was Secil. She was still deeply in thrall to John and had been to the double funeral for his parents.

"They put me on the stand and they was badgering me, making me feel like I did something wrong. I was a nineteen-year-old single mom, going to school full time and working. I had to go there, I was subpoenaed."

Asked about John, she told us: "I was defensive because, in a way, in my sick little mind, I loved him and I didn't want to hurt him." She did not reveal that his sexual abuse of her started when she was fifteen, and she admitted to us that she did not tell the true story in court.

"Young Secil lied about him because that's how she felt about him. But adult Secil would not have," she said.

David also learned at his trial, for the first time, that Rob Biggerstaff was not his biological father.

We spoke to Andy Dazey, the foreman of the jury, and he told us that the testimony he heard has lived with him ever since, describing its impact on him as he showed us round the modern St. Louis County Court building where the trial took place, visiting it for the first time in twenty-three years.

"I have never set foot in this room since then." Pushing open the glass doors into the courtroom, he pointed out the black leather chairs where the jury sat as he relived the trial for us.

"I see David's face all the time. David's face never leaves." Hearing about the crime was very difficult for the jurors. "You couldn't help but be intimidated by the severity of the charges. It was a horrendous crime, to stab your grandmother and grandfather in excess of twenty times. This is not a quick, sudden death; his grandparents suffered a very violent, slow, painful, brutal death. And we were deeply troubled with that, it weighed into our hearts. When we were shown the pictures of the crime scene, there were some jurors who literally had to close their eyes."

One of the first witnesses was John Barnett, and Andy described the uncomfortable atmosphere in the courtroom when he took the stand.

"It was eerie, shocking. It was very observable that there was a very distant relationship between them."

For David, it was unnerving seeing his abuser again. "All the courage I had mustered to face the trial just left. That childhood fear, that sense of helplessness, came back. It was just him being there, that presence. That's the person who had control of my life, physically, emotionally, mentally, psychologically. So the moment he came in I felt helpless again. I didn't hear half of his testimony, I was numb."

The prosecution cited as evidence the murders were premeditated the fact that David took the car, that he had discussed this beforehand, and that he took money from Leona's purse.

"Our first decision was his guilt, but he had made written confessions, a video confession, oral confessions," said Andy.

"He was brutally honest and the confessions were eerily similar. He used two words that stuck in most of our minds. When asked why, he said, 'I snapped.' We had to try to come to a decision about what those words meant. We were troubled about what we did not have answers for. It's not just what we heard but what we didn't hear... You kept asking yourself why there was not more effort put in by the defense team. It was as if it was a slam dunk; everybody, including David's team, said he was guilty."

Even with so little argument being presented by the defense, it still took the jury twelve hours to reach their verdict of guilty.

"Each in our hearts was convinced the verdict was the right one."

The jury then had to decide on the punishment, and crucially, whether David should face the death penalty. It was up to his defense team to present the case for mitigating circumstances. They produced a small number of witnesses, who gave evidence of his terrible early life. But the details were scant.

"None of the sexual abuse, the physical abuse, being a sex toy or a punching bag every day of my life for fifteen years, none of that was presented at my trial," David told us. Speaking of himself in the third person, he said, "The trial was set to go exactly how it was supposed to go for David. The system had always failed David and it was always going to."

"We finally started seeing some people coming forward on David's behalf," said Andy Dazey. "We got snippets of information about what his life had been like."

But for Rita Reames, who had been traced by the defense, it was far too little. A slim, gray-haired woman, she fought back tears as she spoke to us about hearing of David's crimes.

"It was shocking. I did not expect that, especially as these were nice people who had done him no harm. On the other hand, it wasn't as outrageous as you might think when we knew what he had been through as a child. You could tell he would go one of two ways. He was never violent. He was a good kid.

"The trial was the first time I'd seen David since we fostered him thirteen years earlier. I was afraid that he would not connect with me, that he might have hard feelings toward me for not taking him with us. And he was just all happy to see me. After I reunited with David, I got the records and I read everything. That's when I found out the full extent of the trauma that he had been through from when he was adopted. It was an eye-opener."

Rita was desperately disappointed that David's defense attorney used so little material about his background.

"She chose not to use those things. I approached her in the hallway at the court and asked her why none of this was being used to help him, and her only answer to me, which was very curt, was, 'I don't think it will do him any good. I think it will hurt him more than help him.' She just kept walking. I couldn't believe it was not used at the trial, because it was so well documented. It was written down by multiple institutions and people. It does not excuse the crime, but it does explain his mental state. He was less than a man, he was almost a boy."

According to his friend Jason, David had given his defense lawyers a long list of names of people who would appear to speak in his defense, but they were not contacted.

Back in the jury room, Andy described the scene: "Nobody wanted to talk. The severity of what we had to contemplate hit everybody, and I'm proud of the fact that it was that way.

We knew we are going to have to make a decision that is going to have a huge impact on this young man's life."

After ten days, they had still not reached a unanimous verdict. The sticking point was the need to establish that David had carried out the murders after "cool deliberation." Andy and two or three of the others took a long time reaching the point where they could make the choice of the death penalty, and in the end, Andy was the one who held out the longest.

"I remember getting up from the table and walking to the window, holding back the tears. I had to make the decision. Eleven had already done it. Am I there? Have I come to the firmness in my heart to say this guy shouldn't live? And I finally did."

Andy showed us where he stood, his back to the other jurors, as he wrestled with the decision.

"I could not reconcile in my heart of hearts the fact that one could impale a knife and be so rational as to say, 'I got to continue this and I'm going back to the kitchen to get another knife.'"

So the verdict was recorded: David was sentenced to death on both counts of murder, despite a letter from John Barnett and both his sisters to the judge, requesting the death sentence not to be imposed.

"I heard the first sentence," David said. "I didn't hear anything after that because I dropped to the table; it was like my world was over. I knew that I deserved something, but I didn't know what. But the weird thing that I've never admitted to anyone before: it was a relief. I mean, I knew I was going to die and the pain was going to end."

Rita Reames, having made contact with David again at the trial, has remained a constant in his life ever since.

"I knew I wasn't alone," he said. "Death Row was a lot easier with Rita and her husband Ed. She stuck by my side."

Rita, who now lives in Georgia, visits him at least once a year. They used to write letters but can now email, and he sends her cards, always addressing her as "Mom."

"He never forgets a birthday or Mother's Day," said Rita, showing us the cards he hand-decorates for her.

Rita told us that she has often thought about what would have happened if she and her family had not left St. Louis when they did.

"If we had kept David, would all this have happened? Yeah, it occurs to me. But on the other hand, would we have kept him until he was an adult? I don't know."

Some old school friends also made contact with David. "The more support I had, the more willing I was to live. Death Row started to become a place I could call home, but it was a place where death lingered."

David was always on the mind of Andy Dazey, the jury foreman. He kept track of David's appeals, and knowing that he was still on Death Row, in 2013, after years of deliberation, he wrote a letter to him:

I have never previously reached out to you but I can promise you that I have thought of you often during the past fifteen years, and have prayed for you many, many times. I have reviewed the trial in my mind and prayed on the wisdom of our decision. I have asked that God grant you faith, and strength in his mercy. I am sure that you have relived the events many times, as young men we all act imperfectly at times. Unfortunately, for many reasons which I suspect I am not aware of, you made a very serious mistake that day. Please always remember: each of us can be forgiven.

Andy went on to tell David that the case had made him realize how lucky he was, and to give something back, he had been providing tuition for children from difficult family backgrounds.

Please accept this letter for which it is truly intended, not judgmental, simply compassionate. I hope this letter offers you a small form of condolence. Stay strong.

Talking to us about it, he explained that he was conflicted about sending the letter.

"Firstly, I didn't think he wanted to hear from me. I didn't want to come across as judgmental or to force him to relive bad experiences. I can't say exactly why, but there was just a point when I said it's time… When I wrote the letter I was still comfortable with the fact that the decision we made was the correct one."

The letter arrived as David's legal team were putting together the material for a hearing to reassess the death penalty, and the lawyers contacted Andy. They asked him to look through the dossier they had compiled on David's early life. "As I was reading, I kept having flashbacks to the questions some of us had in the jury room. Why had we not seen David's defense team present all this? I vividly remember getting more and more upset with what had happened to David. I thought David did not get a fair deal. I was very upset that the abuser did not have to suffer his own consequences. I think when you inflict sexual abuse and harsh corporal punishment on your own child, you should be held accountable."

Andy went on record for the hearing: "It certainly would have caused me to pause, and more than likely this young man should be held accountable for the death of his grandparents, but not the death sentence. You have to be careful who you condemn to death. How do you weigh all that David had to suffer? David needed a very serious sentence for doing the crime that he did, but in my mind he was certainly not deserving of the death sentence."

He described feeling "duped" by the evidence presented at the trial, and is confident that several other jurors would have felt, had they known all the facts, that the death penalty should not have been imposed.

"I now feel I can connect the dots and say I understand. It doesn't justify the crime, but I understand how someone could potentially just snap."

One of David's lawyers for the appeal was Elizabeth Carlyle. She told us, "In the first trial, justice had not been served because David's story was really not told. And I think before a jury says to a person that they are going to ask the state of Missouri to kill them, his story should be told.

"He was in a difficult place at that point. He never denied that he had killed his adoptive grandparents, so that wasn't the argument. The question was whether the crime was first-degree murder or second-degree murder because the killings weren't deliberate. Under Missouri law, this means there was no period of cool reflection, however brief. That was the argument. Our goal was to get him life without parole." Elizabeth visited David at the Potosi Correctional Center, which houses all the Missouri Death Row prisoners, where David still lives.

"As an attorney you work with clients whether you like them or not. But I liked David immediately. One of the things that struck me immediately was that this man had a remark-ably chaotic and horrible early life.

"There was certainly a lot that was left out at the trial. We started to go through all the stuff we had. We began to make lists of who we wanted to talk to, getting investigators to talk to them. This was all stuff that should have been done at the trial but wasn't. It's tragic but it also made us real angry."

Much of the evidence the legal team uncovered about David's early life had never previously been seen. A vital witness at the hearing was David's teenage friend Jason Kingdon. When David went to jail, Jason was also in trouble with the law and had served a minor prison sentence. He was told that his record meant that he could not contact or visit David—an error on the part of Jason's lawyer, but one that meant that he did not see or hear from David until David's lawyers contacted him.

"I got a call from my brother, who said a private investigator wanted to talk to me about David. We talked for a long time, and he told me he was seeing Eric. And Eric was key. Whatever I could tell them, Eric could corroborate. I just wanted to set up the perfect backdrop for Eric to take the stand."

Elizabeth and her colleagues tracked down members of the DFS staff, including a social worker who had expressed misgivings about John Barnett even before David was fostered by him. They found the reports of his therapy sessions, in which the psychiatrist noted John's domineering behavior toward David and recommended he should not be returned to John's home. They traced David's birth mother, and she made a video for the hearing, confirming her lack of a role in his life. They drew up the paper trail of the numerous attempts made to alert the authorities to the threat posed by John Barnett.

"There was information about this guy that should have made them uncomfortable, yet he ended up adopting three boys. David was the first. There was sexual and emotional abuse. John Barnett was just not the guy who should have been raising three boys, boys who were needy and traumatized," said Elizabeth.

"At the trial it was mentioned that there had been complaints about David and his brothers being abused, but they didn't go into the whole pattern of it. Some of the people we talked to had testified at the trial, but when we talked to them in more detail, it was clear there was a more significant story.

"Anytime David turned to get help, he didn't get it. And finally he'd gotten pretty desperate. What we said was: Look at this man. Look at the fact that by the age of nineteen, which is not very old, he had gone through a great deal of trauma. He wasn't in a position where his full moral and reasoning facilities were available to him. I'm sure David is the first to say his victims should not have been killed. But what we were arguing was that the jury should have heard all this before they made the decision to give him the ultimate penalty.

"We all know, as a matter of common sense but also science, that the way you were brought up and what happened to you when you were really young affects the way you are able to function in the world. And because of his early situation, he was just not in a position to make a cold-blooded decision to do this."

Jason was delighted to have the chance to give evidence for David. David's legal team was keen for him to tell the story of how David had erupted so violently when they had the fight at the tennis courts years earlier.

"It showed how David snapped, and how quickly things could transpire."

Although not seeing David for sixteen years is a matter of great regret for Jason, it played well for him at the hearing. "It helped my credibility because the judge knew I hadn't gotten together with David to come up with some scheme." Jason was one of an impressive list of witnesses, headed by David's foster brother Eric. The hearing also brought David into contact for the first time with two of his biological brothers, one of whom has continued to visit him.

Another witness was an old school friend who had stayed the night at David's house when he was younger, at the time when David was being abused by John. He gave testimony that, waking in the night to find David wasn't in the room, he went to get himself a snack and heard David whimpering and saying, "Stop" and "It hurts."

Secil appeared and corrected the lies she told at the trial about her relationship with John Barnett. In the intervening years, she has qualified as a family nurse practitioner and acquired a doctorate in nursing practice. She's married and has two daughters as well as David's son. She is intelligent, articulate, and has overcome the bad start she had in life. In the words of director Zoe Hines, she is "a force of nature."

Another witness was the rookie cop who had failed to take action after Eric visited the police station with the incriminating photographs. He admitted the system failed and that because he was new in the job, he had to accept the advice of his seniors. But he was now a very senior member of the police force, who now take allegations of child abuse much more seriously. He said the memory of the case, and his instinct that John was lying, had never left him.

The legal team defending the death penalty verdict showed a video taken immediately after the murders, when David talked through the crime scene for the police. This was used as evidence that David had time to stop his rampage and to counter his assertion that he has no memory of the killings or the filming of the video.

By the time the hearing was over, Elizabeth and the rest of David's legal team felt confident that if the jury had been presented with all the evidence, they would not have condemned David to death. She was proud of the witnesses who came forward to tell David's story. When the news came through that the judge had ruled in favor of lifting David's death penalty and commuting his sentence to life without parole, Elizabeth Carlyle rang him immediately.

"It was exciting. He was very grateful, very appreciative of us for hanging in there."

When Jason heard the news he was in a shopping mall. "I just screamed really loud, and I had a lot of people looking my way. My heart was rejoicing because I knew that a great injustice had been undone."

Jason, his brother Mike, and their parents have become staunch supporters of David's, and keep in contact with him by phone and with visits.

"Jason and I are still very close," David said. "We're closer. We are both fascinated about what goes on in my mind. Why does anyone's mind block traumatic events?"

After spending hours talking with David about the crimes, Jason gave us his interpretation of what happened: "When I first visited, it was tough. He finds it hard to talk about, and when I first visited him he burst into tears a lot. I truly, honestly think David doesn't know why he couldn't control himself. He didn't go there to kill them. He had no ill will toward them. It was like the culmination of all that happened to him in his life. It came down to this one moment when he was the most vulnerable. He was finally going to tell them. The police didn't help. School counselors didn't help. Nobody helped. But these were the people he thought loved him. He was finally going to tell them what John did to him, to Eric. He told me that in the midst of the argument, his grandfather had a look of shame in his eyes, like he knew that what David was saying was the truth. But he wasn't coming out and saying it. He could tell that they were hurt and offended. They didn't want to hear it. There were no open loving arms.

"In that terrible moment, David lost his humanity right there on the spot. He just snapped. It was the ultimate loss of love in his life. It was about John and Eric. It was about his whole life. Every stab wound was for John."

Jason countered any idea that the crime was premeditated.

"Why would even a stranger stab the people multiple, multiple times in such a heinous, brutal way if they're trying to steal a car? It's a crime of passion, and I can't believe how all of this was just swept under the rug. It doesn't make any sense if you look at it as a robbery. David has never changed his story."

The hearing also brought David back into contact with his brother Eric, about whom he still felt guilty.

"There are still pieces of me that feel like I failed him, but he has assured me that I didn't fail him."

Rita Reames told us, "David did finally meet his birth mother and he got excited for a while, but she dropped out of the picture. She's died since. That was another big disappointment for him."

John Barnett died in 2017, and was never charged with any offenses against the youngsters in his care. After he retired from teaching, he worked as a school bus driver, an occupation

that raised eyebrows among those who knew of the accusa-
tions against him.

In line with our protocols, we needed to present a fair
picture of him, and we interviewed a friend of his. John was
not known to have many friends, but the boys and Secil all
remembered Fred Domke, his now ex-wife Lori, and their two
children. Fred delivered the eulogy at John's funeral, and at
first only agreed to allow us to film him rereading it for the
camera. On the day we filmed him, he relented and talked to
us more about his old friend.

In the eulogy, he described John as "an accomplished and
cultured man... He was extremely well informed and had a
vast knowledge of current events. John was also wise. He had
the wisdom to discern what his life was all about, and that
was kids. He gave up the big salary and taught kids, many
of them disadvantaged, data processing. He became a loving
foster father and adoptive father... He was a loving, caring,
generous father, and they [the boys] had the opportunity to
live and grow and do well."

Fred told us that he had known John Barnett for almost
half a century and considered him his best friend.

"He was witty, funny, great to be around. I have never
delved into the allegations. You couldn't have known John
better than I knew him. I was in his house, I knew his kids. I
can generically say that this was a really nice man who was
trying to do right by some kids that had a troubled start in
life, and I admired him. He was a great guy, and I don't need
to know any more. I already know it. So if somebody sees
something other than that, how would they think they know
better than I did, when I spent forty-nine years with John?
How could that be?"

Film director Zoe Hines was conflicted about John's death the year before the film was made.

"John Barnett was never publicly tried for the offenses he committed. The fact that he was dead allowed us to explore what had happened without becoming embroiled in legal arguments, but it would have been interesting to see John held accountable for what he did."

David's behavior in prison has been exemplary. He has taken up educational opportunities and now has two degrees. He became involved in the church when he was on Death Row, and is a committed Christian. He has taken part in a dog-training program.

"There's a lot of violent people in there and he has learned to get along with them and to be a peacekeeper," said Rita Reames, who is proud of the way he has dealt with his long incarceration.

We filmed David a second time, three months after our first interview with him, and we challenged him about what he remembered of the murders in view of the police video of him recounting what happened.

"The day before [my arrest], I was drinking, I was smoking marijuana, I was tripping on LSD. My mind could have forgotten a whole bunch of things or purposely blocked something out. I cannot remember step by step what happened. I remember the beginning and I remember the result was horrifying. The beginning I was in a conversation, trying to explain to them, 'Hey, I can't go back and live with John.' I did not have the direct words to point a finger at John: 'Hey, John did this to me.' I don't think I had those skills at that time. But that day, in my own way, I believe 100 percent a part of me was trying to say what happened.

"There's not a day that goes by that I don't think of Clifford and Leona. They live in my heart. Leona...I believe that if she was standing in front of me, she'd give me a hug and say she understood, she forgave me. So would Clifford."

He told us how he now feels about his abuser.

"I don't hate John. I didn't hate John then. I still love John for what he tried to do. I forgive him. He had his own problems, his own things that he couldn't overcome. So he gave in to his desires, whether they were psychological or physical, sexual. I understand he battled demons. I still respect and appreciate the fact that he tried to be a dad, even though he had monsters. That's the only way to put it."

David agreed to tell his story in our film not, he insisted, because he seeks sympathy.

"I only want understanding. I want people to know what really happened. The system is broken. I've seen statistics that show 80 percent of prisoners have spent time in foster care. It's because those kids are never given a chance. I'm one of those kids.

"I deserve where I'm at, I deserve the situation I face every day, and I'm blessed to have it. When I heard that I would have life without parole, I felt they had literally put me in torment, as I would have to live the rest of my life like this. But that's not so much the case anymore.

"Twenty-three years watching countless friends, guys, mature, become good people, dedicate their time, help me change, help me grow, not let me give up. There's a connection between prisoners of: 'Hey, we know you messed up, we're no different than anyone else. We're not going to live in our regrets, but we're going to live with them and push forward.' The strongest bonds and the most love I've ever had were from other Death Row inmates. They have turned my life from waiting to be executed into one where I can now live productively in prison until hopefully I can be a productive member of society."

David's friends also believe that he deserves a chance of freedom, and there was an appeal in April 2020 to have his sentence of life without parole overturned. The appeal was rejected by the Missouri Supreme Court. His supporters are currently running a petition to help him secure a parole date.

For Zoe, the reward of directing the film has been that it has brought a groundswell of support for David, and he has written to tell her that the film of his story has changed his life for the better.

"After the show aired, suddenly everyone was saying this case is awful. I'd been saying it for a year, while I worked on it. Now David is in contact with people who understand what he has been through and it has made a positive difference for him," said Zoe.

2

INTENDED EVIL

CHARLES "CHUCK" THOMPSON

"It was a whirlwind relationship. We were at bars five, six nights a week. We had a lot of fun. We used to go out and play darts, shoot pool, every night. I never meant for her to get hurt. I loved her."

Charles "Chuck" Thompson adjusted the microphone and leaned forward toward the camera, positioned on the other side of the reinforced glass window of the Death Row visitors' room at the Polunsky Unit maximum-security prison in Texas. Wearing a white sleeveless prison jumpsuit, he smiled confidently as he recalled good times with his ex-girlfriend Dennise Hayslip. He has spent more than twenty years on Death Row waiting for execution, having been convicted of the double murder of Dennise and her then boyfriend, Darren Cain.

"I first met Dennise on my twenty-seventh birthday," he told us. "After work, I grabbed a six-pack of beer and walked to a friend's house, and we were hanging out, drinking the beer. About thirty minutes later there was a knock at the door, it was Dennise. We sat around and drank some beers, got to talking, and there was a little chemistry right away." They went to a bar together and later spent the night at Dennise's apartment. According to Chuck, two weeks later he had moved in. It was a drink-fueled relationship.

"This lady could shoot pool, she could shoot darts. She was the life of the party. She had been divorced and she was thirty-eight years old and kind of having all the fun she'd missed out on. That's what she used to say. I was twenty-seven and I thought she hung the moon. I was in love with her; we had a lot of fun."

He admitted that the relationship could tip into violence. "We had a couple of spats. There was one time on St. Patrick's Day: she hit me and I hit her and I regretted it. Man, I regretted it. I was drunk and I just lost my temper and slapped her a couple of times. She had a black eye and I think her lip was bruised. It was nothing I was proud of. It was the first time I'd ever hit a woman in my life."

He gave us his version of what happened the day he shot Darren and Dennise. He claimed to have spent the weekend on a friend's boat doing drugs and drinking: cocaine, weed, and beer.

"She thought I was out with girls on the boat. She was upset, so she went out and slept with the bartender, and she told me about it, and we worked things out. We were very much back together when this happened. The prosecution tried to portray me as a disgruntled ex-boyfriend, and that was not the case. We went out to the bar on Wednesday night; it was our usual Wednesday night spot. We played darts. It was steak-and-potato night for five bucks. One of the staff who worked there and a friend testified about us being at the bar, closing the bar as we always did on Wednesday, and then coming home.

"This gentleman [Darren] called at between 2.30 and 3:00 a.m., saying he wanted to be with her again, so we ended up getting into a fight. The sheriff came and told us both to leave, so I went home. I had a house about three miles down the road."

He told us he had met Darren a few times at the bar, Kelly's Ice House, where Darren was a bartender.

"I never had a clue that he was seeing my girl. He gave us free rounds of drinks and it didn't occur to me why. I just thought, wow, this guy's being really cool to us. Apparently she'd been in there a few times for lunch and was seeing him."

Chuck claimed to us that he returned to Dennise's apartment at six in the morning to pick up paperwork he needed for his new job selling pools, which he said he had left there. He claimed he phoned her before going round.

"This gentleman was there in bed with her so we got into a verbal altercation and one thing led to another, and from what I can recollect he grabbed a French knife out of the kitchen block and he began threatening me with it and the pistol came out. I believe I had gotten the pistol out of her closet as I was packing my stuff and telling her I was leaving. So [he] told me I needed to go, and I said I am not going until you put that knife down. What happened next is kind of a blur to me. I was still hungover, still a little drunk, but from what I remember he came at me. I shot once, twice, and then we fought. I remember us fighting and the gun going off and she got hit. I don't remember how that happened because we're tumbling around and we're fighting over the pistol. It happened so fast and then the next thing I know, I check her, I thought she was dead. I picked up the phone and called 911, it didn't go through. I ran, I left, I freaked out."

Darren was dead at the scene, but Dennise, who was shot through the cheek, shattering her jaw and almost severing her tongue, was able to stagger to a neighbor's home and hammer on the door. The neighbor called the police and ambulance service, and Dennise was taken by helicopter to hospital.

According to Chuck, he went to a friend's house, his injuries were bandaged, and he passed out for a few hours. When he woke, his friend told him she had seen the crime reported on a local television station. The footage showed Dennise sitting up on the stretcher trolley, her head forward to stop the blood choking her. He said the sight of her alive made him cry with relief. He rang his father, who picked him up, and together they went to the police station and Chuck handed himself in. He was charged with the manslaughter of Darren, and aggravated assault on Dennise.

But what happened later that day changed everything.

Dennise's brother, Mike Donaghy, was the first family member to reach the hospital, and he spent the day by her side.

"I was at work when my wife rang me to say that Niecee, the name we always used for Dennise, had been life-flighted to the hospital. Driving there, I heard on the radio that there had been a double shooting, one person dead."

When he arrived at Memorial Hermann Hospital, he found his sister had been booked in with a false name because Chuck was still at large. A nurse told Mike that Dennise's injuries were not life-threatening, but she was "not a pretty sight." Mike found her sitting up, leaning forward.

"She was asking me for something to write on. She squeezed my hand and I said, 'Did Chuck do this?' and she nodded, an emphatic nod. Then she wrote, 'Call my boss, tell her I'm going to be late. Call Felix [her ex-husband] and let him know.' She asked about Darren and I asked her, 'Who is Darren?' and she made a gun shape with her fingers. I said, 'He shot someone else?' I guessed that was the person I'd heard on the news, so I said, 'He's dead. He passed.' And you could see the look in her eyes."

The medical report recorded Dennise's status as: 'sitting upright,' 'denies difficulty breathing,' and 'eyes open.'

Mike talked to the surgeon.

"He told me she was hurt bad but they were going to clean up the wound, try to reattach her tongue, all this stuff. I went to the rest of the family; nobody else had seen her because they didn't get there in time, and I told them, 'Everything's going to be OK. She's going to survive. She's probably going to have a speech impediment and she's going to have scarring on her face.' They said there were going to be other surgeries down the line, and that's what I told the family. Then, about eight or ten hours later, they came in and told us that she's in a medically induced coma and we're not sure if she's going to be brain damaged. That hit me like a ton of bricks, because I felt responsible for telling everybody it was OK. The picture of her, sitting up on the gurney, is etched in my mind forever."

Something had gone badly wrong. A breathing tube that was keeping Dennise supplied with oxygen was dislodged from her windpipe during the preparation for surgery. Her brain was starved of oxygen for between five and ten minutes and she went into a coma. For four days she was kept alive on life support, but when her family were told she was brain dead, her thirteen-year-old son and her mother took the difficult decision to switch off her support. Dennise died three days later.

It was a catastrophic result for her distraught family, but also for Chuck, who seven days later was taken back to court.

"They told me they're dropping the manslaughter of Darren and the aggravated assault charges on Dennise. I looked at the bailiff and asked him, 'What does this mean?' He said, 'They're fixing to tell you. They're introducing capital murder charges.' I looked at him and he said, 'That means the death penalty now, boy.' I thought the death penalty was just for espionage or treason. I thought, 'This is crazy. I didn't kill her, the hospital did.' Yeah, it was pretty sad. I loved the lady and I still think about her every day."

If Dennise had survived, and Chuck had been tried for manslaughter, the maximum sentence that could have been imposed on him would have been twenty years in prison. After Dennise's death, he was charged with murdering her and Darren.

After the first interview with Chuck, director Zoe Hines and the crew had to wait a statutory ninety days to be allowed back into the prison to talk to him again, and during this time we explored the background to the whole case, talking to family and friends of the victims, as well as Chuck's defense lawyer and two jurors.

Dennise had one son, Wade. She worked as a nail technician, with a large clientele, many of whom became more than customers; they were her friends. We talked to Wade, twenty years after his mother's death, and he told us about his early life and what had happened to the family by the time his mother was shot.

"My mom was a very kind-hearted individual. She taught me everything I needed to know about compassion. She was unorganized and at times scatterbrained, and she didn't always make the right decisions, but my mom was very loving and caring. There's no doubt she had a passion for being my mom."

His uncle, Dennise's brother Mike, who kept vigil by the bedside on the day of the shootings, agreed: "She was a great mother, a great wife, and a great sister."

In his study, Wade pulled out a photograph album full of family snaps to show us, as well as condolence cards and newspaper cuttings about her death.

"She was a fun-loving woman. She had a few beers, she spent a lot of time at the bingo hall and horse-racing track. My dad did his own thing. He was in a band. He had his own hangouts and his own friends. A lot of the time I rolled with Mom. I had fun at the horse track; I learned how to bet on horses. I was twelve or thirteen when my mom and dad divorced," he said, holding up the last photograph of the three of them together.

"They had a very passionate but tumultuous relationship. They fought a lot, all verbal, lots of screaming, lots of temper tantrums. There were never any physical altercations. I spent a lot of my formative years under the bed with the dog. As I got older I became more of a peacemaker. I think they loved each other so much they couldn't stand each other. My childhood was great: I had two parents that loved me a lot. At the same time, it wasn't the ideal middle-class family setup."

He described his mother as heartbroken by the divorce from his father, Felix, a country-and-western singer.

"But she needed to move on with her life because they weren't really good for each other. I think she went through a kind of mid-life crisis at that juncture. She was thirty-eight, approaching forty. It was a little bit daunting for her."

Dennise embarked on the new phase of her life, losing weight, changing her hairstyle, and partying. Her brother Mike described the change in his sister.

"I think she wanted to spread her wings and fly...she felt like she'd been held down for seventeen years. That's where the trouble started."

"She went out quite a bit," Wade continued. "I felt the effects, I was resentful about her going out... Sometimes I felt I was more of the adult and she was the child. She was staying up late and then doing a full ten-hour day working. She was taking a lot of caffeine, not eating. She was trying to be twenty-two in a thirty-eight-year-old body. I was oftentimes left on my own."

After the divorce, Dennise and Wade moved into a rented four-bedroom house, which they shared with a friend of his mother's, her two daughters, and a nanny. Wade wasn't happy, and he didn't get on with the two girls or the other adults.

"I just wanted to be left alone. I kept my own little supply of food in my closet, and my grandmother was smuggling food to me. It wasn't the best setup."

He met Chuck when Dennise started dating him, and before long, he was aware Chuck was staying at the house.

"I was a little defensive from day one. This might be something any child feels when their mom has moved on from their father. My mom was very happy when she first started dating Chuck. The simple fact that he was twenty-seven and she was thirty-eight made her feel like she could get somebody young.

"They would go out on a regular basis, more nightly than anything. They had a few local beer joints or bars they would go to. I do believe he loved my mom, especially at that point. He tried to talk to me but we didn't have much in common.

"I began to dislike him relatively quickly. There were a couple of nights he'd come back drunk and I could see my mom was visibly upset. I started talking to my mom about Chuck and how it was impacting on me. I did not sleep much, my school grades suffered. In fact, they gave me the nickname "The Sloth" because I slept a lot in class... I had to explain to her that I didn't really like having him in the house. I think she wanted to embrace that, but at the same time she didn't have the courage to end it. I believe she felt stuck in the relationship. She could feel the walls closing in and she had to do something, but was very conflicted, most probably because she did feel something for him.

"I never actually saw him hurt her, but I'd seen the effects. A couple of black eyes that were blamed on various excuses. I'd seen him punch a hole in the wall."

His uncle Mike met Chuck with Dennise, and together in public all seemed well.

"I just thought he was a boy toy for my sister, she was having fun, didn't have to answer to anybody. But I never saw the real Chuck. He was nice, but it was all fake. He was a con artist."

When Mike tried to warn her, Dennise told him to keep out of her business.

Wade was so worried that he spoke to a youth counselor at the church he attended and to the vice principal at his school. His grandmother, his father's mother, had been a constant support to him throughout his life, and she could see his schoolwork was suffering and he was staying up too late. A case conference was called, attended by Dennise, Wade's grandmother, and his youth counselor.

"There was a great deal of tears, a lot of remorse and regret that it had come to the point that a member of our church had stepped forward to say, 'We've got to do something about Wade or I'm going to call child services.' So a lot of mixed emotions and embarrassment."

Wade made the difficult decision to leave Dennise and move in with his grandmother.

"It was very hard. I was very in tune with her feelings, I don't want to hurt her feelings or drive her further into the despair I could tell she was feeling. But I also knew she needed a shock to wake her up. I moved in with my grandmother, to level my grades, get a good night's rest, eat well. But most importantly, I needed my mom to shake out of it and distance herself from the things that were pulling her down."

Another crucial factor, he told us, was finding weed on the bedside table on Chuck's side of the bed.

"My mother's no angel. I'm not saying she was partaking in any illegal drugs—I mean she probably was. But that was ultimately one of the larger episodes that triggered my exodus from the house."

Living with his grandmother, Wade never met Darren, Chuck Thompson's other victim.

"I did not learn of his existence until the morning of the shooting. As far as I know, Mom and Chuck had broken up. She had gotten her own apartment and moved out from her roommates. She appeared to be trying to get her life back in order."

It was at this new apartment, in a smart block with grounds landscaped with lush vegetation in the Spring area of Houston, that the shootings happened. From descriptions offered by Chuck, Missy Cook, who was with Dennise the night before she died, and Jim Kelly, Darren's employer, we pieced together the events leading up to the murders.

The area is a middle-class, respectable suburb in Northwest Houston, close to a busy area with bars and nightclubs. Dennise and Chuck had a few regular haunts where they were well known, including a bar called Bimbo's, which advertises itself as 'The Friendliest Bar in Texas,' and where they spent that evening.

"Bimbo's is a local watering hole. It's a landmark, an icon dive bar. It's darts, pool, hanging out with friends, dancing, BBQs, bands on the patio, sitting around playing cards.

Everyone come to Bimbo's," said Missy Cook, who was working behind the bar when she first met Chuck.

"He was very attractive, tried to be charming, but also very manipulative. As a bartender, you need to be on cue if something ain't quite right. It was just: Keep an eye on this one. He's a loose cannon. He'd show up late, halfway inebriated. He wanted to ask you questions about yourself, your life, so that he could try to get inside to try to figure out how to work you."

Missy met Dennise a couple of years before her death. "She was freaking incredible. She was one of those people you meet and you start talking to her, five minutes into the conversation you just felt like you've known her forever. She was your sister, she was your aunt, she was your best friend, she was your childhood playmate. She just had this personability; you just felt right at home. You felt like you had known her your entire life. We had children the same age and we'd talk and her eyes would light up. She loved her son.

"Dennise and Chuck seemed a very odd couple to me. He was younger, and he was a complete fucking idiot. And she was so pulled together and disciplined, even though she had fun and let her hair down. He was always aggressive, overly protective.

"I never saw Chuck hit Dennise, but I did have her come into the bar one time with a black eye, late at night. She said, 'Look, this is what he did.' The bar was dark and she said, 'Look, I've got a lot of makeup on.' I said, 'What are you doing with this guy? He drinks too much, he's doing cocaine. Get away from this guy.' I think she kept trying to back him off a little bit."

Missy saw them in Bimbo's frequently, several nights a week. She also knew Darren, who would call in when his shift at Kelly's Ice Bar ended to play darts.

"He was a sweetheart, a sweet, outgoing guy, very attentive to Dennise, to his friends. I most definitely thought they would have made a better couple. I didn't know there was any type of relationship between them; she hadn't divulged that to me."

On the day before the shooting, Missy had worked a dayshift and then stayed on to play darts and eat steak. She and her husband were drinking and shared a table with Chuck and Dennise.

"It was a normal night. Who knew what was going to happen?"

Jim Kelly, the proprietor of the bar where Darren worked, took up the story after Chuck and Dennise left Bimbo's. Darren was at work that evening, and he asked his boss if he could take time off to go to Dennise's place.

"I knew that Dennise was having some kind of conflict with Chuck and he was refusing to let her break up with him. Darren asked me...he said Chuck had threatened her and he wanted to go over to protect her if he showed up. I said, 'OK, go ahead.' To this day I regret that decision," said Jim.

"I told him to be careful. He called me later; they had a confrontation and Chuck was taken to the ground by Darren. And Darren whupped him, from what I understand. Then he said, and this is typical of Darren, 'Chuck, you know this is stupid, because she's not going to date you. She's dating me. If I let you up will you drink a beer with me?' This is what he told me on the phone. And from my understanding, they had a couple of beers and talked things out. Darren called me and asked if he needed to come back to work, and it was slow so I said no."

Neighbor Kathryn Page later testified at Chuck's trial that

at the time of the first fight she heard screaming and shouting and called the police. The deputy who went to the scene
told the court that by the time he arrived all was quiet and
nobody wanted to file charges. He escorted Chuck away from
the apartment complex, warning him not to return.

Early the next morning, Kathryn Page's son heard gunshots
as he was leaving for school. Shortly afterward, Kathryn heard
someone beating on her door and found Dennise sitting on the
ground, bleeding from the mouth, and gasping for breath. She
made a sign with her fingers like someone shooting a gun.
Dennise was rushed to hospital by helicopter.

Jim Kelly got a call from a friend on the police force who
told him that Darren was dead and asked if he had contact
details for Darren's parents. Jim went to the scene and saw
Darren's body: "I didn't want him there by himself." He
visited the scene again with us, and we talked to him against
the backdrop of the apartment where Darren died.

"It's hard to describe when you're looking at a kid you've
known for a long time. I'd known his parents for thirteen,
fourteen years. He was just a wonderful kid, you'd be proud
to have him called your son. He wasn't afraid to work. He
was in college and was working two jobs. There was a lot
of times when the bar was really slow and I'd see Darren
in a corner doing his homework; he was very conscientious
about school. He had a pet cockatiel that would sit on his
shoulder, cute as hell. Everybody loved it, everybody loved
Darren."

Jim met Dennise when she came in with one of her girlfriends, and she would bring Wade to family events at the bar.

"Darren was very excited at meeting her. They'd only been
together a few short weeks when all this happened. He was

excited, she was excited, everybody was excited because it was two really nice people getting together," said Jim.

"I think he cared a lot for her. I think when they met, the sparks flew. And I think she cared for him. She had dumped Chuck because he was a creep. They were the exact opposite. If you could put this guy here and this guy here, you got an achiever and you got a loser. What kind of person would shake someone's hand and then come back hours later and murder two people?"

Mike Donaghy is angry that after the first confrontation between Chuck and Darren, the police allowed Chuck to walk away.

"I still don't understand... Domestic violence, these days it's zero tolerance. Take all three of 'em to jail, then they would all have still been alive. But they escorted Chuck off the property at 2:00 a.m. and he came back four hours later and shot 'em both. That made no sense to me."

Chuck insisted throughout our time with him that the shooting was "a love triangle, a crime of passion," and that he acted in self-defense. It is an important legal point, because one possible defense against a manslaughter charge (which he originally faced) can be that the incident was a crime of passion, but this defense is ineligible against a capital murder charge.

"I ask myself all the time, 'Why did he have to attack me?' I guess he felt he was defending her. He was seeking to take my place in her bed because I was out with her that night," Chuck told us.

Wade was in a science class when he heard about the shooting from his school's youth pastor.

His reaction was, "I knew instantly who had done it. I

didn't have to be told. I said out loud, 'I knew this would happen,' which is the wrong response, but it was instant. I felt like she was headed down that direction, somebody would lose their cool and she would pay for it."

The youth pastor explained that another man had been shot dead, but that Dennise was at the hospital and was probably going to be fine. Wade even went back to his classes. His father picked him up at the end of the school day and they drove to the hospital, still under the impression that Dennise would pull through. The next time he saw her, she was on life support in intensive care.

"Every time her body convulsed, her eyes would open and there was a brief moment when I was thinking she would come back, but she never did. She never came back around. It would be some months before I felt an ounce of anger. I felt sadness that my mom had gone."

Three days after the shooting, the family were summoned to the hospital to decide whether Dennise's life support should be turned off. Wade and all his grandparents were there. The others asked him if he wanted to wait longer.

"I said no, because we were essentially at the crossroads where we knew there was no coming back." Dennise survived for a few days and died one week after the shooting.

The church and the local community rallied around Wade. The local funeral director laid on everything the family wanted, and would not charge; Darren's boss, Jim Kelly, organized a fund that raised enough money to pay for Wade to continue at the private school he was attending and to fund him for his first two years at college. Donations came from clients of Dennise's, some of whom had moved away and not seen her for years.

We filmed Wade and Mike at Dennise's well-kept grave,
where the headstone features their favorite picture of her.
"There was a fantastic outpouring of love," Wade told us.
"The whole family came together. The church holds about
seven hundred people, and it was pretty full. My dad was
a wreck; the love of his life had died, and now I'm older I
realize that there was regret on his part." Eleven years later,
Wade faced more heartbreak when his father died. "I had a
lot of people...Mike and Cindy [his uncle and aunt] leading
the charge with my grandmother. They really stepped up and
made sure I had a fair shot at things.

"In some ways, it feels like it never happened... You know,
to remember someone's voice, you have to put it into context.
And I no longer have the context that I remember her voice in.
I can't hear it anymore. And so, in some ways, it's as though
she never existed."

When he was fourteen, Wade had to appear in court at
Chuck Thompson's first trial. Throughout the hours we spent
talking to Wade, he showed a remarkable ability to empa-
thize with the feelings of other people, including the man who
killed his mother, taking his time to answer questions fairly
and considerately. But as a teenager, the trial, in front of a
packed courtroom, was the first time he felt anger. "On the
witness stand I realized that the weapon, the pistol, was sitting
in front of me, actually pointed toward me, so we had to have
that removed."

Mike testified that, although she was unable to speak,
Dennise had confirmed that Chuck shot her.

One of the witnesses who appeared before the packed
courtroom was Diane Zernia, the friend to whose home Chuck
fled after the shootings. When he arrived at her house, having

thrown the pistol away, Diane was getting her daughter ready for school. Chuck fell asleep in her living room. In her testimony she told the court that when he woke up she joked with him about his black eye, the result of his fight with Darren. She said, "I hope the other guy looks worse." According to her testimony, Chuck replied, "He does. I shot him." He told her he had been beaten up in a fight, and that he returned, kicked in the apartment door, and shot Darren four times. He told Diane he also shot Dennise, and, she said in court, he then said to her: "I can shoot you too, bitch."

The defense later challenged Diane's evidence, producing as a witness a friend of hers who testified that on the day Chuck was arrested, Diane told a different story: that Chuck had been upset and crying about the shootings.

The central part of Chuck's defense in Dennise's case was that he did not kill her, the hospital did. Ellis McCullough, the lead defense lawyer, told us, "The trial, I thought, hinged entirely on the interpretation of the medical evidence; that the cause of her death was by her treatment at the hospital. The state's insistence that the standard was: 'What if the victim had no medical care whatever?' I consider this to be ludicrous. There's almost no injury that can't cause death if left unattended. It was a nasty wound, but they had everything there to save her life and knew how to do it. It just didn't work out. She didn't die at the scene. She didn't bleed to death. In my opinion, with ordinary medical care she would have survived."

The defense team brought in Dr. Paul Radelat, a vastly experienced pathologist, as an expert witness to testify about the medical evidence.

"The thrust of the defense was that this was not a lethal wound, and that she died because of this unfortunate event in

the hospital. It was my job to substantiate that claim within
the bounds of integrity. Although she would not have died
had the wound not taken place, if this therapeutic misadven-
ture had not happened she would probably, in reasonable
medical probability, survived. It [the bullet] didn't impact any
vital organ: the heart, the brain, the lungs. It didn't produce a
wound so serious that bleeding to death over a short term was
a serious possibility, I thought."

He did not blame the medical staff.

"Doctors are not magicians; they're not all-knowing;
they're not perfect. They've had more training, generally
speaking, than the man or woman in the street, but they are
still human beings. I don't think they covered up. It's easy
to make a mistake. I'm not sure any blame, as I understand
the word, should be apportioned to the medical personnel.
They intended no evil. The shooter, I think we can safely say,
intended evil."

The defense asked the jury to find Chuck guilty of murder,
but not capital murder. But after three days of the trial, the jury
determined Chuck *was* guilty of the capital murder charges he
faced. The second phase of the trial began in order to decide
whether or not he deserved the death penalty.

As part of the prosecution case, the lawyers aimed to establish that he was an ongoing, dangerous threat to society, and
they produced his criminal record going back to his early teens.

Letters that Chuck had written while in prison were
produced, and fingerprint evidence was given to prove they
came from him. He signed them "Chuckster Killer." The
court also heard a tape recording of a prison interview Chuck
Thompson gave, while he was out on bail, to a man he believed
was a hit man available for hire. Unbeknown to him, the man

was an undercover cop, and he was wired to record everything Chuck said. The first part of the tape had Chuck giving the "hit man" explicit instructions as to where the gun was. He threw it into a creek when he fled after the shootings, slowing his car on a bridge and tossing it in. With the information from the tape, the police were later able to recover it.

The tape went on, with Chuck making arrangements for Diane Zernia to be murdered.

"There's a witness in this case I need taking care of... I just need you to get rid of her. She's the state's witness. She's the only witness they've got."

He agreed a price of $1,500 with the "hit man," then gave details of how to find Diane Zernia's address, including the detail that her mailbox was painted in a black-and-white cowhide pattern, the make of car she drove, and when she was at home on her own.

"She's about forty-eight, fifty years old. She's a mother; she's got a fourteen-year-old daughter... I don't want her talking any more. She's already talked."

The prosecution also produced a handwritten list, drawn up by Chuck, of the state's witnesses, including details of their addresses, their habits, and their jobs. Top of the list was Diane, and third, behind the undercover cop who recorded him, was Mike Donaghy, Dennise's brother, who testified to Dennise's last communication. The fourth person on the list was the prisoner Chuck believed had set him up with the undercover cop, and the word written next to his name was "snitch." The list had been given to another prisoner, who told the court that Chuck asked him to "either kill them or persuade them not to be there [in court]."

Mike Donaghy was shocked. "He had me on the hit list,

where I worked and lived, that I played golf. He wanted to have me killed! This was eerie. I had no idea until right before the trial. The district attorney called me right before I testified. What was he thinking? He was going to take us all out, but it don't make no sense. You're still going to go down."

In mitigation, the defense presented a picture of Chuck's background. He took us through it when we met him. His early childhood was spent in Texas, but his family moved to Colorado when he was in his teens. He moved between the two states after school, and had two children with an ex-girlfriend.

"I had a good upbringing, never went without anything. My drug use in my teens was one of my main problems when my life went wrong. I started using drugs at twelve. It started with marijuana and drinking, then I was doing mushrooms and acid and kept on progressing, doing bigger and better drugs."

He had criminal convictions from the age of thirteen, having stolen to fund his habit. When he was sixteen he spent two years in a youth correction unit. He claimed he was clean and law-abiding until a relapse when he was twenty-five, which caused his relationship to break up. He was arrested a few months later for smuggling illegal aliens across the Mexico border, and could have faced up to thirty-four years in prison, but he avoided jail on a legal technicality.

Listening to Chuck Thompson's defense, Wade said, "I started getting angry, because I was hearing some of the excuses being made...a ton of excuses. Which is under-standable; I mean you're on trial for your life, so you're going to defend it, even when you're very wrong. But as an adolescent with hormones raging, I felt a great deal of anger... I do remember making eye contact. His eyes felt very cold. When I looked at Chuck it was like he was looking right through me, as if I wasn't there. It just felt like I was glaring into the enemy."

Wade felt then as he feels now. When we asked him who killed his mom, he answered decisively: "Chuck! Shooting her in the face with a gun...he killed my mom. I look at it as a gunshot wound that was caused by an individual with the intention to harm somebody, and I've never wavered from that. The hospital did not kill my mom. The hospital was given the situation to save her and was incapable of doing that."

Again, Wade showed a remarkable capacity to put himself in the defendant's shoes, deliberating over his responses. "I felt that Chuck using the hospital defense was a logical step. I would have done the same. But if I make a mistake, I step up for it. I think it would have been better for Chuck if he had just said, 'I messed up. I put her there.' But claiming, 'I never meant to kill her...' It's very hard for me to accept that argument. You put a gun to her head and you pulled the trigger. I was annoyed that he was choosing to blame the hospital, but again, knowing that he knew his life was on the line...I mean, if my life was on the line, I'm going to scratch and paw and do anything to try to survive."

Mike Donaghy said emphatically, "The hospital didn't put the bullet in her head. Chuck did. I blame Chuck for her death."

Missy Cook told us she was angry that she was forced to appear as a defense witness, having been subpoenaed by Chuck's lawyers to give evidence about Chuck and Dennise being together that evening. She had no doubt about Chuck's guilt, was incandescent with rage directed at him, and would have been happier testifying against him.

"It threw a light on me, people saying, 'Oh, Missy's defending him.' That was never the case. I would have loved to have thrown him under a bus. Dennise and Darren's friends were staring holes in me at the trial, looking daggers at me, hating me, because I was a defense witness. I remember feeling like I was going to have a nervous breakdown."

It was at 8:00 p.m. on 16 April 1999, the fifth day of the trial, after a whole day spent deliberating, that the jury's verdict came in: Charles Thompson was sentenced to death.

Harrell Rodgers was a member of the jury, and one thing that sticks in his memory, he told us, was the sight of Diane Zernia on the witness stand.

"She was the most frightened person I've ever seen. I mean, she's a very thin lady to begin with, and she was just pale. Her eyes were as big as silver dollars and she was scared to death. She was frightened of this guy. We thought a lot about the fact that if somebody had been successful in carrying out this murder for him, he would have had no remorse whatsoever that we could see. He would have been elated to get rid of her, along with a list of other people he wanted to kill."

Harrell, an academic at the University of Houston, told us that the tape of the conversation with the undercover cop "was a real turning point for me. I was not thinking he deserved capital punishment. But this was really scary. It was the first time I realized this was not just a drunken brawl. This was a guy capable of enormous evil.

"The jurors I think had pretty well accepted the fact that if he had not shot her in the face, she would not have died, so he was guilty of taking her life. Our primary issue was whether he was a continuing threat to society, and there were things that came up in the trial that convinced us that this guy was a really dangerous person."

Ellis McCullough summed up his feelings about the verdict: "A trial is a kind of beauty contest. Who looks the best? Who sounds the best? Who's got the prettiest case? Well, you're sitting in a jury and what do you hear? Drunken jerk comes into a house, kills one guy, shoots another who subsequently dies, admits to it, and then tries to get the witnesses killed. Do you care about anything else?"

Wade knew that the prosecution would ask the court for the death penalty for Chuck.

"I felt comfortable with it. I felt vindicated by the fact that the state laws allow for it. I believed it to be the right step." Wade faced another court ordeal nearly four years later, when his family started a civil suit in his name alleging malpractice against the hospital, a case they lost. Wade, who was eighteen on the final day of the trial, was never keen on pursuing the case.

"It was trying to establish that the hospital had made some mistakes. But I have never abandoned the idea that what put her in hospital was a gunshot wound to the face, committed by this man. She's not in the hospital if you don't shoot her."

But for Wade and all the other witnesses in the case against Charles Thompson, the legal torments were not over.

In 2005, more than six years after Chuck was sentenced to death, there was a second trial, not to assess whether Chuck was guilty or innocent, but to examine the punishment phase of the first trial. It was ordered because Chuck's lawyers had successfully pleaded that the evidence of the undercover cop was inadmissible, arguing it had violated Chuck's civil rights. He had not known he was being tape-recorded when he talked to the man he believed was a hit man, so it was entrapment.

"It's kind of ironic," said Mike Donaghy. "We violated *his* civil rights!"

For director Zoe Hines and assistant producer Mel Wong, getting hold of a copy of this controversial tape to play in our film was difficult, but they persevered.

"We had evidence lists of what had been used in court," said Zoe. "We could see references to the tape recording, but we couldn't find it among the official evidence, so we embarked on a chase around Houston trying to locate it. We were there just after the hurricane in 2018, and all of the evidence in one court facility had been destroyed when the courthouse flooded. So they were pretty busy, and here we were, pestering them for this piece of evidence. I can vividly remember just sitting outside the criminal courthouse. Nobody was answering the phones, so we literally doorstepped the clerks, and eventually we were told the tape was at another facility on the other side of town.

"We got straight into the car and got over there, and a wonderful woman called Barbara came to our aid. She had the look of a studious librarian, and in her spare time crocheted stuffed animals to sell for charity; it was hard to reconcile her appearance with the fact that she was the custodian of a huge haul of violent murder evidence. We picked her up one Sunday and drove her to the facility to get access to the box, and there was the tape."

In order to be able to play it, Zoe had ordered an old cassette-tape player from Amazon. Luckily it worked, and they were able to record the chilling words on the tape.

At Chuck's second trial, the details of the crime were heard again, with the same witnesses, but in front of a different jury, and without the evidence of the hit list and the undercover recording.

"The defense did target pretty heavily that she died six days later in hospital," said Kristen Merttens, the jury foreman. "To me, that was irrelevant: he shot her in the face."

Kristen regretted that the trial focused so much on Dennise's death in hospital.

"He did murder somebody else first. I think Darren was lost in the case. I don't think his death was brought up as much as Dennise's, and I feel bad for his family. I wholeheartedly believe that he went there to kill Darren and he went there to kill Dennise."

Kristen thought that to give Chuck Thompson a life sentence rather than execution would be "a gift. He's narcissistic, he really enjoys the attention."

For Chuck, the confirmation of the death penalty was a serious blow.

"It's the worst experience of my life," he said. "You think it's worse the first time; it's even worse the second time. My mom and my grandmother were sitting there crying."

The retrial took place when Wade was at college, aged twenty.

"This was harder for me. I was older, coming into my own. I had a car, paid my own insurance, had my own apartment, mobile phone. I was really going somewhere in life."

The trial threw into relief how much he missed his mother, how proud she would have been of him, how she would not be around to see him marry one day, have children.

"I am not angry anymore. But I do feel that his sentence is appropriate and just. If the law changed, I would support the law. But ultimately this is the path that was written for him. I'm completely capable of empathizing with him and understanding some of the thoughts that might have gone through his mind. He has children, he has his parents. There's a lot of complex emotions on all sides, but ultimately I don't feel any different than I did at thirteen. I hope he understands the domino effect he has set in motion."

It's a sentiment shared by his uncle Mike.

"I forgive him. If you can't forgive, you are going to carry that hate with you forever and it'll eat you alive. People do stupid stuff. The blink of an eye can change your life, and that's what happened; changed three people's lives and then changed all the families' and friends' lives forever. I don't hate him. Maybe I should, but I don't. I won't forget. You are where you are for a reason. Capital punishment is the law of the land here in Texas. Two separate juries found him guilty and put him on Death Row. If the law changed, I'd be OK with it, just as long as he never gets out."

Jury foreman Kristen Merttens remembered that after the verdict, the judge spoke to the jurors and she asked the question, "Is there any possible way he's going to be able to get out?" She was worried that her name had been published. The judge assured her it was impossible.

Yet Chuck did get out. Just days after his trial ended and the death sentence was confirmed, while he was waiting to be transferred to the Death Row unit at Polunsky, he managed to escape. He is proud of the way he did it, and in the hour and a half we were allowed to spend with him on our first visit to the jail, he spent a large amount of time talking about it. He detailed how he managed to smuggle his court clothes into an interview with his lawyer. He changed out of his prison uniform quickly after the lawyer left, used a key to release his handcuffs, and walked confidently down several floors of the Harris County Court building. He jumped on a train, traveling on it for four days into Louisiana, where he found help with food and clothing by posing as a victim of Hurricane Katrina. He was arrested after getting drunk and phoning a girlfriend in Australia from a phone booth. She had already been tipped off, and kept him on the line while police closed in on him.

Wade was in the parking lot outside his office in Dallas when the district attorney's office rang him to say that Charles Thompson had escaped, and Wade was offered police protection. He turned it down.

"I did not think he was a real threat to me. It was a shock that he got out in the first place. He walked right out of jail, and that's quite a feat. But it's ironic that he succeeds and then he gets caught at a liquor store making an international phone call to someone he knew would be a target. He gets drunk and they catch him!"

Mike Donaghy, whose name had been on the hit list, also got a call from the DA, and was told not to worry. But because he was concerned about his wife and children, the family went away for a few days. He too shared Wade's feeling that Chuck "is not real smart. You don't stop at a liquor store if you are on the run. But I was happy that it was over, that my mom could just relax and we didn't have to watch our backs."

Chuck clearly glorified in the success of his escape, but we decided not to make it a major feature of our film, as we were more concerned with presenting a balanced view of the crime itself.

We played excerpts for Wade and Mike from the tape recording we made of Chuck. They challenged many of the details in Chuck's version of events.

"It's an easy excuse: blame the hospital," said Wade. "She's not in the hospital if you don't shoot her. The truth is you held a gun to somebody's face and you pulled the trigger. And the reason why we know it was held close is because there are powder burns on her cheek.

"If there was a pistol in the closet, it was not hers. And he didn't go into detail about how the doorframe got smashed. He says it was just a blur. He fired five times, and when he [Darren] was on the ground, he put a bullet into the back of his head. How is that a blur? That's pretty clear, pretty intentional. There's no way he checked her and thought she was dead. She was very animated and very much alive. She had to go to the neighbor for help.

"I feel this is like a five-year-old, when you caught them doing something wrong but they continually maintain they didn't do it, even though you literally just saw them do it. It's the rest of the world knows, but even so, you're going to stick to this lie. Just sad; I hate that, because I think there is an opportunity for some real forgiveness here. But it's hard to forgive somebody that won't give up. It's very obvious he is not prepared to admit guilt. He says, 'I didn't do it, it wasn't intentional, I wish she was alive so she could testify.' That's just a convenient truth. We do have some written proof that she did testify, right before she died." Mike believes the shot to his sister's face was deliberate, aimed at scarring her for life.

"He put the bullet in her face. It was not in a tussle. In my mind, she was trying to hide. He shot her in the cheek because he knew her vanity, so he put it where everyone can see it. He didn't even own that he killed Darren. He tried to make out it was self-defense or an accident. He's grasping at straws."

When we returned to see Chuck in the Polunsky Unit, ninety days after the first interview, he continued to stress that he had not intentionally shot Dennise.

We told him what Missy had said about Dennise trying to rein him in, get him off the booze. She also insisted that Dennise was living on her own at the time of the shootings, which he countered with a list of the times he spent with Dennise that week.

"Monday night we bowled in a league together and we got drunk, Tuesday night we went to a bar. Wednesday night we went to Bimbo's... So yeah, in Missy's testimony it was the same old 'happy couple doing their Wednesday night' thing... I was tanked that night. I was doing shots, mixed drinks, beer, I was pretty drunk."

We challenged him as to why other people had told us that the relationship with Dennise was not the way he portrayed it.

"I guess because we had some fights, we broke up sometimes."

He told us that he rang Dennise before turning up at 6:00 a.m.

"If I was intentionally going to do this, why would I call first? I went to the pay phone and called her. I told her, 'I have to come and get my work stuff,' and she said she was trying to sleep. I said, 'Is Darren there?' and she said no. So I said I'd be there in five minutes and hung up."

He said he went to the kitchen for his work papers then went to the bedroom to collect some clothes, which was when he realized Darren was there.

"So when I see him there, that's when I started in on her. We had words."

We asked him why everybody we spoke to said he kicked the door in when he returned at 6:00 a.m., and his response was that he got in through the patio door, not the front door.

We also challenged him about shooting Darren in the back of his head.

"You're in a situation where somebody's turning a gun and trying to shoot you and you're fighting over it and it's going off, bullets are flying in the wall, in the pantry door; there's bullets everywhere. In that situation, you don't just say game over... You're fighting for your life... But she got in the middle of the fight over the gun and that's how she got shot. It was two men fighting over a woman that got in the middle of it."

When we told him that both Wade and Mike were angry when they heard him say he wished Dennise was alive to testify for him, and that they felt he was only concerned about her survival so that she could help him, he insisted that not only would Dennise have testified at his trial had she lived but she would have visited him in jail.

"She was that kind of lady. She would have said, 'Was it worth it?' and I would've said, 'No, it wasn't.' I wish that she could've told the truth about what happened, that's what I meant. I would've liked for her to tell them the truth about what happened, because nobody believes what I have to say, apparently. I would've liked to see her go on and live a productive life, be a grandmother to a grandson, see him graduate college. I understand he grew up without his mom. I tried to express remorse. I'm sorry for what happened. I have said before to the Cain and Hayslip families that I have no ill will toward them and I have remorse for what I did, and don't know what else to say."

His answers were composed, confident, and articulate, but he was unprepared for hearing the undercover tape recording again, and he begged us not to use it in our film as it had been ruled inadmissible in court.

"It was an ethical problem for us," said Zoe. "But the tape was publicly accessible. It was in the public domain; we had the right to use it. We're not a court of law. We took legal advice, and we were told we could include it."

Chuck was visibly uncomfortable talking about it, and clearly surprised that we had tracked it down. He told us that he was set up, that he went ahead with meeting the under-cover cop because he believed Diane Zernia had changed her statement, and that the prisoner who had been given his hit list was a state informant. (This allegation was rejected when he tried to use it in an appeal.)

"What they were trying to do was create future threats to society, showing that I was trying to act violent toward the witnesses. It's embarrassing, what can I say? It's confused. I'm a drug addict, alcoholic, made a bad decision and another bad decision and another bad decision. I was upset that she changed her statement; I felt that she was lying. It's nothing I want to talk about really... That's why I had a retrial, because what they did was illegal."

He regained his composure and laughed as he asserted that his jail escape demonstrated that he is not a future threat to society.

"Ha, ha. I think I kind of debunked 'future threat to society.' I was running around in the free world for four days. I walked past little old ladies in front of shopping centers getting out of their cars. I didn't carjack 'em. I didn't rob anybody. I didn't assault anybody, hurt anybody. But if you listen to any capital death penalty trial, they try and put it into the jury's head that 'he's a future threat, he'll kill again.'"

Faced with the fact that Wade and other members of Dennise's family feel the death penalty is the right sentence and should be carried out, Chuck again laughed and said, "How is my execution, twenty years later, going to make them feel better? How is victimizing my family by me being killed going to make them heal? The death penalty just creates a whole new set of victims, that's all it does. To carry a torch for someone to die for twenty years? I couldn't hate somebody that long. It's not in my blood. You know what they say about hate. It'll eat you up inside."

As we packed up our gear and said goodbye to Charles Thompson, he added his final message:

"I'm not the same man I was twenty years ago... I just need another chance."

Shortly afterward he rang Zoe.

"If you put that [the tape] in the film, you are signing my death warrant," he said.

This phone call resounds in Zoe's memory. "Momentarily I thought: Is there a world in which I am contributing to someone's execution? But it is part of his story. I would say it was more fool him for thinking that we wouldn't dig that far."

Wade is planning to attend Chuck Thomson's execution. "That will be fairly tough," he said.

Mike Donaghy, his uncle, will go with him.

"I told Wade I would go with him. I have no desire to watch another human being die, but just to comfort and be with Wade, I'll do that. Wade is amazing. From fourteen years old he had to do everything without his mom. He persevered through all of that and came out on top, which doesn't always happen."

Wade also faces the prospect of having to explain to his son, Walker, who was eight when we filmed, the reason his grandmother is not around. "The older he gets, the easier it will be for me to explain. He'll ask his own questions, and we'll tackle that. Nobody wants their kid to be sad. Protecting him from sadness is something we can't do, but it's something that we can minimize. He never met his grandmother, so it won't carry the same weight. But I want him to understand the weight that bore on me. Not in a way that I want him to share it, just to know what I have been through."

3

TRAPPED

LINDA COUCH

"He was so different when we were just dating. But once he had that ring on my finger he changed into a monster. I probably would not have ended up here had I just went ahead and divorced him. I'm a good person. I made a mistake, but I can't change that mistake. I took a life. It was an accident. I wasn't out to get him."

Linda Lee Couch, a slight woman in her mid-sixties, was talking to us from the Ohio Reformatory for Women in Marysville, Ohio, where she has spent more than thirty years for murdering her abusive husband, never wavering in her claim that his death was an accident. The pretty, dark-haired young woman whose sensational trial dominated Cincinnati news channels in the eighties now has gray, curly hair, her eyes defined by rims of black eyeliner, her eyebrows vividly painted on. She was wearing a prison uniform, a dark-blue sweatshirt with the green collar of her regulation shirt on show. As she spoke to us, her head and hands shook slightly as she relived the events that led to her imprisonment.

Linda was sixteen and pregnant when she married twenty-one-year-old Walter Couch. Born and raised in a working-class family, the trauma that dominated her early years was the death of her father when she was five.

"Even to this day, if I think about my dad I start crying."

Her mother married again when she was twelve, and by her own account she got on well with her stepfather.

She met her future husband at a wedding reception: "The more we talked, the more we seemed to have in common, and from there it took off. He was clean cut, very good looking; I was amazed he even wanted to date me. We went out and had fun. It didn't take long; I guess within a month he proposed. And of course I said yes, and I should have thought it out better, but being a teenager and thinking you're in love... Now I wish I had never met him."

Before her pregnancy, Linda moved into the three-story house in the blue-collar Price Hill area of Cincinnati where Walter lived with his parents, Walter Sr. and Dorothy. Telling her mother that she was moving in with him and that they would marry was "the hardest thing. She thought I was out of my mind. I told her we weren't getting married right away and she said, 'I hope not, because sixteen is just too young to marry someone you don't really know.' Unfortunately, I didn't listen."

When they started dating, Linda was still in high school, and Walt used to pick her up from school, but after she moved in with his parents she had to drop out because they lived further away. She took a correspondence course to complete her high school education.

She and Walt had been together for five months when they married. Her mother and grandmother were very upset, especially when she soon became pregnant.

"At first it was OK. Walt was very caring. But when I was pregnant his whole attitude changed. When I was going through morning sickness, he would go off with his friends. He was so against having a child. He pushed me down the stairs when I was pregnant. Thank God there was no damage. I went to the doctor immediately to make sure. When I got back from the hospital, all the parenting was left to me. When she cried, he would get angry."

Walter was the youngest of four children, and the only boy. He was the apple of his parents' eyes, and the fact that he was partially disabled made him even more precious to them. He was registered as blind because he suffered from retinitis pigmentosa, which meant he had no night vision. He also wore hearing aids because he was deaf, and an accident had damaged his spine, leading to a succession of back operations.

His parents did not want him to marry Linda, and she told us that she never got on with Dorothy, her mother-in-law, although she had a better relationship with Walter Sr. After Roxanne was born, the teenage Linda felt Dorothy wanted to take over the care of the baby and was constantly giving her advice.

"I couldn't do nothing right, wasn't raising my kids right. Many a time, me and my mother-in-law almost came to a fight. She would say, 'That's not right, this ain't right,' and in the end I said, 'If I want your advice, Dorothy, I'll ask for it.' I was so happy to have this child. It was like a precious gift to me. But not to my husband."

Two years after Roxanne's birth, a second daughter was born, followed by a son after another two years.

"Walt hated Roxanne, my first one, the most. I never could understand it. He would say she was fat and he would make her do exercise all the time or go up and down the steps for an hour. We would have fights over that because I was really starting to get worried, because every time she would do the slightest little thing, he would beat her with his belt and leave welts on her bottom. And I would soak her with baking soda to take the welts down. He never touched the other two; it was always Roxanne and me.

"I didn't understand it, but I do now. Roxanne looked like me, and that's why he had a hatred. I didn't know what to do. I've tried to defend her many times, and I just got the same. I'd get beat up. I've been punched, I've had black eyes. He cracked my nose. Walt was brutal. If I'd seen this side of him before, I never would have married him. I didn't know then that he was very angry, controlling."

Stuart Powell, the director of the film we made about Linda's story, was unprepared for what Linda told him next.

"We weren't able to have much contact with Linda before filming, so we went in blind, without too much background information from her side," said Stuart. "This bit of her story hit me like a hammer; I hadn't expected to hear it, it didn't come up at the trial."

Linda said on camera that Walt would bring friends to the house. He did not drink, but his friends did, and she claimed that he watched and laughed while his friends raped her, starting when she was eighteen.

"One night I was awakened by being shook, and when I opened my eyes all his friends were in the bedroom. I asked, 'Why are they all in here?' And he said, 'Well, they want to have a part of you, too.' They would come late at night and he would not let me know they were coming, because if I'd known, me and the kids would have been out of the house and wouldn't have come back until they'd gone. This was the worst time in my whole life. Anytime his friends came over, this would happen.

"I talked about divorce with him, and that did not go over well with him at all. He said, 'If I was you, I wouldn't even think about it.' I went to the police one time and told them about the abuse, and they did nothing. I had even gone as far as calling an attorney to talk about divorce. I did not phone from the house but from a phone booth. Walt knew that I was going to go back to my parents until I could get a place of my own. He told me that if I went back to them, or if I spoke to them about what went on in the house, he would kill them. They kept pleading with me to leave and I just could not take that chance that they would get hurt, and my grandparents too."

The prison allowed us to talk to Linda in a large empty room, and somehow the emptiness and bleakness of the setting underlined the story she was telling when she talked about her unhappy marriage.

"I just felt trapped. Slowly but surely he was bringing me to a breakdown. The entire time I was married I felt trapped. I was alone. I knew Walt didn't love me. He didn't really care about the kids. And I was scared for my oldest, Roxanne. It was just Roxanne and me... I lived a life of terror with him, and a person can only take so much before you can't take no more.

"I couldn't do anything without him knowing where I was. He had everything timed, how long it would take to go from one place to another. If I went to the school, I would call and let him know I was there. Or if I was just going to the grocery store down the street, I had to call him.

"One time I took the children to a movie they wanted to see so badly. We were watching the movie when the usher came up and said, 'Are you Mrs. Couch? Your husband's on the phone.' And the kids all said, 'Oh, Mom, you forgot to call Dad...' And when I went to the phone, he gave me thirty minutes to get back home. When we got home, I told the kids to stay in the car and lock the doors. I went into the house and he beat the hell out of me and he said, 'I guess next time you will call me when you get there.' That's how my whole life was. I was more in prison there than I am here," she said, gesturing to the prison walls. "At least I got some freedom here."

Linda told us about a friend she had at the time, in whom she had confided a lot of information about the abuse. Unfortunately, when we tried to trace the friend, we discovered she had died. One of the neighbors who knew the family confirmed to us that Walt was a controlling husband, but they were not willing to say it to us on film.

Linda's description of being "trapped" is echoed by Roxanne, her daughter.

"She said she felt trapped, but by what she did that night she trapped a lot of us. She was looking for her freedom, her escape. She wanted out."

We met Roxanne in Ghana, West Africa, where she moved in 2016 and now lives with her third husband and toddler son, near the house they were building for themselves. Roxanne was busy with her ten dogs and had settled happily into a completely new life.

"I fell in love with this country, with the people it's a people country," she told us, strolling along a sandy, palm-fringed beach, her hair in braids. "I have always loved animals and I could never have them growing up. So when I could, one dog led to another, and I have a house full of them."

There are parts of Linda's story that Roxanne corroborates, but other parts where she fundamentally disagrees with her mother. She described her early life with her parents.

"They should never have gotten married. Their marriage was a disaster from day one. She never lived on her own, ever. She went straight from her parents' house to my father's house, living with his parents. She didn't have the chance to grow up. She was unmarried, pregnant, very young, and he felt like he had to marry her. It was a powder keg waiting to explode."

She remembers witnessing her father being violently abusive with her mother from the age of about five or six.

"My father was a headstrong man. It was his way or the highway. There was no gray area with him. He had rules for me, and rules for her, and she doesn't like rules. He had a temper that could go from zero to eighty in a split second. One little thing could set this man off. He would hit her. He would shove her down to the ground. I saw it myself many times. I've seen him throw her up against the wall. I've seen the bruises on her. And there's no denying the hand marks, around her throat at times. As the years went on, it got worse and worse.

"The thing was his physical size. He was a force to be reckoned with. He doubled her height and weight. And it got pretty nasty, to the point where I would just run back upstairs because I couldn't stand to watch it. I would try to hide under a pillow."

Roxanne wiped away tears as she relived the violence in her childhood home. She confirmed that she took the brunt of Walt's anger.

"I would be beaten every day, on my hands, my backside, my legs, my arms. It didn't matter. He would take his belt off and beat me to the point where I would just lay down. I wasn't what he wanted. He wanted his first child to be a son. I wasn't pretty enough. I was too big. My grades weren't good enough for him. So anything I did wasn't good enough for him, and he made me aware of that every day. I got used to it. I had to deal with it. I was a kid.

"He would beat me with his hand, with a stick; one time he broke the antenna off the back of the television and he beat me with that. I think I was singled out because as a kid I looked just like my mother. Everybody said it. I was her mini-me. I think for him it was almost like taking it out on her.

"The side everybody else saw was a good man, a man who would do anything to help you. They all thought he was a great man, such a loving father, because that is what he portrayed. But it was all show. It was like one big magic trick. What they saw was an illusion created by him for everybody else."

But Roxanne did not agree that Walt had complete control over Linda.

"She liked to spend money on herself. When she went shopping, it was like therapy for her and she felt better. She would get her hair done, and makeup, and new clothes. She liked to show off, to flirt. She loved attention, and that gave her a boost she wasn't getting at home. She would buy for us kids too, so that my father thought that's what she was buying."

Roxanne describes herself as being very close to her mother at this time. She told us her mother was borrowing money, withdrawing cash from their bank accounts, taking out car loans, running up credit card debts. As a child, she was trained from the age of about seven or eight to check the mailbox before her father did, and to remove any letters from banks or credit companies. She believes that by the time of the murder, her mother was in dire financial straits because the bank was no longer prepared to deal with her unless her husband came in to see them.

"I was with her when she went to the banks and withdrew the money," Roxanne said. "She told me, 'Don't tell anyone.' I was her confidante and best friend, she had nobody else to talk to. I became the keeper of secrets. She knew it was all going to crumble in front of her. He would have discovered what she had done. She got scared. There was no coming back from that. I don't know what he would have done, but it would not have been good, for any of us. She had literally backed herself into a corner."

Roxanne adamantly denied that Linda stood between her and Walt to protect her and took beatings for her.

"She *never*, ever, ever took anything for me," she said. "Linda's concern is always about Linda, not about me. Never has been about me. No, no, no, no, no. She literally would turn around and walk out of the door."

She also challenged her mother's allegation of being raped.

"We would have heard them. Our bedrooms were above theirs, and if they were having a party we would have heard it. For her to say they basically raped her, that just didn't happen."

When they were first married, Walt had a job in a factory, but after an injury, he received compensation and an insurance payout. The family lived on this money and Social Security payments. When she was twenty-eight, Linda decided to go to college to train to be a nurse. She saw it as an escape.

"Of course, Walter didn't want me to go to school by myself, so he got into the nursing program too," she said. It was only a matter of time before Walter's serious eye problems meant that he was asked to quit the course.

"He wanted me to quit and just stay home with him, and I said no, I'm not quitting. That was the first time I've ever said no to him. He could not stand that. Walt had blue eyes, but he was so mad his eyes were black. That's how angry he was. I knew then: 'Oh my God, I'm in trouble.' There was just no way he would allow me to continue to do what I wanted to do. That's the only thing I ever wanted to do, be a nurse. Well he shattered that dream."

Linda claimed to us that this row precipitated the killing, which happened while the children were out of the house and staying with their grandparents down the road.

"That's when he stormed into the bedroom, where we had a new-purchased gun. It was supposed to be for protection if something ever happened, if somebody broke in or anything. And he had the gun, and I knew if I didn't do something I was going to be killed. All I could think about was: 'Oh my God, if he kills me, what's going to happen to Roxanne?' I truly feel she would have been killed. I went after him, and of course he was a big man. I knew there would be no way I could wrestle the gun from him, and the only thing I could think was to kick him in the groin. And he bent over and let loose the gun a little bit, enough that I could grab it.

"As I was backing away, I tripped over the back part of the bed, and as I was falling, the gun went off and I shot him in the head. And that's where I panicked... I said, 'Get up, get up,' and he wouldn't answer me. He wasn't moving. I cautiously took my foot and budged his arm a little bit and checked his pulse.

"I knew he was dead. That was the beginning of my nightmare. I think I passed out a bit, and when I woke up I thought nobody, especially his parents, will believe this was an accident. I wasn't totally right, I wasn't thinking straight. When the police showed up, I told them everything, I didn't leave anything out. I gave them the gun; I let them know what happened."

This is the version of the killing that Linda gave when she was arrested and which she has stuck to ever since, throughout her time in prison and at our first meeting with her. There is another version, which subsequently played out at her trial, during which the prosecution presented a damning timeline to argue that Linda's actions that night were carefully premeditated and that Walt's death was no accident.

What isn't contested is what Linda did next. She dragged Walt's body down four flights of stairs to the basement of the house, where she wrapped it in a large rug. She told the children and her in-laws that Walt had stormed out after a row, leaving the family. She did not appear to be unduly distressed; in fact, she embarked on a spending spree, using credit cards and loans to buy a new car and new furniture for the house. She took the children away on holiday to Gatlinburg in Tennessee, a resort village where they stayed in a cabin and went sightseeing.

Roxanne, who was twelve at the time, admitted that when she first heard her father had left home, she felt relief. "I knew I wouldn't be beaten anymore. But in the back of my mind it didn't feel right. But as children we were taught not to question."

When they returned from their holiday, there was a pungent smell from the basement, and Linda had to do something to dispose of the body. The carpet was wet and heavy, and Walt was a big man, so the bundle was more than she could manage on her own. She asked a neighbor for help, a man who lived next door and had always found the Couch family pleasant and helpful, and who owed them a favor because while he and his family were away they had looked after his property. The roll of carpet had already been loaded on to a dolly when he arrived, and they struggled to get it upstairs from the basement. The neighbor, who had no idea what was inside the carpet, asked why Walt wasn't helping, and Linda told him her husband was out of town. When they got it to the garden, the neighbor offered to put it out with the trash, but Linda told him to leave it.

Unable to dig up the hard ground of the vegetable patch in order to bury her husband, she hired a small tiller, a machine that prepares ground for planting. Unable to start it, she asked Walt's father to help get it going. Unwittingly, he was helping her bury his son. Linda dug out a shallow grave while the children played around her in the garden. Did they help dig the grave? Linda maintains they didn't, but Roxanne, the eldest, told us she did. She also claimed that a local man, who Roxanne said had a flirtatious relationship with Linda, had helped with the digging, but when we tracked him down he denied it.

It was ten days after Walt's death, 23 October 1984, when Linda's plot unraveled. Walter Sr. and Dorothy had finally had enough. Armed with evidence that Linda had committed fraud, changing the deeds of the house into her own name, they accosted her and publicly accused her of murdering their son. A loud argument started in front of the house, and a neighbor across the road rang the police because she thought Walter Sr. was attacking Linda. Within minutes, two police cars were on the scene. One of the first cops there described it as mayhem, with the grandparents shouting and screaming, the children running around, and Linda being very quiet.

We were taken through the events of that afternoon by Larry Whalen, then the assistant police chief in charge of the Operations Bureau of the Cincinnati Police Department, who was also soon at the scene. He was on his way home when he heard a call over his radio that sounded like a typical domestic dispute, a family argument that was out of control.

Larry drove us along the road and showed us the outside of the house where the Couch family lived, parking against the curb in the same spot as he had all those years ago. The tall building is still painted red, as it was at the time of the murder.

"It didn't seem to be anything out of the ordinary. I saw a uniformed police officer chasing a person, and the person was the deceased's father, Walter Couch Sr. The police officer had him under control at the end of the driveway. They were yelling. There was a lot of confusion, a melee going on, and the mother was shouting, 'She killed my son, she killed my son.'"

We walked with Larry around the side of the house, and he pointed out the plot where Linda had buried her husband, a narrow strip alongside a double garage.

"There were several people in the backyard, a couple of family members, some neighbors. They were looking into what had been a vegetable patch over the summer. It was a level and even plot, just turned over lightly, as you would after a season of planting."

One of the policemen who had arrived earlier told Larry that Linda had confessed to shooting her husband, blurting out that it was an accident. The policeman's instinct was to get an ambulance quickly in order to save the victim, but when he asked Linda where Walt was, she replied, "You're standing on him." At that point, the officer found a spade and started to dig in the vegetable patch until he could see the carpet and smell the body.

When Larry arrived, he looked at the hole.

"They had excavated down several feet. There was a rug and a bright piece of garment, a towel or something, exposed, and you could smell death. Death has a pervasive odor. It's clinging. It sticks to your skin and hangs in your nostrils. It's not pleasant. And you knew there was a body in that carpet."

Larry remembers Linda as "kind of calm, kind of stoic about the whole thing. Usually there's more emotion at the time of a confession. You know that she realized all the things she had done to cover up were falling apart, and usually at that point they become distraught and the emotion and tears take over, but I didn't see any of that."

Linda showed one of the police officers where the gun was, in a drawer in the bedroom.

Walter Sr. was briefly arrested and taken to the police station because he had been making threats to kill Linda, but the police quickly realized the situation, and he was not charged with anything. The next-door neighbor who had helped Linda move the carpet from the basement came forward and told the police of his unwitting involvement, and he was also briefly arrested until his story checked out.

By this time, the news of the murder was out, and the street quickly filled with spectators, camera crews, reporters, and photographers. By using the upstairs windows of adjoining properties, television crews were able to record the makeshift grave being carefully excavated by volunteer prisoners from a low-security prison and the remains of Walter Couch being wheeled out to a police vehicle. For five or six days, the street was full of police cars, camera vans, and ghoulish sightseers.

It was Joe Ackerman's wife who first rang the police. The Ackermans lived across the road from the Couches, and Joe told us about the stir the case made in the neighborhood. "I called home to tell my wife I would be late, and she explained she had called the police because she saw Walter Sr. getting physical with Linda Couch. She was saying all the police were there and there was a helicopter flying over. Then we began to find out, little by little, what was going on."

He described the area as quiet: "Everybody keeps themselves to themselves. But if there was trouble, we would notice, and there was never any kind of trouble over there.

They seemed a fairly normal family. Nothing ever stood out about them or their activities. They just did normal family things as far as we could tell."

For the three Couch children, the events of that day were traumatic. When the police arrived they were taken into a neighbor's house, and their father's cousin broke the news to them later that their father was dead.

"It was a shock because we'd been told he packed his bags and left. Then to find out that he's been here all the time, in the basement, wrapped in that old rug that we buried in the backyard. It hit me: What have we done? So it really hurt me," said Roxanne.

"We were all three of us interviewed by the police, but within a couple of hours they realized I was the keeper of secrets, which is what one of the detectives nicknamed me. They interviewed me several times over the next months. I guess I helped solidify the case, which was purely circumstantial. I know she never in a million years thought I would tell her secrets to anybody, let alone the police. She thought I would keep her secrets forever, but I realized I couldn't.

"I was sad that my father had been murdered, because, regardless of his temper and what he had done to me, he was still my father. My siblings had a different relationship with him, they loved him very much. For them, the hurt was deep. We were told our mother had been arrested. That whole day was one shock after another, and we were trying to figure out where we were going to go. We had no idea where we would even end up that night."

In the immediate aftermath, the children stayed with their grandparents, and eventually Walt's parents were given permanent custody of them, a decision that Linda opposed from prison.

"They raised us until we were grown," said Roxanne. "They put us through school and college. They did a good job. It was a loving home and they made sure we had everything we needed. My grandparents adored their only son. They were devastated. My grandmother was never the same. My grandfather was crushed, but he had to stay strong for my grandmother and make sure the three of us were all right."

She credits her grandparents with exposing Linda's crime.

"She thought she had gotten away with the murder," said Roxanne, "but she didn't count on my grandparents."

Pat Dinkelacker was working in the Hamilton County Prosecutor's Office when the case came up, and he and another attorney were assigned the case. We interviewed him in his office; by the time we met him, he'd been made a judge in the Hamilton County Court.

"It was a big deal at the time. It was on the news. I had done murders before, but this was big. I took my role very seriously. We worked hard at putting it together to present to a jury to get a conviction of aggravated murder."

Aggravated murder is a more serious offense than murder and carries heavier sentences. Premeditation is one factor that turns a murder into an aggravated murder.

"She claimed it was an accident, that there was a struggle between her and Mr. Couch and the gun went off accidentally. I did not believe that defense. As I sit here today, I do not believe that defense. I do not believe, in any way shape or form, that Linda Lee Couch accidentally killed her husband. I truly believe that she did it with prior calculation and design, and I believe I will go to my grave believing that. She wanted him to die. She shot him and killed him," said Pat.

"We took nothing for granted. We knew we had to get all

the pieces of the puzzle together. The forensics showed that he was shot in the back of the head, rather than the chest or the arm, indicating a struggle. It was an execution shot. He didn't see it coming."

Pat and his colleagues drew up a timeline and examined Linda's behavior in the days leading up to the murder. They found out she committed forgery, transferring ownership of the house, which originally belonged to her in-laws, into her name. She also arranged for the children to be away for the night, and she bought the gun.

"The deed was made out to Walter by the parents in 1983. It gave everything to Walt, nothing to Linda Lee Couch," said Pat. "She got hold of that deed and she cut it, glued it, retyped parts of it, and deeded it to Linda Lee Couch. She took it in and had it re-recorded in her name. Walter Couch Sr. didn't buy what she said about her husband, he kept after her: Where is he? What's he doing now? When's he coming back? And she would repeatedly lie. And he went to the recorder's office and looked up the deed, and he saw that it had been tampered with. He knew that was not the deed he presented. That was another red flag that told him this isn't right."

The next step, according to the prosecution, was the purchase of the gun.

The gun was bought by Linda from a well-known Cincinnati department store, Van Leunens, and the salesman who served her gave evidence at her trials that she did not seem to know what kind of gun she wanted. Having chosen one, she had to return three days later to collect it, because the store ran security checks when selling weapons. He was able to identify her clearly, because it was unusual for a woman to buy a gun, and because half an hour or so after collecting it, she came back in and asked one of the staff to show her how to load it. It was the following day that Walt was shot. According to Roxanne, her father was "totally against guns. We never had one in the house before."

Then, the prosecution claimed, Linda had to get the children out of the way.

"On the night he was murdered, she told the children a story that wasn't true to get them down to their grandmother's house. That was part of her plan. The kids could not be around if she was going to execute her husband. She knew exactly what she was doing," said Pat Dinkelacker.

He also argued that her actions after the killing were evidence of premeditation: "What does she do after the shooting? Did she call an ambulance? Call the police? No, nothing like that. She takes and hides the body. And that's part of the process of prior calculation. I do not believe it was an accident in any shape or form."

Another significant factor for him was that Linda "lied repeatedly to Walt's relatives, his mom and dad. She went so far as to make a missing-person report."

When Linda came to court, almost a year after the murder, it was a sensational local news story, with cameras in the courtroom and film coverage on all the local television stations. We were able to get a copy of the court video. One of the most shocking pieces of evidence was that Linda's children had unknowingly helped with the burial of their own father. The evidence that she had hired a tiller gave rise to another lurid headline: "The Tiller Killer."

Linda sat at a table, flanked by her attorneys, clutching a rosary under the desk. She was calm most of the time but occasionally wracked by sobs. The video footage showed her, in a white dress, re-enacting for the jury her struggle to get the gun from her husband. The media coverage was tough for the Couch family.

"You could not help hearing about it," said Roxanne. "Everyone was talking about 'the backyard burial.' Our grandparents protected us from the media, and they asked that our names should not be used in the newspapers or on the television news. When I gave evidence, they just said 'the oldest daughter,' and they did not show me on the video of the trial. I owe that to my grandparents."

Linda was tried twice, because her first trial resulted in a hung jury: one member of the jury could not agree with the others on her guilt. At this stage it would have been possible for the judge to declare the case over, but the prosecution, with the strong backing of Walt's parents and family, pressed for a second trial. At this one, the jury was unanimous.

Pat Dinkelacker said that, although "mention was made of some abuse at her trial, the defense did not produce any evidence. She did not provide any witnesses, There were no exhibits to substantiate her claim. We did not even take extra steps to rebut her claim, and I don't think the jury bought it... We deal in proof in our system, and there was no proof... As for the rape, we heard nothing about that. She tried to represent herself as the woe-is-me type of person. She was praying with her rosary during the trial, and I've got nothing against people praying. But in my estimation, she had a plan to present herself as a victim. Did I see her as a victim? Absolutely not. I believe she did not want Walter Couch around."

One member of the jury, Clint Eckberg, chose the same term used by police chief Larry Whalen to describe her demeanor: she was, they both said, "stoic."

"Seeing Linda Couch at the table in the courtroom, there's the initial feeling of sympathy and concern for the individual. How could they possibly have gotten themselves into this situation?" said Clint.

"But as the case unraveled, and with the evidence presented, the thoughts in my mind go more to this being a pretty cold-hearted act, that children were used to take the next step. It's just shocking. Inhuman. Carrying him out in a carpet and putting the carpet into the grave out in the backyard would certainly, I think, stay with you for life."

By contrast, Walt was presented by the prosecution as "a good man. He certainly didn't deserve the end he received. I know that he must have been a pretty good guy, because that family was devastated by his loss," said Pat Dinkelacker.

Giving evidence at both trials was difficult for Roxanne, who testified for the prosecution and had her fourteenth birthday on the day the sentence was given. Facing her mother in the courtroom was the last time they saw each other.

"I know she never thought for a million years that I would tell her secrets to anyone, let alone the police," said Roxanne. "She knew that without me on her side, she basically had nobody left. I was supposedly the one friend she had. So for her to see me up there, I'm sure it felt like a great betrayal. I betrayed everything she had told me not to tell anyone."

The defense's case was that Linda was mentally unbalanced when she shot Walt, but the evidence of premeditation held sway. When sentence was passed, she was given a life in prison for aggravated murder, with a mandatory twenty years to be served before she could be considered for parole. For Linda, "it was like being shot myself."

The prosecution was pleased with the result.

"She put herself in that situation. There's a person that's dead, no longer a son, a father, a friend. It's tough. It's not TV, it's the real world, and real people are involved. This stuff affects families big time," said Pat Dinkelacker. "There is no question: on March 13th, Walter Couch took a bullet to the back of his head."

When she talked to us, Linda explained her actions immediately after the murder.

"I wasn't thinking straight. I was not in my right mind. I took my husband to the basement because I didn't know where to put his body. I had to think about where he would want to be, if he really wanted to be buried in the yard. That's the only reason it took a couple of days."

She justified choosing the back garden as his burial place: "Living with my in-laws, which I did when first married, before they moved up the street, was not a good situation, and I tried to get Walt to move. The strange things is, the entire time I was married to him, all he ever said was, 'I will never move out of this house. If I ever die, I want to be buried in my own backyard.' I gave him the last thing he wanted. I know it was wrong. If I could change anything, I wouldn't have done that. I would have just gone to the police right away.

"But when the police did show, I told them everything. I gave them the gun and I told them my emotional thinking at the time. I said he was an abusive man and I was scared to have a gun in the house because of that, but he insisted." She said she did not get the children to help dig the grave. It has caused Roxanne distress ever since, even though she has been reassured that none of it is her fault. "Still, in my heart, it is just like: How would you not know? But I didn't know. I felt horrible, because I knew I had helped her. I didn't kill him, but unbeknown to me I had helped bury my father in the cold ground. It stayed with me for a long time until I literally just had to forgive myself. My siblings were too young, the shovel was too heavy for them, and the ground was hard."

Linda was stunned by the sentence, and for her, "coming to prison was probably the hardest thing to deal with. I had a breakdown and needed psychiatric help."

She was supported by visits from her stepfather, her brother (by the time she went to prison, her mother had died), and from her friends. She had brief contact with one of her daughters, and she met one of her grandchildren. She also had a brief exchange of letters with Roxanne, but Roxanne terminated the relationship.

"She blamed everyone else. She blamed my grandparents, my father; she even blamed the children because of the stress. She never once blamed herself, took responsibility for her own actions. So I quit writing to her. That door is now locked and I will not open that door again. She likes to tell stories, she likes to get sympathy. She will tell anyone anything if she thinks she can get something from it. She doesn't know the difference between truth and her lies anymore, because she's told so many lies to so many people."

She talked of the profound effect the killing had on the whole family.

"Me and my siblings, we went through our trials and tribulations. I think the way my father treated me about my weight triggered eating problems, and I gained a lot of weight and became unhealthy. Eventually I took matters into my own hands and I worked at it.

"Linda's actions that night destroyed an entire family. We have all lived good lives, but it took time, because we all had our own demons. You'd think, because of what we went through, we would be close, but we really aren't. We have gone our own ways. We don't speak to each other or see each other. We have our own families. She [Linda] will never know what she has missed out on. She has nobody to blame but herself.

"I cannot forgive her, and that hurts me to say because she is my own mother. But this was done cowardly and premeditated. I really don't think anyone in the family will forgive her. I don't want her to be paroled. I don't want her to be outside again. She's not sorry for what she'd done."

We asked Roxanne if she has forgiven her father for the beatings he gave her.

"That's hard. I have the scars on me, up and down both my legs. That's a constant reminder. So it is hard to say that I have forgiven him, but I have."

She has found peace in her new life in Ghana.

"I have a lot going for me. What is past is past, and that's not my concern anymore. She'll end up dying there, and I don't think anyone in his family would want any less. If she was truly unhappy, she could have just left. People do that. They pack their bags and go. But she took the coward's way out."

This sentiment is echoed by Pat Dinkelacker.

"She wanted a different life, but instead of choosing the normal thing, a divorce, she opted to take his life. I'm not aware of anything that justified her actions."

We played him the tape of some of the interview Linda gave us from prison, in which she made the allegation that she was raped by Walt's friends.

"Anybody that claims they've been raped, that's a serious thing, it has to be taken seriously. Why didn't we hear this in 1984? Why are we hearing it now? As far as the beatings, why are we hearing it now? If you've got black eyes and a cracked nose, you need to do something right then and there to make sure he didn't do it again. Why all of a sudden, many years later, are we hearing this for the first time? What she is saying now in no way conforms to what she said then. I'm not going to say that she's lying, that's not my job. But I would be very, very skeptical about the things she is saying now," he said.

He agreed with Roxanne that Linda was telling the truth was when she said she felt trapped.

"I think the evidence shows that she clearly felt trapped. I think that was certainly one of the biggest factors as to why she took the life of Walter Couch. I've not seen her in over thirty years. But I know what she did. It wasn't a spur of the moment thing. She planned it. She buried him in the backyard. That's callous. A mom of three children taking the steps she did. I do not think she needs to be back in society... I think she should spend the rest of her life in prison."

During our second interview with Linda, three months after the first, we asked her why the extent of the abuse and the rape allegations did not come up at her trial.

"My attorney advised me not to say anything about the abuse from my husband. I didn't understand, because I thought it would have helped me more. But she kept advising me that I shouldn't say anything. She said, without any evidence, your word is just your word, not anybody else's. I truly believe if I'd been able to say what I wanted to say in court, I would not be sitting here today. There were so many things I could have told the jury, I would have had them in tears, but I trusted my attorney."

We played her tapes of Roxanne talking to us, contradicting the stories of rape and of Linda's having taken beatings for her.

"I hate to say this, but Roxanne is lying. I don't understand why...well, maybe I do. Roxanne was under the thumb of my in-laws for all those years that she was growing up while I was in here. Even my attorney said her evidence looked as if it was rehearsed. She didn't look at me. But when she came past me when she was done, I said, 'I love you,' and she said, 'I love you too, Mom.' I'm saying that her testimony was what the in-laws wanted her to say in court against me.

"I did try to protect her, and many times. She may not know this, but I took a lot of her beatings. I still love her, I love all my children. That will never change," she said.

Once again, she denied getting the children to help her with the burial of their father, an allegation that prompted many of the sensational headlines during her trial.

"I didn't ask them to help. They didn't know what was being buried. There was no way for them to help me; it was just too heavy for a child. I was doing the digging in the evening, and they were out there, and I told them to get back upstairs and watch the TV program and I'd be in in a little while. I wasn't taking the body out that evening; that was just the digging part.

"My state of mind was that I wasn't thinking how it might affect the children. I didn't know how it was going to affect me."

We also challenged Linda about the evidence that she bought the gun and that she transferred the house deeds into her name. In both cases she said it was at the instigation of her husband.

"He told me to buy a gun, and I told him it was more his department, but he insisted that I be the one to buy the gun. He put it in the drawer."

She said that the claim made in court, and repeated by Roxanne, that Walt was against guns was wrong.

"His family were from Kentucky and they did a lot of shooting down there. He knew a lot about guns. My husband told me that I should put the house in my name so in case anything happened we would have a place to live."

She also countered Roxanne's evidence that she was running up debts.

"The money was in his name. I couldn't take anything out without him knowing. Over the years, Roxanne was brainwashed by my in-laws to say negative things, because that doesn't even sound like Roxanne. That's pure lies... Negativity has been put into her head, and I can't fight that." We asked her if it was possible, in her state of mind in 1984, that she deliberately pulled the trigger and that it was not an accident. She denied planning the murder.

"I wouldn't say that I planned no murder. I knew something bad would happen if there was a gun in the house. I am just not the kind of person that can think deeply about planning a murder. I didn't mean to kill him. I made a bad choice putting him in the backyard, it just happened.

"If I'd been in my right frame of mind I'd have called the police. I didn't want him dead. I just wanted him *to let us go.*"

She stressed the last four words. Then she said, "Yeah, thinking back, it is a possibility, because of my state of mind, that I pulled the trigger on purpose. But I can't say that as a fact because at the time I was not in my right mind. It could have been because I thought about all I've been through for fourteen years and what Roxanne went through. Because of that, anything is possible."

It is the nearest she has ever come to admitting her guilt. After serving the mandatory twenty years, Linda became eligible for parole. Her appeal was refused; since then, she has applied for parole another six times, and has been turned down every time.

"It's very frustrating, when I have done everything possible within the prison to show that I am not the same person. I got on with my life in here. Each time I went before the parole board, I would answer their questions, and I accepted it. I stayed positive that maybe the next time they will give me my freedom. The answer is always that it is due to the nature of my crime. Well, the nature of my crime will never end. It's always going to be the same. But what isn't the same is me. I've changed. I'm a better person."

Linda cites the fact that for over twelve years she has not been guilty of even the smallest infringement of the prison rules.

"I have a good reputation, not only by the staff but by the inmates. If I get release, I can guarantee they are never going to see me again. I will walk a straight line.

"I've paid my price. I've done these years in prison for trying to save my life so that my children wouldn't be hurt. I have done everything I can possibly do to prove myself, not only to the parole board but also to myself.

"I still hope they will let me loose and that I have a bit of freedom before I die. I really don't want to die in prison. My children are all safe, and they've grown, and at least they are alive. Once I'm released, I'm going to get a job and have my own place and just live out the last part of my life. Whether or not old friends want to see me, or my children, I'm just going to continue to be who I am."

4

MEANS TO AN END

JAMES ROBERTSON

"I accept full responsibility for the way my life turned out and stuff. People always saying how unfair the world is and stuff, ain't nobody ever said that life was meant to be fair. People just got to accept that. There ain't no sense in just being bitter about it. That's life."

The prisoner, a thickset man with a shaven head, wearing the orange T-shirt of a Death Row inmate, was regarded by the Florida Department of Corrections as one of the most violent and dangerous of their 95,000 inmates. His wrists were handcuffed in front of him and shackled to his waist by a restraint called a black box, preventing his hands from moving much. His ankles were chained together.

The room was tiny, ten feet by ten feet, and fifty-four-year-old James Robertson and director Ross Young were sitting face-to-face on hard chairs, so close that their feet could touch. There were a chilling few seconds, after the prison officer escort left the room and before the prisoner spoke, as he eyed the film crew. He gave a wary smile, revealing a mouth full of broken and discolored teeth.

Producer Stuart Powell stepped forward to attach the microphone. Then, as if unleashed, James Robertson poured out his thoughts, angrily and fluently, about the lifetime he has spent in prison, where he'd been sent after the petty theft of a set of speakers when he was sixteen. Violence, fighting, and the ultimate cold-blooded murder of another inmate meant that when we met him, he had spent thirty-seven years in prison, all his adult life, the last four on Death Row waiting for a date for his execution.

He didn't feel sorry for himself, he didn't have any remorse about his crimes, and perhaps unique among the other 2,500 Death Row prisoners in the United States, he had deliberately worked to get himself onto Death Row—including committing a calculated and brutal murder. He had no memories of life beyond the whitewashed buildings, floodlights, watchtowers, and rolls of razor wire of the Florida prison system, apart from those of being a child and teenage boy. He wanted to die, because the alternative for him was to live out his years in the punitive Close Management (CM) system of Florida prisons. It was this that he wanted to talk about, and whenever we tried to steer the interview, he soon came back to his own agenda, railing against the CM system. The prison officer sitting behind the door was alarmed at this sudden transformation in the sullen, silent inmate with a shocking record of violence, who refused to engage with any of the staff, turning his back when they spoke to him. The officer called for reinforcements, and two colleagues joined him, ready to plunge into the room if James's anger tipped from verbal to physical. Our crew did not know this until later.

Regarded as the only way of controlling the most violent prisoners, CM requires they be locked up twenty-three hours a day, with only a brief period of exercise, inside a cage nicknamed the "dog kennel." There is very little contact with other prisoners or staff: food is posted into cells through a hatch, and handcuffs are worn when prisoners are moved around the building. For twenty years, on and off, with breaks when he was reintegrated into the prison population before being returned to CM, James had lived this way, and for him the prospect of death by lethal injection was genuinely welcome. He did not relish becoming one of the aging, infirm, older prisoners, regularly bullied by younger inmates and prison officers.

He spoke quickly and with few hesitations, emphasizing his points by leaning menacingly into the camera and swinging around on the hard seat. When he talked about his decision to get onto Death Row by committing a cold-blooded, premeditated murder, there was a brief pause as he stared at Ross, checking the reaction of the crew to his vehement assertion: "I don't feel no remorse."

Then he laughed as he sneered, "You think that's really something, don't you? Think that's a big deal? I don't have no remorse for what I did."

It was an unsettling moment as he smirked into the camera. For Ross, intent on getting a good interview, the full impact did not hit at the time.

"It was only when I watched it back I felt a chill. Especially after another prisoner later told me, off camera, that James is so violent that if he had taken against me, the prison officers outside the door would not have been able to prevent him attacking me, and although the shackles impede him, they would not stop him," said Ross.

For producer Stuart Powell, being so close to James's scarcely controlled anger was unnerving, and he knew that he was the one who would have physical contact with James, to later remove the microphone, and again when the crew returned for the second interview.

"I had a dream where, when we went back and I was miking him, he bit my cheek," he said.

In telling James's story, we needed to explore his early life, before he committed the crime that sent him into Florida's adult jails, his home ever since. It was two weeks before his seventeenth birthday when he was caught by a security guard as he tried to steal a set of speakers from a shop across from the apartment block where his family lived, on the face of it a petty crime, but one with enormous consequences for him.

James had been smoking dope from the age of eleven. He grew up in a poor area of Orlando that was riddled with drug abuse. The child of alcoholic and drug-addicted parents, he disciplined with a switch at home. A truant from school, he was happiest on the streets hanging out with his friends. He witnessed his father beating up his mother. His mother, a one-time cocktail waitress and stripper, was addicted to prescription drugs, slimming pills, and Valium, and from time to time would disappear for months, leaving her sister to care for James and his two brothers. For a time he lived with his grandparents, both alcoholics, his grandfather a member of the Ku Klux Klan. For James, this life was normal, and he never once blamed his upbringing.

With prompting from Ross, James talked about this early life.

"I had a pretty good childhood. I ate good...I had good parents. Well, they used to fight. But it doesn't really have nothing to do with why I'm here now... I mean, my dad used drugs and drank, and he's even used drugs with me, but I'm going to tell you he never wanted me to use drugs. He only used drugs with me because he knew I was going to use it anyway... They wanted me to do good, to stay out of trouble; they didn't want me to hang out on the streets... My brothers and I, we wouldn't behave, our mom didn't want us hanging

out on the streets all night but we would do it anyway...
They're good parents, I don't blame them for nothing."

James described his childhood as "lower-middle class" and
insisted "it didn't cause me to be what I am. When you say
poor, that's all relative... I've seen extreme poverty." Despite
his claim that the family were not in the lowest category, they
were designated as "economically disadvantaged," and James
was given free breakfasts whenever he attended school, which
was not often.

He was diagnosed as hyperactive: "So I didn't do well in
class, I wasn't learning stuff." By the time he was eleven, he
was using drugs and "skipping school all the time." When
he did attend, he was violent and unruly. His life was "drugs,
partying with friends and stuff, you know. Running around the
streets. I used to love doing that. Mostly pot, smoking a lot of
pot. I did other things. Acid, PCP [known as Angel Dust], but
mostly pot. Using quaaludes and Valium and cocaine, stuff
like that."

Marijuana was his main drug. Whenever he had problems
at home or school, he smoked pot to lift his mood and make
him feel more upbeat. Funding his drug habit meant stealing from his mother and then embarking on a career in petty
crime. His first arrest came at the age of twelve, for shoplifting,
and shortly afterwards he was caught for stealing a bicycle. He
graduated to burglary at the age of fourteen, and then violence
came in: at fifteen he attacked three boys and was sent to the
Florida School for Boys, a reform school that has been branded
as barbaric for imposing inhumane discipline and punishments
on pupils, and which has now been closed down.

He was held there for five months, getting involved in more
violence before returning home. His stay had no beneficial

impact on his behavior, with more arrests for petty crimes following. Then came the charge that led to a lifetime spent in prison.

"I was hanging on the street and I would see some place that looked like I could break into it, get some money for dope." As he recounted this to us, James laughed ruefully, aware that it was a small crime but that its consequences for him have been massive. At the time he was living in Pine Hills, a neighborhood west of Orlando that was nicknamed "Crime Hills" and was in decline and decay, a favorite haunt of drug dealers.

"I had already broke into there and got the stereo. I took it to the dope man and I went back to steal the speakers. He wanted the speakers. So stupid stuff. Petty. I didn't actually get inside. Some security guard caught me and I got into a little wrestling match with him, and I thought I had a knife in my sock. I tried to get the knife out and stab him so I could run off but I couldn't get to it. The security man and his mate were both on top of me. That was it. Cops get there and some cops grabbed me, and after they cuffed me they slammed my head up against the door. They tried to say I assaulted the cop. I didn't assault no cop or nothing. But they dropped the case for assaulting the cop."

While he was being held in custody at the Orange County jail, waiting for his trial, James and two other prisoners escaped and went on the run.

"Me and two other guys, we went through a plexiglass window, a big security window. It was real high up toward the ceiling, about two and a half stories high, and we made a pyramid, and we were able to steeple out by forming a human pyramid. We went on a roof. We jumped across the street and went to an apartment complex."

To escape, James stole his grandfather's station wagon, and it's one of the few things in the whole catalogue of violence that followed that pricks his conscience.

"I felt real bad. That's one of the worst things I ever did as far as I am concerned, you know. I stole his station wagon. It had all his carpenter's tools in there and me and one of the guys, we went up north. I got caught in Indianapolis. I was gone for two days." It was the furthest he ever traveled in his life.

Back in custody, he was charged with burglary, one charge of aggravated assault, and the escape. His mother told the court that his father turned James and his brothers onto drugs and encouraged them to commit burglaries. His grandmother claimed that living with her and his grandfather for the past few months had turned his behavior round.

Their evidence didn't help: for the first two charges he was given four years each, and the escape added another two years. Crucially, the judge ordered that the sentences should run consecutively, so James was facing ten years in an adult prison at barely seventeen. Had he gone to trial at the age he was when he committed the offense, sixteen, he could have been sentenced in the juvenile system, where the emphasis is on rehabilitation. In Florida, adult prisons offer some help for those who want it, but the system is all about obeying orders, and obeying orders was not something James Robertson was prepared to do.

His prison record shows a litany of disciplinary actions for unarmed assaults, threats, possessing weapons, disobeying orders, and being in unauthorized areas of the prison. Over the years, more time was added to his sentence. He got another fifteen years for smuggling contraband; five years for battery with a deadly weapon; five years for introducing a deadly weapon into prison; eight years for attacking a law enforcement officer when he was trying to escape.

"I used to catch a lot of time, stabbed a few dudes. I kind of had a bad attitude. I've had a bunch of other cases. I don't even keep up with them, how many, about a dozen of them or something. I've got a bunch of time, about a hundred years, I guess. Like stabbing inmates, assaulting guards. Tried to escape one time. I went to outside court and I kicked a guard. I tried to take his gun from him. I tried to kill a couple of inmates. You know what happens in prison." Again, he leaned into the camera and spoke emphatically: "They put bad people in prison, that's the reason they're in prison."

But although he maintained that crime in prison is expected, the sheer length of James's conviction sheet is not typical, even in prisons full of hardened and violent criminals. It was his rap sheet that initially made him stand out among the other Death Row killers we filmed.

"James was an outlier," said Ross Young. "The other Death Row prisoners we looked at had four or five offenses on their prison rap sheet. James's rap sheet was as long as your arm. He had spent more than twenty years in Close Management. He was different."

His first few spells in CM ended with him being released back into the general prison population, a life he looks back on with nostalgia.

"I'm a population man. You get friends you can hang out with. You got the kind of guys who are more like you and you can pick and choose who you hang out with, and you can run around the compound. Fresh air! You can be active all day; your time is a lot better. You might work."

Several times when we were with him he spoke of missing the sun, the Florida climate that was the only one he had ever known. But his chances of ever getting off CM ended when, in 1995, he attacked and stabbed another inmate thirty-nine times, knifing him continuously in the chest and neck before being hauled off by prison officers and eventually getting another sixteen years added to his sentence. His victim miraculously survived.

After this, he admitted, his life changed, and he realized that he "probably isn't ever going to get out. I just kind of stopped caring at that point. It's just something you've got to accept."

In 2008 he had racked up seventy-seven charges in his prison career, and then he committed the biggest crime of all: the horrific murder of Frank Hart. At the time, he had been inside for twenty-eight years, and his earliest possible release date was 2038, when he would be seventy-five years old (by which time he would have spent nearly sixty years behind bars). James explained the murder to us by saying he knew he would never get off CM, because of his record, and he had to take back control, change his life. He condemns the CM system as inhumane.

"You fucking start losing your mind on that CM. It's like you're just existing like a damn hermit or a damn rat or something..."

The murder happened in the Charlotte Correctional Institution, one of the toughest prisons in Florida, when James had been moved from the most secure level of CM (there are three levels) to one where he was put in a double cell with another inmate. He didn't like this. He particularly didn't like the cellmate he was sharing with: Frank Hart, a convicted pedophile who had been in and out of prison for fourteen years, and whose habits around the cell annoyed him.

But he has never claimed that any of this fed into his decision to murder Hart. The killing was a means to an end, he said, and the end was to get off CM and onto Death Row.

"So finally I got mad and decided I'm going to go ahead and kill somebody... I'll just kill my cellmate, I felt pretty confident I could overpower him because I had a thirty-minute window. So I went ahead and killed him. He was a child molester and I didn't really want a child molester in my cell. I don't care nothing about Frank Hart, he's nothing. I don't have no remorse for it. It was premeditated. I wanted to get on Death Row. I started to think about it six months before.

"I woke the guy up. I waited until the guard made his round, I nudged him, woke him up, and I had some socks tied up. I started struggling around with him. Eventually I overpowered him and strangled him."

The official report into the murder, in December 2008, added chilling details. After killing Hart, James put the body back on the lower bunk and pulled the bedcover over it. On his own top bunk he read a thriller, *Dial M for Meatloaf*, by the light coming from the window. In the early hours, he lined himself up with the security camera and pulled a series of grotesque faces, then went to sleep. First thing the next morning, he ate his own breakfast and then ate Frank Hart's.

"I wanted to show callousness, that I didn't care what I did."

When a prison officer and a female nurse did their morning rounds at 9.15 a.m. (almost nine hours after the murder), James passed a note to the officer: "I don't want the lady to see it. Hart died."

To his huge disappointment, five months after killing his

cellmate, he was charged with second-degree murder, a charge that does not allow a Death Row sentence. A first-degree murder charge is for a killing that is premeditated, whereas second-degree murder, while malicious, is not pre-planned.

It was a big blow for James. He'd made no secret of his ambition to get to Death Row. With a second-degree charge, he was going to get what he least wanted: a lifetime on CM. He told Ross that one of his motives for getting to Death Row, apart from his overriding wish to be executed, was to have a six-hour visit from his mother. Both his parents visited occasionally in his early years in prison, but by this time his father was dead and his mother was seriously unwell and rarely came to see him. His brothers had not been to visit him for over twenty years and wanted nothing to do with him.

"My mom was getting old and she was fixing to die. I knew she didn't have much longer to live. She was like seventy, but her health was that of a ninety-year-old; she's been smoking all her life, she can't hardly breathe. I know her time is getting near and I want to see my mom, but she'd come up, she'd drive for three hundred miles, and I only get to see her for two hours if I'm on that status [CM]. I wanted to get out on the compound [Death Row], where I could get a regular visit for six hours."

His mother visited him the year before the murder, and James admitted to Ross that it was the one time he cried in all his time in prison. It turned out to be the last time he saw her before her death.

"Because I was on CM, it was only allowed to be two hours. And she's old, and she's got a mask, and she can hardly get around. I was hoping when she come to see me we get six hours. But it was kind of rushed. So it kind of upset me, man, and when that visit turned out the way it was, I got emotional man. I try not to get emotional."

Determined to have his charge regraded as first-degree murder, James embarked on a three-year crusade against the justice system, a battle with the ultimate prize: Death Row. In court, he demanded a first-degree charge. He wrote to five different officials in the State Attorney's Office, setting out his case. He ran through a series of four lawyers, falling out with them because they would not support his determination to be executed. He told state officials that if the charge was not changed, "if I am forced to go another route, I meant what I said," meaning that he would kill again.

In December 2011, three years and nine days after killing Frank Hart, and still facing a second-degree charge, James decided to carry out this threat. He was being held at Charlotte County Jail for a court appearance when he attacked a prison officer after persuading him to open the cell door to take out trash. He'd fashioned a weapon by taking a thin wire off a cleaning cart.

"It wasn't very sharp. There's some kind of gloss on the floors, they're real smooth, so you can't get it sharp. I knew the guards wore shirts that's a tough material. I didn't have a lot of confidence, but I tried anyway. He opened the cell door and I told him to give me the key. I wanted to go to a cell and kill an inmate, open up all the other cells... The rod was flimsy, and I struck him in the rib cage and it bent in half.'

The officer had cuts and abrasions on his chest and stomach, but no serious wounds. James claimed he did not want to hurt the officer, "He was kind of nice, I liked him," but he knew he had to act, because if his cell was searched he would lose his improvised weapon.

"I'd already told them that if they didn't give me the death sentence I was going to kill somebody." He was charged with attempted murder and attempted robbery, and again he insisted to investigators that his motivation was entirely to do with getting a death sentence.

"I want nobody to feel sorry for me. I just want to get my death sentence and go on down the road, get out of y'alls hair. That's all I want to do," he told them. He repeated that if he didn't get his charge changed, he would look for another opportunity to kill an inmate.

"Any opportunity that presents itself. There's so many people in the prison that I hate, inmates and guards. I don't have a problem finding anybody I dislike."

James stressed repeatedly in our interview that his sole motivation was to get off CM and onto Death Row, something that can only be understood in the context of life inside prison. To explain the difference between the two, we talked to Anne Otwell, a staff nurse who has worked at the Charlotte Correctional Institution since 1992. A small, impeccably made-up woman with neatly bobbed white hair, Anne is at first sight an unlikely person to be working with the toughest prisoners in one of the toughest prisons in the country. She lives in an equally neat redbrick home, the Stars and Stripes flying outside, a sprinkler watering her immaculate lawn, in the upmarket area of Cape Coral on the Gulf Coast, a forty-minute drive from the prison. Her route to work, across the spectacular Cape Coral Bridge, is a journey from the reality of her own life, cooking dinner and walking her little dog, to an enclosed world of jangling keys and stark corridors punctuated with metal security gates, where she works with the state's worst offenders.

"You try to get into their mind but it's impossible. I try to understand but I can't, I never will. I can only accept them for who they are," she said.

When Anne met James for the first time, while he was in CM, several years before the murder, she found him even more difficult and intimidating than most prisoners.

"He was very withdrawn. He did not talk to his peers; he did not talk to the staff." She described him as "a pressure cooker waiting to blow. He was extremely angry, but his quietness was something that was daunting to me. He did not look at you, he looked through you."

She said the staff knew that James wanted to get onto Death Row.

"He made no bones about it. Everyone knew, and when an inmate voices that, one has to be very cautious, because he would stop at nothing to get there...and James stopped at nothing and he got there. Took him a while, but he did it." Anne explained to us the differences between being contained in the punitive CM regime, and Death Row.

"On Death Row, they have their own TVs, sometimes they can have their own bedspreads... They have their own area to exercise, they get more recreation."

Most of all, she emphasized, it is quiet and peaceful, and there is a camaraderie between the inmates that does not exist in CM or in the general prison population.

"In Close Management, the inmates sleep most of the day and they're up all night. They put sheets round their eyes so that they can keep the light out and they sleep all day long... they're fighting with one another, one room to another, all night long. They're angry, they're throwing temper tantrums. Then, during the day, it's quiet.

"In the general population it's noisy: doors slamming, inmates yelling. When you walk on Death Row, you can hear a pin drop. Death Row is literally a home from home. They know they're not going to be executed tomorrow; they know they are going to be there for maybe twenty years. In all the years of being in prison, this is the most stable place. Nobody's going to move them. The system constantly moves inmates, and they hate it. When they're on Close Management they can be moved to another Close Management prison at any time, and they don't like the upheaval. But on Death Row they don't move. They like the stability, bizarre as it may seem.

"The living conditions are not much better in our eyes, but for James it would be like going from the slums to Beverly Hills. By the time they get to Death Row, there's no more bucking the system. They have come home. That's how the majority of them look at it. They love Death Row."

To provide an all-round picture of James, we asked him to name any friends or relatives who we could talk to. It was difficult: the people he hung out with on the streets as a teenager had long since moved on with their lives, his parents were dead, and his two brothers had turned their backs on him years before. He nominated Bobby Lynch, a prisoner he has done time with in different Florida prisons since the late eighties, as a friend. We interviewed Bobby at Jefferson Correctional Facility, where he was serving eleven years for burglary.

Jefferson is a medium-secure jail, and in contrast to James, Bobby walked into the large interview room unaccompanied by a prison officer and with no handcuffs or shackles. He wore his own tracksuit bottoms and pristine white trainers with a blue prison top, the V-neck revealing a chest of amateur-looking tattoos stretching to his neck. Rangy, slim, with a grizzled gray beard, he walked with a confident, bouncing gait to the chair set up for the interview, and immediately confounded the idea that he was a friend of James Robertson.

"He's a piece of shit," he said, unequivocally. "I can't imagine why he would say I'm a friend. I don't have an intimate knowledge of James Robertson, but as far as interacting with him on a daily basis, I know him pretty good. I've messed up. I've come to prison, but if I give you my word, it's good. I'm not going to pick on someone that's defenseless. That's not his outlook. He thinks if he can do something and get away with it, he'll do it. And for me, that's a coward.

"If I see somebody picking on an old man or a young dude that's green, I got a problem with that. It bothers me. It don't bother him."

Bobby referred to James by his prison nickname, "Chickenhead," throughout the interview. He said that James's reaction to any problem, however small, was to pull a knife, despite a code of conduct that applies within the prison walls.

"There's certain things you stab for and certain things you fight for. If somebody breaks in your locker, that's a stabbing offense. If somebody contacts your family and tries to do something with your family, that's a stabbing offense. But you don't want to just kill somebody to be killing them. But the first thing Chickenhead's going to do is grab a knife... He loves a knife, his first thought is a knife. He looks for an opportunity to hurt people.

"He's got no ethics. Chickenhead don't care what anybody thinks about him. He don't care if you think he's a piece of shit. I can't think why he would say I am a friend. A friend is somebody you can count on for moral support, emotional help. That dude's not my friend, he's not my drinking buddy.

We've hung out in a crowd. Eight or ten people, standing around the rec yard, sitting there bullshitting or whatever.

"He's violent. He is capable of crossing you out. He's killed. He will kill again, there ain't no doubt in my mind, if he gets the opportunity. That's the type of dude he is... There's a total lack of self-control. He's unfeeling, it's like he's dead inside. Like he has no heart... Chickenhead's problem is his violence. That's why he's done so many years on CM. If you're super violent, the guards got to keep an eye on this guy. It's easier to put him in a cell, get him out of the way. Chickenhead's always going to be a threat to the people around him. That's the way he lives. Every camp [prison] I've been to with him, he's stabbed somebody."

Like James, Bobby had also done part of his sentence in CM, and he spoke to Ross about the need to handle your time in there.

"Don't let the room take control. That room will close in on you, sitting in that room every day, getting out only for three showers a week, recreation only two to three hours a week. So if you let it, it will take control.

"There's things you can do: you can get books, you can learn. When you're in that cell, you ain't got nothing to do but focus on you. People have to come to grips with themselves. You ain't got no choice: you've got to meet yourself head on. If you let it, it will break you mentally."

Bobby challenged James's assertion that he knew he would never get off CM.

"If you want to get off CM, all you have to do is what you're supposed to for a certain period of time. They don't ask you to do anything special."

We also interviewed Mark Desisto, whose life crossed with

James Robertson's by chance, but who became a pivotal part in his crusade to reach Death Row. After he had dispensed with the lawyers who found it impossible to support his plea for execution, the state allocated him a new attorney. Mark was "on the wheel," meaning he was the lawyer whose name came up on the duty roster of public defenders. He's a well-established Florida lawyer, and when we met him he was looking forward to retirement, puttering around on his river cruiser (called, with some wit, *The Defense Rests*) after a long career representing young offenders and criminals and fighting motoring charges and personal injury cases.

He lives in Port Charlotte, a beautiful town on the Gulf Coast of Florida that is regularly named as one of the best places to retire in the States. The town is constructed around miles of man-made, tree-fringed waterways, geometrically laid out and lined with luxury homes, all with perfectly manicured lawns leading down to boathouses. Filming on Mark's boat and next to his pool, where he relaxed throwing a ball for his pet corgi, made for a stark contrast with the background James came from. But Mark had plenty of experience with clients who'd had difficult starts in life, and felt compassion for them. He'd been into every prison in Florida to see clients, including seeing prisoners on CM and Death Row. But he admitted he had never encountered a prisoner like James.

"The first time I met him he was in lockup at the courthouse, for a hearing for him to change attorneys. I was coming on as his attorney. I had very little time, a minute or less, to see him. He was charged with second-degree murder. I quickly asked him if it was accurate that he was seeking the death penalty.

"He told me he was. I didn't know what to expect when

I first met him, but he seemed happy to know that I already had a bit of information [about securing the death penalty]. I told him I would look into it more. I've never been hit with that. I asked myself: Can this be done? Can someone actually plead for the death penalty? I realized it could be done, and I started the ball rolling because I knew that was his desire. The main part of the job is doing what clients want as long as it is lawful. Everything he asked me to do was lawful, so even though I might not have agreed with it, I was ethically bound to do it. I had to take that road and travel it for him or with him, because he was asking nothing I wasn't able to do for him."

Mark spoke to a couple of James's previous lawyers, and they told him that James was level-headed, not disruptive or violent in meetings, but that he could not accept that the death penalty was not on the table. Having learned about James's background, Mark told us that he believed James deserved some sympathy.

"He had a lot of bad cards dealt to him, some of his own giving, but I think some were probably there that he didn't justly deserve. Based on his background and his family setup, it would have taken a lot for him to overcome a lot of things he had to face.

"He certainly made mistakes; I think every human being does. The average person makes a mistake, they pay their price, and move on with their life. I don't see him as this evil person who must be killed, but that's his choice. I don't see him as this person who has no redeeming value.

"He's the one that committed the crime that meant he was incarcerated. But when you look at his family background, he didn't have all that much choice at the age he was, and then you start looking at what happens once you're inside the prison, especially in a Close Management situation.

"I guess if I had to use one word to sum him up it would be 'sad.' It's a sad situation. He's an individual with a totally different mindset from anybody else I ever ran into in my life. But I've never run into someone who's been essentially locked up their entire life. He sees life through a different prism. He never had a life. There's things he'll never see in his life that we all take for granted.

"The other clients I've had, the longest amount of time on Close Management was eight or nine months. I've never heard of anyone that's spent nearly their entire life in Close Management."

He also believes that it is an act of mercy to kill James. "I'm sure that's how he sees it. His only other choice is to get older, suffer more, put up with more of what he's been putting up with for the last twenty or thirty years. Things he could handle at twenty or twenty-five years old...but in your fifties and sixties you're not going to be able to take as he gets older, becomes more frail. It was getting harder and harder for him, both physically and mentally.

"I asked him straight out: 'Why would you want to have the death penalty? What's your reasoning?' He said, 'I look at the guy that's in the cell across from me. He's going blind, he's sixty-five, he gets pushed around more, he gets messed with by more people, guards, inmates. I don't want that kind of life. I used to be able to do the violence, now I'll be the one that's getting the violence done to me.'

"I can understand he wants to put an end to it. I don't see the prison system changing or it getting any better for him, so it's an act of mercy. There's no question in my mind, if I had the same two choices, I would make the same choice as him. I would not want to spend the remaining thirty or forty years of my life in Close Management... After I looked at everything, it made absolute sense to me."

Mark put together a case, and in October 2012, the state of Florida finally gave James what he wanted: he was charged with the first-degree murder of Frank Hart. He immediately pleaded guilty and demanded to be sentenced to death, making a statement to the court that if he could go to Death Row, he would no longer hurt anyone, but if he didn't get a Death Row sentence, he would continue killing or trying to kill.

To help the judge decide on a sentence, A pre-sentence investigation (PSI) report into James was prepared by probation officer Mike Gottfried. It was the last report that Mike, who had worked for the prison and probation services for twenty-three years, prepared before his retirement. Mike enjoyed this part of his job, and when we interviewed him we found him a conscientious person who worked hard at presenting a balanced report to the court. He had only two weeks to write the report before James's trial. "Cramped but manageable," he said.

A PSI looks at an offender as an individual, not simply as a list of criminal convictions, taking in their socioeconomic background and family history, and it includes the views of the victim's family.

"What I'm doing is turning one-dimensional into three-dimensional. Everybody knows him as a sheet of paper: facts and figures. They don't know the inside: Who is this person? That's what the PSI is trying to do," said Mike, who spent an hour and a half with James.

"I didn't pay any attention to what I heard about this

inmate because I wanted to go in totally objective. He was rather laid back. I knew he was dangerous, I'd been told. There was a deputy sitting outside the room. I didn't want him inside because it might make a difference in how Robertson responded; he didn't like authority. I felt he was coopera- tive: he didn't act nasty, he didn't give me any reason to feel uncomfortable. He came across as determined. He knew what he wanted. He had one thing on his mind; he wanted the death penalty.

"He spoke with a tone, not of indifference, but a tone that he already knew what he wanted. If the judge actually sentenced him to life without parole, that would have been harder than a death sentence. The writing's on the wall: he had nothing to look forward to. He had no crosses to tick off on the calendar. So he was making a new calendar, a death calendar. He was going to cross off the days until he got what he wanted, death. Because getting old in prison is a sort of living death.

"He didn't come in as a Close Management inmate. He *made himself* into a Close Management inmate, one of the most dangerous, because he would not conform and it was unsafe to keep him in the general population.

"In Close Management, you are dealing with hard-core individuals, and when an inmate has his back up against the wall, a lifer, a person who is never going to get out, they become dangerous. They are the worst inmates in the prison, so bad that they cannot live in the general population.

"What do they have to lose? I truly believe they become hard- ened, aggressive, even more dangerous. James Robertson... became more calculating, cruel, heinous. Close Management is a horrible existence, but it doesn't slow James down, it gives him new drive. Frank Hart, his cellmate, was a means to an end. He was making a statement." Mike is reluctant to condemn the Close Management system. "It's extremely easy to criticize, but people who have never been in a maximum-security prison with hard-core inmates don't understand what you have to deal with." One of the most striking aspects of James's case, for Mike, was that "you're dealing with a person who has never lived as an adult in the outside world. And that's tough for people to understand... Violence is a part of James Robertson because violence was a part of his upbringing. You say to yourself: How could we release him back into society? As that kind of person?"

There were no members of James's family available for Mike to talk to, but he was able to speak to Frank Hart's family, who supported James getting the death penalty on the grounds of "an eye for an eye."

Mike's official report recommended the death sentence but stressed "that this recommendation is made in no way to reward this inmate by recommending the sentence that he so desperately wants."

Interviewed by us four years later, Mike stood by his recommendation and emphasized again that it was not a reward.

"It was what he wanted, but society, on the inside and the outside, was being protected, because he would have looked for another way to make his statement."

Reports from two mental health experts, a psychiatrist, and a psychologist concluded James was sane. Three years and eight days after the murder, he finally achieved his goal: he was sentenced to death.

The obvious question, which we addressed in the film, is why, if he wants to die, James hasn't committed suicide in prison. Suicides in Florida prisons amount to an average of fifteen to twenty a year.

Nurse Anne Otwell said, "He didn't kill himself because he's narcissistic. He's not a cutter [self-harmer]. He couldn't hurt himself because he loves himself. He's fulfilling his dream. That's what he wanted, Death Row.

"He wanted to be on Death Row to show everybody that he made it. It's just like going to medical school and then you graduate. In his mind, he graduated to Death Row. He wants to make something of his life that everybody will remember. His death would be something that would be front-page news, in his mind... Being on the row, you are somebody, you wear a jumpsuit that says Death Row on the back. In his mind he is a celebrity."

Mike Gottfried agreed with Anne Otwell that James would never kill himself, but for a different reason. "James would see that as a cowardly way out, and James isn't a coward."

Bobby Lynch, on the other hand, held that if James genuinely wanted to die, there are ways to do it, and he did not believe that James really wanted his life to end.

"Get up on the top bunk and dive off, swan dive. Get your razor blade and in three and a half minutes you're dead," he said, demonstrating with a slash of his hand across his own throat. "He ain't tired of living. He ain't going to kill himself. He's seeking attention."

The story of James Robertson could have ended with his move to Death Row, where he waited to be given a date for his execution. But something remarkable happened in his life, something that has not changed his determination to die but which has affected the way he lives. Two years after he moved to Death Row, he received a letter from his cousin, Darrell

Mosher. Darrell, who was too young to have many memories
of James before he went into prison, shared a similarly tough
upbringing. His mother and James's mother were sisters, both
of whom Darrell described as "wild, didn't pay the bills, left
the boys to their own device without any discipline."

Darrell also had problems with alcohol and had spent time
in prison. But he had turned his life around and was inspired
by his newly found belief in God to reach out and make contact
with James. He knew his cousin was in prison, but he didn't
know he was on Death Row.

The relationship he'd developed with James made him a
natural choice to include in the film, but initially Darrell was
reluctant to be filmed. With so few people—apart from officials (a probation officer, a nurse, a lawyer)—talking about
James, Darrell was important to us in order to establish an
all-round view.

Eventually, the two-man crew of Stuart Powell and Gareth
Morrow took a chance and flew from Florida to Tennessee,
where Darrell and his family had been living for the past twelve
years. Landing in Nashville, they drove for four hours through
snow blizzards to reach the Mosher home in Greeneville, a
small town in the foothills of the Appalachian Mountains.

After a few minutes talking on the doorstep, Darrell agreed
to be filmed, and he explained on camera how he, his wife,
and their children became part of James's life: "We don't force
ourselves to be his family, it just came natural. I had to give
it a shot, and trust God, and it turned out to be a blessing for
all of us.

"When I was a teenager, I knew he was inside, and whenever I talked to my aunt, his mother, I always asked how
Jimmy was doing. I looked online and I just called Florida

State Prison and asked what I had to do to write to him. I wrote him a letter, about half a page long. I was nervous writing to him, not knowing what kind of person he was. I just knew I had to write him, let him know who I was and that I was sending him twenty dollars a week. That's all I said, and that if he wants to write back, he's more than welcome.

"So he wrote back and he didn't remember who I was. He knew my brothers. His first letters were abrupt and he cussed a lot. [After a while] he said he hoped I'd be in his life forever: 'But you'll probably be like everyone else, come into my life for a month or two, then leave.' Then, a year or so later, he wrote, 'I'm comfortable now, I know you're not going to leave me.' When he wrote that he'd only ever existed and never lived, I cried. I thought about it a lot. He has never had a job, anyone to love him, never been with a woman."

Having spent some time in prison himself, Darrell understood the need for money to pay for extras like deodorant and clothes, and because James had no way of earning money inside, and no family support from outside, he missed out on buying these small luxuries.

"I didn't know his story until well after we started writing. I mean, I knew he was there for murder and I figured it was an inmate he killed. But I didn't know the circumstances. Picture a seventeen-year-old boy, frail, blond hair, blue eyes, going into prison with guys doing life, twenty years. I can only imagine what he went through. If you protect yourself, you get punished. You got to do what you can to survive. You don't get a manual for surviving prison.

"The guy's been in prison all his life; it's just been one heartache after another. He had a hard life growing up, and then straight to prison when he was sixteen; it got even harder.

"I think it's been a wasted life. I mean, they [his mother and father] may have loved him, but I think there's different levels of love. There's parents that just love their kids to death, and that wasn't the case with his mom and dad."

The Mosher family produced bundles of letters and cards for us, sent to them by James, or Jimmy, as they called him. The three children had cards and pictures drawn by him; he wrote to Darrell's wife as "Sis," and he called Darrell "bro," describing him as "the only true brother I ever had," and signing off with "I love you, brother."

The family were filmed sitting round their dining table looking at these cards and letters, written in perfect, child-like handwriting and sometimes illustrated by James. Darrell read out a birthday card: "Darrell, I'm so grateful that God brought you into my life. You're the best friend I ever had, and more than that, you are my brother. The Lord has instilled love inside your heart that shines through. I love you."

A card to Darrell's wife, Naomi, read: "I want to show my appreciation for what a wonderful job you do raising three adorable children, for the sacrifices you make as well as being a loving, nurturing mother."

James's appreciation of a good family life contrasted starkly with his own experience, and in the letters he said several times, "I've never had a family, never had anybody to love, nobody loved me."

The family visited James in December 2016, traveling to Florida State Prison from Tennessee. The time they spent together vindicated James's campaign to get to Death Row: they were with him for two six-hour visits, on a Saturday and Sunday, and James was able to hug them, have his picture taken with them, and hold the youngest child in his arms. On the second day, Naomi and the children left halfway through the visit, so that Darrell and James could have time together without distractions. A photograph of the two of them together shows an uncanny family resemblance.

"I felt it was important for him to meet my wife and kids. I wasn't worried about bringing the kids to meet him. I felt that if I didn't take them I'd be robbing him of something. He was loving with them, just like an uncle. He's never been around kids.

"It was very hard to leave. There was a lot of love shown. I don't know how many times I hugged him, especially saying goodbye. I could see his eyes were watering, but of course he had to hold it back, being where he was."

Darrell believed he'd seen a side of James that others don't see.

"I don't think anybody's ever seen the good side of James. He's been locked up pretty much all of his life, so yeah, I've seen a side of him that nobody else has. He can't show that side in prison, I guess he would be considered weak if he did. You've got to build up an image in there that you're tough. There's no love shown in there, and you can't trust anybody. You go in there and show no tears. I think the love we show him has changed his life. It's like his heart has been softened."

The relationship changed James's behavior.

"He knows that if he gets in a fight or something, he can lose all that he's got: visits, letters, the commissary [where he can buy goods with the money he gets from Darrell]. He's been thinking before he acts now, and that's something he's obviously never done. Love does that," said Darrell.

"I've talked to him about trying to get off Death Row so he has more time to spend with us. But I was being selfish asking for that, as he'd rather be executed than spend another forty years in prison."

Sixty-five days after our first interview with James, when the prison authorities allowed us a second interview, our crew again drove under the arch announcing Florida State Prison, along the drive with well-tended lawns each side, to the low-rise buildings of the prison, searingly white in the Florida sunshine.

At this second interview, we too saw a different side to James. The tension of the first visit, with the angry, emphatic outpouring of his feelings, was gone, and James was calmer and more relaxed, smiling openly. There was a shaky start: Initially it seemed as if he would refuse to do the interview. A prison officer told the crew that James was not prepared to leave his cell because he had not received any follow-up letters from us after the first interview.

We had written to him, but the letters had not gotten through the prison system. Luckily, Ross had copies of them with him, and he was allowed to sit with James in the wide, beige-painted corridor, outside the empty cell designated for filming, while James read them, with the other two members of the crew and a prison officer looking on.

"It was tricky, but when he could see we had been trying to stay in touch, he relented and agreed to be interviewed again," said Ross. "When I talked to him on camera, there was a softness that we had not seen before."

James, who had grown a stubbly beard between the interviews, spoke about the experience of having a newfound family.

"I can't even express in words how good it feels to have somebody that cares about you like that. It's a good feeling."

When Ross asked why he chose Bobby Lynch, who clearly did not like him, as "a friend," James's reasoning was lodged in the very short amount of life he had known outside prison. Bobby, he said, had lived in the same areas of Orlando, and knew some of the people he used to run around with. That had been nearly forty years earlier, and for Bobby there had been life outside prison, but for James it was all he had ever known of a world beyond the razor wire, and he seemed to cherish his few memories.

"How much do you think about the life you didn't get to lead—the life outside?" Ross asked him.

"I don't even really think about it. Man, it's over. I mean that's been over with, I stopped thinking about that a long time ago."

His happiest time, he said, was "just hanging out on the streets. Just wandering around."

Ross thought that the choice of Bobby as a "friend" was not a naive one on James's part.

"James is smart. I think he wanted us to know what he was like, the unvarnished truth. He's not in any denial about how violent he has been, and I think he knew Bobby would tell us."

At this second interview, James stressed that he is happy to face death.

"I've already accepted it, a long time ago, and I don't blame nobody but myself. I'm ready to go. I'm tired of living in humiliation every day. Fuck that. I'm happy.

"You all think that's a big deal, that Death Row... And I'm not going to get real scared when the time comes, I ain't going to be nothing like that.

"There ain't nobody up on a cloud wearing a robe and

saying, 'I'm going to make everything fair.' It ain't like that, man. I got to face the music.

"I look forward to [the execution]. It's like getting a transfer. I already know how it's going to be. I've been doing time here since the eighties. I already know how they do the whole procedure and everything. They come up and put some sort of cast that they wrap around you to keep your arms from moving, because they think you might start struggling or something, which I wouldn't do. Maybe they just do it to sensationalize the whole bit. To make it wild, like strapping them up like Hannibal Lecter. I don't know." He looked straight at Ross and laughed at the comparison with Hannibal Lecter, but it was with a wry, amused expression, unlike the menacing, mirthless laugh of the first interview.

"But I'm OK with it. All they do is shoot a damn needle. I'd rather have a needle stuck in me than be electrocuted…but I could go either way. All that shit you read in the newspapers about how inhumane—that's a bunch of bullshit. I mean, come on, man. They shoot some damn chemical, knocks you out, and puts you to sleep, you don't know what the hell. You aren't feeling nothing."

Ross's conclusion, after spending two hours interviewing James, is that he genuinely wants the death penalty and is, in his own way, happy on Death Row.

"I think he is at peace. The way he explains his decision, it is entirely rational. If you divorce it from the evil of the act, the murder of Frank Hart, it makes sense."

Mark Desisto agreed, and told us he was glad for James to have the chance to die rather than live out his life on CM. Mark is determined to be there when James is executed. He will join a group made up of journalists, relatives of the victim, and other observers.

"I will go, I've wanted to do it from the very beginning," said Mark. "I'm thinking I'll probably be the only friendly face he'll recognize there. I've made a promise to myself that I will definitely go to make sure he does recognize someone on his side was there... someone who allowed him to have what he wants."

With his cousin Darrell re-entering his life, it looked as if there would also be a member of his family there.

"I will definitely be there. He needs somebody there. I don't want to be there, but I know he wants me there," Darrell said. Sadly, since making this promise, Darrell has faced problems in his own life, and he is no longer in touch with James on a regular basis.

So it looks as though Mark, the lawyer who fought for him, will be the only friendly face when James Robertson finally faces the end he has fought for, his execution.

5

PYRO JOE

JOEY MURPHY

"It's something I never intended to do. I wish I didn't do. If there was anything I could do to change it I would, but there's obviously not..."

In his locker at Richland Correctional Institution, a prison in Ohio, Joey Murphy has a fading newspaper cutting taped to the door. It shows the grave of the woman he murdered in 1987, a seventy-two-year-old widow called Ruth Predmore. Tending the grave is Mrs. Predmore's niece, Peggy Kavanaugh. The photo reminds him daily of the woman whose life he took, and also of the woman who helped to save him from the death sentence.

After twenty-three years on Death Row, Peggy Kavanaugh's testimony was a crucial part of Joey's appeal for clemency, an appeal granted in 2011, when, just a few days before he was due to be executed, his sentence was commuted to life imprisonment.

In the film, we were able to use the video of Mrs. Kavanaugh's testimony to the death penalty board. When she talked about meeting the man who killed her aunt, she said: "When I first met Joey I was looking to see a hard-nosed criminal. But when I learned about his past life, and how abusive it was, I steered away from that. Our system has let him down terribly, as it let my aunt down. I feel he is remorseful. I want the board to know how angry I am at the whole system itself and what it has done to my family, and to Joey and his family. It wasn't just Joey on Death Row these twenty-five years, I sat on Death Row and so did my family."

Mrs. Kavanaugh gave evidence that her aunt, who was violently murdered by Joey, would not have wanted him to be executed. She stated that her cousin, Ruth's daughter, who has since died, was also fervently opposed to the death penalty. And she too, as the next of kin, did not want Joey to die for his crime.

Clemency is the final appeal of a condemned man, and it's granted in less than 1 percent of all death penalty cases. It is very rare for it to be granted purely on the basis of extenuating circumstances: appeals are usually based on doubts about the evidence or the legal proceedings at the trial. Joey's was a truly exceptional case. The death penalty is supposed to be reserved for "the worst of the worst."

We wanted to know if this term could be applied to Joey. Was this the right definition for the man who, at the age of twenty-one, savagely slashed the throat of an old woman who had always been kind to him? He was a young man who from the age of six had been housed in seventeen different institutions, and was known to the police as "Pyro Joe" because he was responsible for a spate of fires and had been diagnosed as a pyromaniac by one of the many experts who had been assigned to his case.

What was said with great conviction by several experts who dealt with Joey throughout his troubled childhood was that his *background* was "the worst of the worst," a story of dire poverty, physical, sexual, and emotional abuse, in which a child of with learning disabilities was scapegoated by his whole family. Joey's was a world in which his alcoholic father sold him to be raped at the age of six in return for a fifth of moonshine liquor; a world in which his mother beat him so badly that, frightened of the reaction of his social worker to the scabs and welts on his back, his father tied him down, poured petrol on him, and set his back on fire to hide the abuse.

Joey and his family lived, for most of his impoverished childhood, in Clay County, West Virginia, in a squalid shanty town of tar-paper shacks where, even among dirt-poor neighbors surviving at subsistence level, the family were pitied outsiders. Tar paper is a roofing material made from cardboard waste coated in tar to make it waterproof. For Joey, his parents, three brothers, and one sister, home was a crude, three-room hovel made from a frame of lengths of wood covered with this tar paper, which offers some protection against rain but is not windproof and offers no heat insulation. The shack was freezing cold in winter and too hot in summer.

There was no sanitation. They took water from the creek for cooking on a coal stove and for washing, and large five-gallon drums were littered around the house for the family to use as toilets. The stench of urine and feces was overpowering for outsiders, but the Murphy family were inured to it. Cockroaches, flies, and rats shared their home. Garbage was strewn inside and out, where rusting household appliances lay among burst sacks of trash buried in the encroaching scrubby vegetation.

We were able to find a photograph of the actual shack where the Murphy family lived, which was burnt down before they moved away. The wooden structure is blackened and rotting, the tar paper hangs in tatters, the weeds and bushes are reclaiming the land.

Joey was the third of six children. His mother, Stella,

was fifteen when she became pregnant with the oldest of the siblings, and at seventeen married she Jerry Murphy, the father. She was in a hurry to get away from her own family, where she was one of thirteen children and where, after the death of her father, when she was ten, she felt unwanted. Four years after her son, also called Jerry, was born, she had a daughter, Drema, followed by Joey and his three younger brothers, Deris, David, and Michael.

"They had no income, no plans, no electricity, no gas, no phones," Joey told us when we met him at the prison. He is now a middle-aged, gray-haired man, wearing a prison denim shirt over a black T-shirt. He is softly spoken, and his whole demeanor is gentle and slightly effeminate.

His mother, Stella, was diagnosed with a brain tumor when he was a child, which required frequent hospital treatment. Joey's father, Jerry, was a hopeless alcoholic, with liver damage that caused him to be admitted to hospital several times. He had two nervous breakdowns. During one of them, he climbed on the shack roof, played with the TV antenna to change channels, and went days and nights without sleep or food. After his second breakdown he was diagnosed with schizophrenia and held in a psychiatric unit for some months after suffering hallucinations, probably due to alcohol-induced psychosis.

"The sort of person my father was, if I didn't see him drunk I would think something was wrong with him because I've always known him to be drunk and he was abusive when he was drunk. He didn't care. And then the next day he wouldn't remember."

We were able to interview one of Joey's family members, his youngest brother, Michael, who is six years younger than him. Michael explained he could talk to us because he is no longer in contact with the rest of the fractured family, who have turned their backs on Joey. His father and sister are dead, and so are all four of his grandparents.

"It was important to talk to him because we wanted to present the family's story, not just Joey's version of it," said Ned Parker. "Although he endorses some of Joey's story, he has a different take on aspects of it."

Michael underlined the hopeless alcoholism of their father:

"When he couldn't get no alcohol he would literally go to the bathroom and get a bottle of rubbing alcohol and take a couple of swigs and get sick. But keep drinking it. We could spend a hundred dollars on a microwave and the next day it would be missing—for a two-dollar bottle of wine," Michael said.

Over the years, Jerry and Stella divorced three times, but always remarried. A lot of the friction between them was over Jerry's homosexual relationships, and he lived with the family on and off, disappearing for days at a time on drinking binges. He never worked, and traded the family's food stamps for alcohol. Both he and Stella were keen to keep Joey with them because they received extra welfare payments due to his mental disabilities, which his mother deliberately exaggerated to the authorities.

"My parents would always say I was 'retarded' but I didn't know what it meant. I just thought it was something to do with the way I was but I didn't know what mental retardation was," Joey told us. "My mother was receiving a Social Security check for my retardation. I was never allowed to play with the other kids. My mother told them I was sick and if they played with me or talked to me they would end up sick too. I was always alone."

His earliest memory is of being tied up all day when his brothers and sister went to school.

"My mom would always blame me for her hardship because we had nothing and we were always considered to be bad people. The school bus would have to stop in front of our house to pick up my siblings and they would say the area stank, which it did but we couldn't smell it because we were used to it."

Whether or not it was because he was intellectually slow, Joey became the scapegoat of the family from a very early age. As a baby, when the shack caught fire, his parents escaped with the two older children and went to his grandmother's house. The grandmother reminded them about Joey and they went back for him; luckily he was unharmed. All the children were whipped with belts, extension cords, or switches, but Joey was beaten more than any of them, for minor offenses like his younger brother David spilling milk, for which Joey took the blame. He took the blame for most things that went wrong, and he was regularly beaten two or three times a day. The other children also beat Joey up, and David remembers stabbing a steak knife into Joey's head and thinking it was funny to see it sticking out.

"Our mom used to say Joey was her worst child," said David in a statement for Joey's clemency hearing. "I remember when I was six or seven my father told me not to play with Joey because he was retarded. I did not understand what my father meant."

One of the social workers attached to Joey's case when he was thirteen wrote in her report:

Joey was continually blamed for deeds that his brothers performed and at least on one occasion he was charged with actions of the adults in the family. His family was comfortable not only blaming Joey but also taking the stance that he had always been 'bad' and there was nothing to be done about it. Joey never received the emotional or practical support from his family, and his relatives deny any responsibility for his problems.

Although he was beaten more frequently than his siblings, none of them escaped their father's physical abuse: Jerry would chase his children down the street throwing rocks at them; he chased his oldest son with a hot iron and a scythe; and he held Deris by the hair while he kicked him. David confirmed that Joey always received the worst beating.

"We would all compare welts, but Joey got the worst of the beatings." His mother was still beating Joey when he was twenty years old.

The most shocking instance of abuse came after a particularly savage beating by his mother, which left his back and his legs livid with bleeding wounds. Joey's social worker was due to visit the following day.

"She told my father you have to fix this 'cause she's going to be here tomorrow and she's going to see it and she's going to take Joey away and we won't get his check this month," Joey said. "So my dad said he'd take care of it. And he took me out back and he tied me down to a set of box springs. And after he'd tied me down he put gasoline on my back and set me on fire and I was screaming bloody murder because it burnt so bad even before he set it on fire because the gas was going into the cuts on my back. I just blacked out, I was in so much pain. The next day when the social worker came I was told to sit in the doorframe and don't move."

Joey's case was well known to the social worker, and she

had agreed a code with him that he should wink at her when something was wrong. He winked, and she insisted that he walk back to her car with her.

"She said, 'Come on, honey,' and then I wouldn't get up so she came over and put her arms round me to pull me up and I just screamed out because the shirt was stuck to the burns on my back and the skin just peeled off."

His mother claimed that Joey had backed too close to the stove and set his shirt on fire, and that she was going to take him to the doctor but had forgotten. The medical staff kept him in hospital as long as they could, because they knew he would be going back to his abusive family.

Although the family claim that Joey began playing with fire at the age of three, social workers believe that many of the fires that caused the family to move home several times, exchanging one tar-paper shack for another, were started by his father or other members of the family, but it was easier to blame Joey. It became a self-fulfilling prophecy, because Joey soon developed his own relationship with fire.

"One time my mother was making me clean and I spilled something and she said she was going to whup me. And when she whups you she don't like to stop, so it's really bad and there's blood involved. I accidentally set a stack of clothes on top of the stove because I didn't know the stove was on and it set the kitchen on fire and caught the wall and roof on fire. And here comes a bunch of fire trucks and police; the sirens was going, the lights was flashing, and we had to go stay somewhere else, and I realized that my mother had forgot to beat me. So I learned from an early age, if I set a fire I'm not going to get beat. So a lot of times I would set a fire either to the house or the outhouse or abandoned garage or something in order to escape punishment because that's what I've taught myself to do.

"When I was little it was my rescue. As I was getting older, listening to the fire trucks and police sirens and the lights, it was like relief. Finally someone's here to help. I was sent to an institution and they ran a test on me and said that I was a pyromaniac, which is a person who gets excited by fires, but that wasn't the case at all. No one knew why I really set the fires."

Diagnosed as hyperactive at the age of six, Joey was prescribed Ritalin and other drugs, but his mother gave them to him "upside down," preferring to keep him subdued during the day, then tying him down at night. He slept on the floor, lashed to her bed to prevent him wandering around the house. Through the broken wooden floor of the shack he could see snow and dirt.

"I always thought that was normal for if you have too many kids and not enough beds," he said.

A neighbor remembered him as barely able to talk, but he would turn up at her home and say, "Me hungry," and her mother would feed him. Stella, his own mother, did not include him at mealtimes because she claimed he would be less active if he was starved.

"Sometimes my sister would steal a can of apple sauce from the kitchen and take it up on the hill and bust it open on a rock and feed it to me. My mother would say if we don't feed him he wouldn't have any energy and he would not be able to run around and be hyper. So she'd sometimes go days without feeding me and my sister would try to make sure I didn't die of starvation or something... My sister took care of me."

When he first attended school, teachers reported that he did not have adequate clothing or nutrition, and that he ate "like he was very hungry." He stole vegetables from neighbors' gardens and ate them raw. His family was described by an expert on the area as being "one of the poorest families in one of the poorest counties in the country."

Sexual abuse began when he was five or six.

"The first time I remember it was a man called Al. He made alcohol, he was a moonshiner. And my dad loved going there and getting drunk. He'd give him food stamps for alcohol and get drunk and one day he took me with him. We went to a bus that was abandoned by the road and that's where Al made the moonshine. And my dad took me in the bus and said he wanted some alcohol and Al said he don't have none and my dad said, 'Well I got my son here and you can have your way with him and just give me a jug of alcohol.' So Al took me to the back of the bus where he had a mattress and undressed me and I wasn't thinking anything of it. And then he got undressed and laid me on the mattress and got on top of me and raped me anally. And I was screaming for my dad, 'Please help me, Dad, he's hurting me.' And he'd just sit in his chair drinking his alcohol and act like he couldn't hear me. And then after he grunt like a pig and got off of me, I ran out of the bus and ran home butt naked. And it was about half a mile away.

"And when I got home I was yelling, 'Mom, help me, help me,' and then whenever I got to the house she came out on the porch and I said, 'He hurt me, he hurt me.' Then my mom took me in the house and whupped me cause she thought I was playing in the creek and took my clothes off and got cut by glass and that's why I had blood on my buttocks and the back of my legs."

As well as the moonshiner, Joey was raped by a family "friend" who was hiding from the police in their shack. He was also abused by at least one other older man.

When we played Joey's brother Michael the tape recording of Joey talking to us from prison, Michael disputed some of it. He said he didn't remember Joey being tied to the bed. He confirmed the children all got whipped by their mother.

"But she didn't tie us down or nothing like that. I don't think Mom would do that. I've gotten whipped and I've gotten yelled at but I took it as a punishment. Back then that's how everyone was punished, I guess. A lot of kids didn't get punished, and you can see a big difference in the way they act."

Michael remembered Al, but not Joey being sold to him— he would only just have been born when Joey was six. He said that Joey was conflating two stories:

"I remember Joey telling stories, most of the time they're not true, but there's some truth to it. Dad did take Deris to Charleston and sold him to a whorehouse. Mom found out where he was and got him back. But Joey confused Dad trading Deris for him being traded for wine."

He remembered Joey being on fire, but claimed it was Joey who was responsible, while the rest of the family were in another room.

"Everybody was in the living room, he was in the bedroom. Mom took him to the emergency room. He's been saying that since the trial. That was his defense to get off Death Row."

Michael said that if Joey's account of his childhood were true he would feel even sorrier for him.

From the age of six, Joey was in and out of many different psychiatric and correctional institutions across four different states, never staying long anywhere. He was tested constantly, and always recorded an IQ in the bottom 6 percent of the population, a score which was probably inflated: a more accurate scoring system placed him in the bottom 1–2 percent, with an emotional and developmental age well below his chronological age. He was assessed as exhibiting "borderline mental retardation" and was functionally illiterate.

"When I went to an adult hospital for the mentally ill, that was the first time I've ever seen a real toilet and be able to use it, or a real shower. That was the first time I ever brushed my teeth or washed my face."

A home tutor appointed to visit the Murphy home to teach Joey made three visits and then refused to go again. She reported that while she was trying to teach Joey, the rest of the family were constantly walking through the room and "children were throwing knives into the walls and putting things in the light sockets." When the house burnt down the family moved again and did not tell the school services where they were; Joey's stunted education ended completely.

A social worker who was involved with the family said, presciently, that "until a felony is committed or a family death occurs, it is doubtful that this pathological family will change."

Social workers struggled to find a suitable place to deal with Joey's acutely disturbed behavior. In at least two institutions he was sexually abused by staff members, in one of them on numerous occasions. "Sexual submission became his way of surviving," said a clinical psychologist who later assessed him.

"Joey was moved constantly, placed on and off heavy medications, and was unable to develop roots in either a social or educational sense. Essentially, he was left to survive as best he could within the West Virginia mental health and foster-care systems. He had no positive role models. Most relationships were very brief and based on fear," said his social worker. "Like any person of limited intelligence and social skills, he was easily victimized."

Joey told us about the abuse:

"I was sexually abused whenever I went to the institution. I thought it was something everyone deals with, puts up with. I was happy because they fed me, they clothed me, and I wasn't getting beat every day and I was able to sleep."

Seven months in one facility, Dayton Children's Psychiatric Hospital, was beginning to have a good effect on him: his skills were improving and he seemed to be developing more respect for the feelings of others. But before he could make more progress his father arrived and took him away; the family were desperate for the extra money they received for him.

"Each time I would go home the family would be all happy to see me, but after the social worker would leave, my mother would get all my new clothes and shoes and tell me that I don't need them because I don't go to school, and she'd give them to my siblings and then everything would be back to normal where I was getting beaten, hit every day, and not able to eat and tied down to the bed.

"At one time when my social worker brought me home, we stopped at a store and she bought me a bunch of clothes and a big trunk to keep 'em in. And my mother did what she always does. She got everything and gave it to the other kids so they would look nice going to school. And she put the trunk at the foot of the bed and put me in it. That way she knew I wouldn't be able to get out at night and run around or do anything. And little did she know that was more comfortable than sleeping on the floor."

As Joey told us this story he smiled broadly, recalling this small victory.

He also told us about one of his only "happy" childhood memories, a rare occasion when he rebelled against his mother's treatment of him. One Christmas his grandmother told him that his mother had been saving the Social Security checks she got for him and that she had been shopping to buy gifts for all the family. His grandmother told him to look forward to it.

"So my mother did stack up a bunch of presents under the Christmas tree and it was the first time we had a Christmas tree. And she got to passing out the gifts and she got to the last one, which was a really big one so I knew it was mine. But then she took the top off and it was a TV. She said, 'This belongs to everyone.' I said, 'What about me?' And she said, 'You don't go to school, you don't need none, you're sick.' So it hurt me really bad and I started to cry so hard I could hardly breathe and felt like I was going to pass out.

"I just ran out of the house and she's yelling behind me, 'Joey, get back here. Don't you dare go to your grandmother's and tell her anything.' And that's what I did, I went to my grandmother. And I was crying so hard I couldn't talk."

When his grandmother found out what had happened she went upstairs and came down with a wrapped present. It was a flashlight, and Joey recognized it as one his grandmother had had for years.

"So she forgot too. She wrapped it up just to give to me. And she had a pack of batteries and she said, 'If you ever get lost and need to find your way back to me, this flashlight will lead you.'"

On his way home, Joey opened the back of the flashlight to put the batteries in and found a ten-dollar bill with the words "I love you" written on it. When he got home, his mother told him, "You better go to bed, you're going to get the beating of your life tomorrow. I told you don't go to my mother's house."

Joey spoke back to his mother for the first time in his life. "I walked in and I said, 'Mom, I don't care how much you hate me, how much you starve me, how much you beat me, one day you're going to love me because that's all I want. I want you to love me because I love you.' And I put the ten-dollar bill on her chest and walked out."

He spent the night curled up outside the front door, and the next morning his mother told him to get into the kitchen.

"Then she tells me to sit at the table with the others and we had breakfast together and they was looking at me like: What's going on with Joey? Why's he sitting at the table? Then she gave me her plate and had me sit at her place at the table and she gave me breakfast and that was the first time she ever cooked breakfast for me. And she told the other kids to get ready for school and me and her went shopping with my grandmother."

It was one of Joey's few happy memories, and years later, on Death Row, he drew a picture of the Christmas tree, the flashlight, and the ten-dollar bill.

At one point he was being held in an institution in Colorado, and when he was released his social worker was unable to trace his family. They had moved from their shack in West Virginia to a house in Marion, a city in Ohio, without telling him. He was a teenager, so he was given a bus ticket to Marion and the address, and left to find them. The move was a huge step up for the family: the house had running water, sanitation, and electricity. As his brother Michael said: "We changed worlds."

"We moved to Marion when the house we lived in Caledonia [Clay County] burnt down. Marion was a nice city. Our house had a bathroom in it for the first time. And there was two bedrooms, a living room, a kitchen, and a dining room," Joey said.

It didn't take long for the family to reduce their new home to a dirty hovel. Once again, outside the house became a junkyard of discarded equipment, sacks of trash, cushions bursting open and spilling their stuffing, making it an eyesore among the well-tended small houses on the street. Inside, flies and cockroaches infested the place.

Joey's brother Michael described the house in Marion: "You could open the cupboard and you'd have to wait for the cockroaches to go away before you could reach in for food. It was just that bad... The paint was peeling, the windows were busted, the stairs were busted. The porch was crooked. Cockroaches everywhere. It smelled awful. The basement would flood. We never really had anything. Going to the store and getting a bag of chips and bringing them home and everybody eating them and that's what you had for dinner. If you could find something to eat you were lucky."

Back with his family in their new home, according to Joey four older men began sexually abusing him, a situation he came to regard as normal.

"When we were young and spent time with a particular man, who was a child molester, he would take Joey out back into the bushes," said David. "I did not know why this man was taking Joey into the bushes at the time, but I believe he was molesting Joey."

Joey says his mother knew about the abuse from these men. It wasn't until his trial and his subsequent life on Death Row that "I learned it's not normal."

We spent a long time in Marion, a faded, down-at-heel town, built around industry that declined in the seventies. The center of the city is decaying, as an out-of-town mall has robbed it of retail life. We spent days trying to contact people who had known Joey and his family, or who had known the victim, Ruth Predmore. Most were reluctant to talk to us.

Michael Murphy still lives in the same area of Marion, the front of his house punctuated with seven stars-and-stripes flags, a brindle dog tied on a long leash to his front porch. He took us on a tour of the area, showing us a bar where his front teeth were knocked out in a fight and the neat clapboard house where Joey's victim, Ruth Predmore, once lived.

Michael remembered Joey as "a troubled kid. Stealing or whatever. He'd get sent away, six months at a time. He would catch a fire or he killed a dog. He killed my dog Snoopy, threw it under a truck. Another time he had a dog hanging. He'd get whippings for it. And that didn't do nothing to Joey.

"There was multiple fires going on in Marion, a whole bunch of buildings getting burnt down, and it was all over the newspapers about an arsonist and it turned out it was him. From what was told to me, it was like I liked candy when I was a kid, he liked fire."

When he was eighteen, Joey went to prison for eighteen months on arson charges—he was charged with fourteen counts and pleaded guilty to three. In prison he spent most of his time isolated in his own cell because of disruptive behavior. When he came out he joined up again with his girlfriend, with whom he already had a daughter and later had another child, born at the time of his arrest for murder (his girlfriend later married again, and he has no relationship with them).

Soon after his release, his sister Drema was injured when a car she was traveling in was hit by a train. Marion, like many American cities, has train lines that run through the city without controlled crossings for traffic. According to Joey's account, the whole family, and particularly Drema's husband, believed that she needed better medical care than the local hospital was giving her, but they needed money for her to be transferred to Columbus, the state capital, and if they didn't get it they believed she would die.

"He said we need to go somewhere and do a crash and grab, just steal something and run out, and we agreed that the item should be a VCR. I said I knew someone who I believed had one, I said it was Ruth Predmore, the lady we had done odd jobs for before."

In our first interview, Joey gave us his account of what happened on 1 February 1987, the day of the murder:

"Miss Predmore was a lady that I did odd jobs for down the street from my mother's house. And she was a very nice lady. She was always kind, giving me work to do, and she would pay me a couple of dollars. Sometimes when I was cutting her grass or trimming around the house or cleaning out the water spigot she would come out with a sandwich and a glass of lemonade."

Joey claims he and his brother-in-law hatched a plan to go to the house, and while Joey was trying to get in the front way, Drema's husband would go in the back way. Joey's story has varied over interviews with the police and others who have talked to him since he has been in prison, and his brother-in-law, who is now dead, was never charged with involvement. This is the version he told us at first.

"So we went down to the house and he was trying the back door and I was trying the front. And I was thinking, if she's in she's going to hear us and she might call the police. So I took a knife out of my pocket and went to cut the phone line, but I didn't know what a phone line was and I was cutting the wire to a lightning rod. So when I went back to the door,

Ruth Predmore was there and she said, 'What are you doing? Get away from here.' It startled me and I was scared so I just swung the knife and I closed the door and I ran, and about two hours later I went back. I was walking real slow and scared, not knowing what to expect, and I opened the door real slow and I could see her body lying on the floor. I was scared but I was still in need of helping my sister. So I went on in and proceeded to get stuff that I thought was of value and exit through the back door. Miss Predmore should never have died at my hands. It should never have happened."

On his return to Mrs. Predmore's house, Joey stole a wallet, a credit card, a jacket, a handbag, and a bowl of pennies. The bowl of pennies he took was for a charity collection Mrs. Predmore was managing as treasurer for a philanthropic organization called the King's Daughters and Sons, and amounted to more than a hundred dollars.

In reply to a question about whether he realized Mrs. Predmore was dead when he went back to the house, Joey said, "I could tell that she was, because she had blood around her and her neck was opened up and her glasses were halfway off and she wasn't moving at all."

Joey claimed that his brother-in-law had also been in the house and told Joey not to tell anyone.

Looking at the trial details, and talking to neighbors who knew the family, his brother Michael, and the policeman who investigated the murder, we learned more. Joey did not tell us the whole story: he neglected to tell us about a note he wrote to Mrs. Predmore a few days before her murder. Although functionally illiterate, he was able to scrawl: "You don't have no phone. I want your money. Put it in a bag and put it in your yard or I'll kill you tonite. No money. No life. Tonite at 8.00."

Michael Murphy claimed the note was his idea.

"Joey asked me, 'If you were going to rob somebody, what would you do?' I said I wouldn't do it. I'd just put a note on their door saying give me all your money and leave it in a brown paper bag. That's what he did, and when she didn't he went in and killed her.

"The lady was nice to me. I would mow her yard, shovel her sidewalk, walk her groceries back from the store. She'd pay me. She's like a grandma to me. And when that happened I didn't know how to act. You know, I loved the woman, and my brother did it. So it's kind of hard to deal with. Your brother and someone you considered like a grandmother."

Mrs. Predmore showed Joey's note to a shop assistant at the local store. More evidence that the murder was premeditated came from an assistant at the local petrol station who gave Joey some wrappers for small coins; after the murder, Joey and his brother Michael parceled up the loose change from the charity collection. Joey offered some to his mother for cigarettes, and tried to exchange some at a garage.

Mrs. Predmore's body was discovered the next day by a supervisor for a Meals on Wheels service. One of her delivery staff had reported that Mrs. Predmore did not open the door when they delivered a meal, and when the supervisor checked, the front door was not locked and the body of Mrs. Predmore was sprawled in the hallway.

The first policeman on the scene was Wayne Creasap, now retired. Stockily built, with a large handlebar mustache, when we spoke to him he said that thinking about the case triggered a lot of flashbacks to the sunny February day when he was called to Mrs. Predmore's house, and his account was of a much more brutal murder than what Joey had recounted to us.

"As soon as I walked in the front door I saw the body lying on the floor, an elderly female on her back. It sticks in my mind; I still see her laying there, like a photograph, there forever. This was a very, very horrific crime. I don't feel it is a case where he accidentally tried to harm her. It's apparent that he stood behind her. The cut on her throat was so deep it darn near took her head off, it was just hanging by a thread. So it took a lot of force. And the blood pattern was all over the walls and on the ceiling. She was laying on her back. The top of her dress was soaked in blood.

"Once we started looking round, we knew there was a robbery involved; something was taken but we weren't sure what at this time. Then we determined all the pennies were gone.

"It was senseless. I mean...she didn't have anything to begin with. Small home, she lived there by herself on a pension. You know, she didn't deserve what she received. The name came up real quick. Joe Murphy was well known to the law enforcement community; a lot of the officers referred to him as 'Pyro Joe.' He liked to play with fire. He was known to set small animals on fire. Small-time thief, just liked to get into trouble.

"He was a bad egg as a kid and it got worse as he got into adulthood. He progressively stepped up his criminal acts as he got older. I have no sympathy whatsoever for him. People tried to help him back in the day, tried to help the family, and apparently he just didn't want help. I mean, you have children services involved trying to give guidance, you had his educators from school trying to get him on the right track. There's only so much you can do. He's just a downright troublemaker. I don't believe he's mentally retarded or mentally challenged. I believe he's using this system to benefit him to save his life."

The wallet Joey stole was found in the backyard of a house

between Mrs. Predmore's house the Murphy family home, two blocks away. The credit card was later found in the Murphy house. Joey was arrested at a trailer home belonging to his aunt Cynthia, who still lived in the area of West Virginia where Joey grew up, where he had fled with his girlfriend.

Photographs from the time of the arrest show a slim, small young man with a mop of dark curly hair.

After his arrest, Joey was assessed by a psychologist for his ability to understand the court procedure he faced. When he was asked what he thought would happen if he was found guilty, he said: "Mom says they'll give me the electric chair."

The psychologist concluded that, although Joey had a personality disorder and was unreliable, unpredictable, and would probably be a difficult client for his lawyers, he was competent to stand trial.

One of his defense lawyers from his original trial for murdering Ruth Predmore, Michael Grimes, later recalled the shock of meeting Joey's family before the trial.

"During my many years working on juvenile and custody cases, I have never seen anything like the living conditions of Joey's family. His family was absolutely the most dysfunctional and primitive people I have ever encountered. It was astonishing. The living conditions were appalling. The filth and stench of the home were beyond belief. A wall in the basement, where Joey's sister Drema stayed, appeared to move when I saw it. Once someone turned on the lights it became clear that the movement was actually cockroaches that had completely covered the wall.

"Joey's father was a staggering, unintelligible drunk. Joey's mother, Stella, was pure evil. She would often direct Joey to commit crimes. It was astonishing to me that Joey had ever been released back into the custody of his parents. I think about Joey and his case often."

Linda Richter was a mitigation specialist who at the time worked for the state public defender's office and was assigned to Joey's case. Her job was to investigate Joey's background and the extenuating circumstances that could, in some way, explain his crime, which would be presented to the court before he was sentenced. Like all the experts we talked to about Joey, she recalled him and his family vividly.

"He needed a lot of help to understand what was happening. He would hear something on the news and become very upset or distraught and we would have to explain what was going on. He really was a weird boy. His personality was like a twelve-year-old; he had trouble expressing his thoughts coherently, and he was very anxious about what was happening.

"Joey's was probably one of the most impoverished and emotionally sterile backgrounds I had come across. Even in retrospect, after many years doing this kind of work, it was a mind-blowing experience to see that individuals lived in this kind of situation. They had many factors working against them, Jerry's alcoholism, impoverishment, drug and alcohol abuse that was rampant in the family. Joey was psychiatrically damaged from an early age. He was known to start fires, to torture animals. But he could also be kind and loving."

The Murphy family resented Linda and her colleagues probing Joey's background.

"They cared what people thought. They were very, very angry with him, putting their family in the spotlight in Marion. We'd arrive at ten in the morning and Jerry was drunk, Stella was chasing children around, the cleanliness of the house was awful: cockroaches, animals, animal feces. It smelled. And this was in Marion, a step up from how they lived in West Virginia."

Linda and a colleague drove to Clay County to see the Murphy's old home and to visit Joey's grandmother, who still lived in a tar-paper shack. They took photographs to show the jury, including one of the burnt-out shack where the family had last lived, which we used in the documentary.

"We're talking of poverty that I have never experienced in my lifetime."

Linda is used to dealing with clients who have been sexually abused, but Joey's father selling him for a jug of wine was the most depraved thing she had ever heard. When she listened to a recording of Joey telling us about the incident she said:

"I've heard this story before and it makes me just as sad as it did the first time. I can't imagine feeling so betrayed and so helpless by the one person in your life who's supposed to be there to protect you and love you and keep you safe. As a child, your sense of safety and humanity is shattered... I don't know how anyone at that young age goes through that kind of violent act and then relates to the world normally. The world is a hostile, mean, scary place.

"The psychologists who worked with Joey thought the amount of rage he was exhibiting, setting fires and killing animals, meant that he most likely had been sexually abused and that the fuel for a lot of that rage spills out into these kind of impulsive and not-well-thought-out murders."

After reporting on his background to the jury, Linda was devastated when, after only eight hours' deliberation, the death penalty was pronounced.

"We worked really hard. I thought Joey had done a terrible thing, but I did not think he was the worst of the worst. His

David Barnett

Rita Reams, who fostered David as a child
and was one of the few caring adults in his childhood.

Secil, who was also fostered by John Barnett, and had a child with David.

Charles "Chuck" Thompson talking to us from Deah Row at the Polunsky Unit in Texas.

The room where Chuck shot both his ex-girlfriend
Dennise Hayslip and her new boyfriend Darren Cain.

Linda Couch as she serves her sentence in
the Ohio Reformatory for Women.

Linda's older daughter Roxanne at her home in Ghana, West Africa.

Linda's husband and victim, Walter Couch.

Pat Dinkelacker, one of the prosecutors on Linda's case.

James Robertson on Death Row. He has been in prision since he was sixteen, and campaigned to get himself onto Death Row

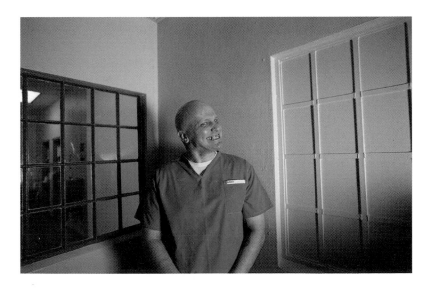

Robertson (right) as a child.

Mark Desisto, Robertson's lawyer, who was pivotal in helping him secure his wish of being put on Death Row.

Joseph Murphy, whose childhood was
described as "the worst of the worst."

The tar paper shack where Joey lived growing up.

Joey *(middle)* with his parents on his birthday in 1970.

Joey's brother Michael.

Joey with Kathy Sandford, whose work was instrumental in getting Joey removed from Death Row.

Kenneth Foster, who drove the car on the night of the murder of Michael Lahood Jr.

Nico Lahood,
brother of the victim,
and at the time of the
photograph the
District Attorney
for Bexar County.

A girl holds a banner
at a protest march
for the successful
campaign to get
Kenneth off
Death Row.

Kenneth's devoted grandfather with a picture of his grandson.

Brandon Hutchison, who finally told the truth.

Michael Salazar, who, like Brandon,
was also given a life sentence without parole.

Michelle, Brandon's ex-wife, who remained
in his life until his death from cancer.

Deandra Buchanan, who killed his girlfriend
and two close members of his family.

Cavona Flenoy, serving a long sentence for shooting a
man she claims was trying to have sex with her.

Kate Webber, who led Cavona's ultimately unsuccessful bid to overturn the decision that prevented her from withdrawing her guilty plea.

Eric Zhand, the prosecutor in Cavona's case.

Stacey Lewis, Cavona's mother who has
supported and fought for her throughout.

Charles 'Billy' Armentrout, who has found a better life in prison.

Billy's stepsister Wendy and stepmother Mary,
who remember his difficult childhood.

Rubin Haman, one of the detectives who arrested Billy.

background was so atrocious. I thought he needed to be in prison, but taking his life was victimizing him one more time."

It was during the trial that Joey first realized that his childhood was abnormal.

"I found that it wasn't normal that my parents were making me sleep at the foot of the bed like a dog. It's not right. And now I'm going to be sentenced to death not even knowing what a real family is like."

His understanding was so limited that when the death penalty was pronounced he thought he would be taken straight out to the back of the courthouse and shot.

The statistics are against Joey ever having a trouble-free adult life: children raised in poverty are twice as likely to be violent in their adult life as other children, and children raised by parents with a substance-abuse problem are twice as likely to be violent toward other children. Children who are sexually abused are three times more likely to commit violent crimes as adults. Almost 80 percent of children who are physically abused and see other members of the family abused, and who grow up in a climate of fear and hostility, go on to be seriously violent themselves.

As one of the many psychologists who evaluated Joey over the first twenty years of his life reported: "He needs a long-term setting where strong external controls to his behavior are present and from which he can learn and internalize such controls to enhance his self-regulation."

Eventually Joey found just such an environment: Death Row.

"I was kind of happy to be on Death Row because I was treated better than I was at home. But I wish it wouldn't have took a victim to get me sent here. I pray to her every day and ask God to watch over her soul, and I know she is watching over and seeing me as well."

After a few years on Death Row, Joey became a committed Christian, working with the clergy of a local church and establishing a good relationship with an older woman in the church who he called "Mom" and who visited and kept in touch with him. He also joined an interdenominational prison faith group called Kairos (a Greek term for "God's special time'), which involves talks, meditation, music, and prayer. He took lessons in stress management, and with help his reading and writing improved.

He was dealt a serious blow when his sister Drema, who had tried to feed him and showed him some affection when he was a small child, was killed in a motorbike accident in July 1994. She was the passenger on a bike that slid under a truck and was dragged along the road. Drema was no longer with her husband, and after her death her four children were split up between different homes. Joey's family, who had visited him a handful of times, cut off all contact after Drema's accident. Joey believes she was on her way to visit him, and so the family blame him for her death.

By the time of his clemency appeal, Joey had been through two state court appeals, a federal court appeal, and a petition to the United States Supreme Court, all of which he lost. After this final rejection, the date for his execution was set, and that's when Kathy Sandford, Pam Prude-Smithers, and their colleagues in the public defender office started work on the clemency appeal, Joey's last chance to avoid execution.

With fifteen large boxes full of paperwork on Joey's background, reports from social workers and institutions that dealt with him, his original trial, and his failed appeals, it was a gargantuan task. They worked hard assembling an impressive list of supporters for Joey's case.

For us, getting Kathy Sandford to agree to talk was key to the film being made.

"We realized there had been such a huge amount of work done by her office. Without her, it would have been virtually impossible to tell Joey's story, not just for her insight, but because of the various other people who would not have spoken to us unless she was on board. All the reports and evidence we have about his awful background came from Kathy's files."

We explained to her that the film would not be judgmental and would not shy away from presenting the other side of Joey's story, notably his brother Michael's contradictions and Wayne Creasap's vivid recollections of a horrendous murder.

Most appeals are based on doubts about the guilt or innocence of the condemned prisoner, but Kathy, who met up with us in a park in Marion, said:

"In this case there was no guilt or innocence question, we were not trying to get him a new trial. We were trying to get him a new sentence. There is no doubt that Joey committed the murder... This was a unique case because our sole focus was on the mitigation, not the crime or problems in prior court hearings. We try to explain how the situation came to happen, and with Joey it was the nature of his upbringing and the fact that he is lower in cognitive functioning and doesn't have particular skills with coping. I do believe that someone with that background cannot be judged by the same standards as someone [else] who doesn't. There is a difference there."

Kathy was surprised that Joey had been given the death sentence at his original trial. She was not convinced that they would get the result they wanted, especially after evidence of his early life had been presented at the trial and in the earlier appeals process.

"We started work about eight to ten months before the execution date, which was October the 18th, 2011. What struck me about Joey the first time I met him was his childlike nature. He was thirty-two when I met him and seemed much more like a twelve-year-old. He was very nice and polite but had childlike mannerisms. He called me often, and I felt like I was his link to the outside world and that he hadn't had someone he could trust and rely on ever, really. And that person, I think, became me. And so I tried to do everything I could to instill trust in him. He was very remorseful about the crime. If he could take it back, he would in a heartbeat."

Kathy knew that a letter from Ruth Predmore's daughter, opposing the death penalty, had been presented at the original trial but had no effect. The daughter, Helen Napper, who had since died, wrote to the court: "I oppose the imposition of the death penalty in this case and believe that justice would best be served by the defendant being sentenced to a term of life in prison without eligibility for parole for a period of thirty years." (At the time of the trial, the sentence of life imprisonment without parole did not exist in the Ohio courts.)

Kathy remembered reading a newspaper interview in which Mrs. Predmore's great-niece, Peggy Kavanaugh, claimed she had never heard from Joey and did not know if he was remorseful about the killing.

"I kept it. And when we had a date for the execution and the clemency hearing I reached out to her. I thought it was incredible that she wanted to meet with Joey and give him a chance to explain to her what had happened and talk about his life with her."

A meeting was set up under the Offender and Victim Family Dialogue scheme run in Ohio prisons.

"And they met, I believe, for three hours. I think when she went into the meeting she was still favoring the death penalty but when she left she said she supported clemency," said Kathy.

Joey described the meeting to us, his eyes welling with tears:

"When I went into the room there was a lot of people sitting at a long table and there was a real quietness in the room. And it seemed to take forever to walk up to the table. She told me who she was and I told her who I was. The hardest question I was asked was why, and that was a very tough question to answer. And it brought on tears from her and me.

"It ended up being very tearful and emotional... I told her that if that's what you want to happen [my execution], I hope you get it. And I just started crying and she started crying and she said, 'Honey, we forgave you a long time ago. Your parents should be locked up, not you. Can we please hug him?' And the warden gave her permission to hug me. She put her arms round me and she said:, 'I love you, honey, and I don't want to see you die.' It was a true, honest, forgiveness hug. And that made us both cry even more."

Kathy believes that presenting Peggy Kavanaugh's testimony was a very powerful part of the appeal for clemency. "There is definitely a chance that had we not presented this to the parole board, he may have been executed. She definitely either saved or helped to save the life of the person who took the life of her aunt... She was shocked and horrified at the life Joey had to endure growing up and with his family."

The video of Mrs. Kavanaugh supporting the appeal for clemency was only received the night before the hearing. In it she stressed, "The system has failed Joey. It also failed my aunt."

Kathy also assembled an impressive list of testimonials in support of clemency for Joey.

"I did not know if the victim's niece agreeing with Joey receiving clemency would be enough. That's why we presented a multifaceted approach. It was twenty-four years after the crime and it struck me as very unusual that everyone agreed to be involved. It completely shocked me. I think his background struck so many people as unique, and in a horrible way. I remember thinking when I read about his upbringing that if he was executed I didn't know if I would be able to continue doing this work, because I thought there is no real justice then."

One of three supreme court justices who voted against the death penalty at Joey's original trial (the vote was carried by a narrow majority of one) joined in the appeal for clemency. Retired judge Herbert Brown said:

"The discussion in death penalty cases often centers around whether a crime can be considered 'the worst of the worst' and therefore eligible for the most severe sanction. In this case, however, I have no doubt that instead it is Mr. Murphy's childhood and background that are the worst of the worst."

Two of the original jurors from the murder trial came forward to support Joey's appeal for clemency.

Notably absent from Joey's appeal for clemency were all members of his family, with the exception of his brother David, who was himself in prison at the time of the appeal, and his aunt Cynthia.

"I do not want Joey to die. I love Joey and would miss him," David said. "I felt sorry for Joey because our parents never showed him any love. Joey was raised unfairly and the people in his life were not good people… Our mom was always money hungry. Joey and I would go through the Good Will boxes in Marion and steal things. We would take clothes and accessories and bring them home to our mom. She would go through the bags of stolen stuff and take out what she wanted. She never disciplined us or told us it was wrong to steal."

One of the mitigation specialists working with Kathy Sandford, Angela Wiley, went to the Murphy home in Marion, Ohio, and spoke to a man sitting outside while three or four children played in the yard. The man confirmed he was Jerry, Joey's older brother, but when he heard why Angela was there he said: "We do not want to talk to you." Stella, Joey's mother, confirmed this, ranting at Angela and shutting the door in her face.

Joey's grandmother agreed to see Angela, but at the last minute she pulled out, and there was a note pinned to her door stating that she wanted nothing to do with anyone inquiring about Joey.

Joey himself, whose reading and writing skills had improved while in prison, wrote to the parole board:

"I did something really bad. I took the life of Mrs. Ruth Predmore. I'm so very sorry and wish it didn't happen. Many times in my life I've wish that I could live that day over so that it wouldn't of happen… I still pray and ask Mrs. Ruth for Forgiveness and I'm still very sorry For what I did. Last month I came face to face with Mrs. Ruth Predmore's Niece name Mrs. Peggy Kavanaugh. We talk for three hours and we both cryed so many tears and she Forgives me."

Addressing the parole board on Joey's behalf, Pam Prude-Smithers said that he deserved mercy because of the chaos and abuse of his upbringing and the fact that he is borderline mentally disabled.

"His father was a raging alcoholic, his mother was an abusive and ineffectual parent. There were no sexual boundaries in the home. At one point Joey's father was having sex with his wife's brother and was also having sex with his daughter's husband. Joey's life was so outside the bounds of what we consider normal that it is shocking."

His appeal was opposed by the Ohio Attorney General's Office, represented by Brenda Leikala. She said:

"I don't discount that he had a bad childhood. I'm not going to say that he had a good childhood at all, because he didn't. He grew up in an impoverished area. However, not everyone who grew up in Clay County, West Virginia, turned out to be murderers."

She countered the fact that Mrs. Predmore's niece, Peggy Kavanaugh, supported the plea for clemency by producing a letter from another great-niece of the victim, Tonya Kardosh. It read:

"The damage has been done and it's obviously irreversible. I believe it is now time to pay the punishment ordered by the state of Ohio. Joseph Murphy has asked for forgiveness. But I believe God will have to make that call."

When we asked Kathy how she felt about the assertion by the prosecutor that Joey's siblings came from the same background but have not committed murder, she said:

"They didn't have the same treatment that he did. He was the scapegoat. He was the one tied to his parents' bed. He was the one sexually abused by various people... They didn't have his low-functioning mental abilities. Joey was born with less than they had and he was treated worse than they were growing up."

Joey's appeal was for a new sentence of life without parole, meaning that he would spend the rest of his life in prison. Just twenty-two days before he was due to be executed, the Ohio governor, John Kasich, commuted his sentence to life without parole. His statement read:

"Joseph Murphy's murder of Ruth Predmore was heinous and disturbing and he deserves—and continues to receive— severe punishment. Even though as a child and adolescent Murphy suffered uniquely severe and sustained verbal, physical, and sexual abuse from those who should have loved him, it does not excuse his crime.

"After examining the case with counsel I agree with Chief Justice Moyer, the National Association of Mental Illness, and the Parole Board's unanimous 8–0 decision that considering Joseph Murphy's brutally abusive upbringing and the relatively young age at which he committed this terrible crime, the death penalty is not appropriate in this case. Thus I have commuted his sentence to life in prison with no chance of parole. I pray for peace for all who have been impacted by this crime."

Joey heard the news from a prison warden.

"He said, 'Murphy, I've got some news. The governor granted clemency.' I almost just wanted to fall down and start crying, and he said, 'Murphy, I don't want no hug,' and I said I wasn't going to hug him."

Kathy Sandford and her colleagues were elated, and when Joey called they were all in tears. For Kathy, the wait had been tense.

"I had complete last-minute nerves, and the night before the parole board recommendation came out I called one of the other team members and said, 'What if we're completely wrong and they decide against Joey receiving clemency?'

So I had a very sleepless night. And when we got the phone call and they unanimously recommended clemency we were beyond thrilled. And then Joey called and he was in tears on the phone."

After being granted clemency, Joey now faces life in prison without any prospect of parole. He accepts it, and knows that his case will never be reviewed again.

"Whatever happens in here, it's better than it was at home. I'm glad to be within the prison system," he said.

"It's sad to think that he is happier in this place that he will never walk out of, and will die in, than anywhere else in his life," said Ned. "He has virtually no adult memories or experiences, nothing else to relate to. Yet he's comfortable with his life."

Kathy Sandford thinks the sentence is right. "Joey's not someone who could function in society if he was given that opportunity. He just doesn't have the coping skills."

Despite his victory getting off Death Row, his family have still not been in touch.

"I wrote to them. I sent her [his mother] more letters and cards at Thanksgiving and Christmas, but she didn't write back. I love my mother to death and I always will. But it seems she's upset that I wasn't executed... It saddens me because I still love my family very, very much.

"I've talked to psychologists and therapists since I've been incarcerated and they tell me it's not normal to continue to love them. But just as what I did was terrible, my family deserve my forgiveness and my love. That's why I continue to write to them even though I get no response and some letters come back marked 'Return to Sender.'

"I have received more love and compassion from the

victim's family member, Peg Kavanaugh, than I have from my family during my entire existence."

The move from Death Row to being part of the general prison population was "mind-rattling" for Joey at first. After more than two decades alone in a cell, he found himself with a cellmate and housed in a unit with dozens of other prisoners.

"It was kind of hard being around a bunch of people... It's hard getting used to the noise," he said. "I would feel like hyperventilating because there's so many people around me that's talking at the same time. But I've managed to get past it. Now I can look at the sky. Now I have a life. I have adapted to prison, and I accept my punishment. I was given a chance and I'm doing everything to make that chance count for something and do something constructive and meaningful. Making friends with inmates and understanding their problems, trying to help."

When we met him, several years later, he was used to this relative freedom. At our second meeting, ten weeks after the first, he appeared relaxed and happy, with a small black-and-white cat which he had on a long lead, and which settled happily on his shoulders, nuzzling the back of his neck.

"This is the dorm cat, Duff. We named him after Andy Dufresne, in *The Shawshank Redemption*, also known Duff as a nickname. He was found when he was four days old almost frozen to the ground with three other kittens. One died and his two sisters were adopted. The person in charge of supervising animals with inmates said we could take care of him. He's a real comfort to have around. He likes to sit around my neck. I walk him every day and we play around in the yard. A lot of people relieve stress and anger playing with him. It's comforting to watch him playing in the grass or chasing birds."

At this second meeting we challenged Joey about not telling us the whole story, especially about the note he delivered to Mrs. Predmore demanding money. He didn't flinch from telling us about it.

"I was riding my bike up and down the sidewalk trying to find odd jobs and couldn't find none. So I thought I would write a note saying put money in a bag in your yard. But it didn't happen. I know it looks bad, and I admitted I wrote it and I admitted I did go to the house a few days later and did what I did."

We also told Joey that, after looking into his case, Ruth Predmore's injuries seemed to be far more severe that those caused by simply lashing out.

"It's probably because it was a brand-new knife, that I had stolen from my brother's collection... There was a lot of blood. She had bled out and it was the worst thing I have seen in my life."

We also confronted him with the discrepancies between his account of his childhood and his brother Michael's. Joey repeated that his stories were true. He agreed that Deris had also been sold by their father for alcohol.

He said the stories about him being cruel to animals were part of his mother's claim for the welfare check.

"My mother would tell people I was very destructive, not only fires but other stuff: I was very hyperactive and killed my dog, animals around the house. It was my mother's way of letting doctors see that something was wrong with me. Then you're going to get Social Security for having a sick child. And by telling stories my mother was able to receive more than three hundred dollars a month, which was a lot of money to a family like ours."

We interviewed Dr. Michael Gelbort, a clinical neuropsychologist, who had done an earlier evaluation of Joey and who gave written evidence for the defense at the clemency appeal.

"The circumstances in which Joey grew up are way, way different from what most people experience... It's unimaginable what he went through. It's hard to relate to it. You can hear the words but it doesn't make any sense. We all expect adults to act like adults, while some adults are unable to act like normally functioning adults because something has happened, either an injury that affects their brain or because of emotional deprivation growing up.

"He was a fire setter, which is probably an outgrowth of the treatment he received from the family... He didn't have a perspective to recognize the abuse. His experience was that this is what my mom and dad do...what I'm experiencing is what most people experience, the life I'm leading is what most people do... It's hard to hold him to the same standard as people who have not had such an aberrant and strange upbringing.

"It's not a matter of whether we feel sorry for the individual. Maybe he didn't have the ability, based on his upbringing, the capacity to do better than he did. I am of the opinion that we come into this world as blank slates and the training we have from those around us.

"I became involved because Kathy Sandford wanted an assessment of how Joey functions. He'll pass the test, he can look reasonably normal, but in terms of nuance, subtlety, dealing with complex issues, if you lined up a hundred people from smartest to least intelligent, he would be way at the back of the line.

"This is not a psychopath. This is not someone who is out

to kill people. This is someone who was a victim himself. It's not that his background made him kill anyone, it's not that anyone who has his background will kill. But they have less opportunity to stay out of trouble. They're closer to the edge. And some of them fall over the edge. He fell over the edge."

When we interviewed Dr. Gelbort, he discussed the discrepancy between Joey's and Michael's accounts of childhood in the Murphy home.

"Often people tell you a story that is other than absolutely true. As a psychologist I never believe what people say as being absolutely true. It is always shaded by our memory. Our emotional needs and our cognition and emotionality enter into how we remember different things. Everything that Joey said, I'm not going to believe hook, line, and sinker. On the other hand, it was consistent enough... I suspect that by and large it is accurate. I'm comfortable saying that the history of abuse he relates is pretty much on target. It would be one thing if Joey's brother said that never happened, that his father would never do such a thing. But the fact that the brother says it happened, just not to Joey. He's establishing that the father is the sort of person who could do such a thing. Michael was remembering it happening to a different brother. Who's to say it didn't happen to Joey too?"

Kathy Sandford is still a friend for Joey, and he keeps in touch with her.

"She's like a big sister for me. She's the greatest," he said.

"I'm still a link to the outside world for him, I believe," Kathy said. "He asks me about other inmates on Death Row who he was friends with for a long time and what's going on with their cases.

"I don't think you can represent someone for so long as

Joey Murphy and not care about them. I care about his well-being. I want him to do well in prison. Just be the best person he can be. Since he left Death Row, he has gotten tougher and he can take care of himself now."

Peggy Kavanaugh, the woman whose appeal on Joey's behalf probably did more than anything to save his life, continued to write to him until her death in 2016.

Joey has never seen the film we made about him, but he has heard about it and is pleased with the letters and emails of support he has received. For us, the email we received from Kathy Sandford saying that the film vindicated her faith in the production's values was a good moment.

We felt the history of abuse made Joey's story different from the others we examined, and it was clear before we met him that this was a case we could get behind; not in a campaigning way, and not taking away from the facts of the murder or the negative aspects of Joey's character, but we felt we could celebrate the fact that he is no longer on Death Row.

6

KILLER IN THE EYES OF THE LAW

KENNETH FOSTER

"I've learned a lot about the LaHoods. The father was a good man, from everything I've learned about the family. The father had three boys, Michael Junior, Nicholas, and a younger brother. I learned Michael had a lot of potential that was cut short. I understand from his family's perspective they kind of view me as responsible. There's a point I had to come to in my life when I realized I put myself in this position."

Kenneth Foster's execution, for the murder of Michael LaHood Jr., was six hours away. He shared an emotional goodbye meeting with his father and grandfather. Refusing to walk to the prison vehicle that would take him to the execution unit, he lay down on the floor and was manhandled on to a stretcher by a phalanx of guards wearing riot gear. As the hour of his death approached, family and friends were driving to the prison where they would witness him being killed by lethal injection. So too were the brothers of the victim.

Inside Huntsville Unit, the Texas State Penitentiary building that houses the busiest death chamber in the United States, preparations were well under way for Kenneth's final journey. In his last permitted phone call, his elderly grandfather refused to say goodbye, buoyed even then by the hope of a last-minute reprieve. But as the old man drove toward the prison, the clock was ticking inexorably toward the hour of his grandson's death by lethal injection.

Nico LaHood and his younger brother, Marc, were also

on the road, making the four-hour journey from their homes in San Antonio to witness the second of the men convicted of murdering their older brother go to his death.

With the time ticking away until Kenneth was due to be taken to the chamber, cell phones began to ring in both cars. Newspaper and television journalists were on the lines: had they heard that a reprieve had been granted by the governor of Texas, Rick Perry? There had been no official contact, and even a call to the Huntsville Penitentiary by Lawrence Foster, Kenneth's grandfather, was not reassuring. Officials had not been notified of a reprieve. Both cars carried on in the direction of the jail until finally the media story was confirmed: Kenneth Foster was not going to die that day.

On what was to be the last day of his life, his sentence was commuted to life in prison with no possibility of parole before he has served forty years.

For Kenneth, the news was delivered brusquely by a prison officer, and within ten minutes he was on a prison bus taking him away from Huntsville to be reprocessed back into the prison system, no longer a Death Row inmate. In prison for more than ten years, he described that day in 2007 as the moment the second half of his life began.

His reprieve was due in large part to a campaign on his behalf, with protest marches, international support, and posters proclaiming "Wrong Time, Wrong Place" and "Sentenced to Death for Being a Driver." The campaign was part of a bigger movement to outlaw all executions across the United States, and Kenneth Foster became the face of the crusade in Texas and a very vocal promoter of his own cause. It dovetailed with the campaign to change the Texas law of parties, which essentially means that an associate at the scene is as responsible for the crime as the person who actually commits it if they know that a crime is likely to be committed.

There was one fact that everyone, including the prosecution, the victim's family, and the campaigners, agreed on: Kenneth Foster did not fire the gun that was used to shoot Michael LaHood in the face from close range, killing him instantly. Kenneth Foster was seventy feet away, behind the wheel of a white Chevrolet rental car. He drove the murderer, Mauriceo Brown, away, then found himself in the dock to be tried alongside Mauriceo and was sentenced to death at the same trial as him. Despite the protestations of the defense, the jury agreed with the prosecution case that Kenneth knew that his friend was armed and was likely to use the gun, making him guilty of capital murder.

On the night of the murder, in the early hours of 15 August 1996, Mauriceo and Kenneth were not the only two in the car driving around San Antonio. Next to Kenneth, who was nineteen at the time, in the front passenger seat was Julius Steen, twenty. In the back were Mauriceo Brown and Dewayne Dillard, both also twenty. Dewayne was on bail for the murder of a taxi driver two weeks earlier. Julius also had pending charges. Kenneth had been given a deferred adjudication (probation) for shooting at another car and seriously injuring two of the people in it just two years earlier. The night had already involved robbing four other people at gunpoint, three of them women. It was not, as a brother of the victim later said to us, "a Sunday school outing."

Yet the whole case against Kenneth revolved around whether he knew Mauriceo was carrying out another gunpoint robbery and would shoot if he was provoked, or did he genuinely believe that Mauriceo was just chatting up an attractive woman: in Kenneth's words, "just goofing around, he liked to flirt." As his devoted grandfather Lawrence put it, Kenneth was sentenced to death because the jury at the trial believed he was psychic.

"Is he a fortune teller? Is he someone that could predict the future of an individual just by observing him? No... It's the one that commits the crime that should be punished," Lawrence said, emphatically.

Kenneth's case, taken up by campaigners against the death penalty, became a cause célèbre because he was condemned to death under this controversial law of parties.

We wanted to explore with Kenneth, his supporters, and those who thought the death penalty was justified in his case, including the victim's family, how much he knew and how much he could be expected to assume about Mauriceo Brown's behavior that night.

For us, three people were crucial to the narrative: Kenneth, his grandfather Lawrence, and, very importantly, Nico LaHood, the brother of the victim.

"It took a lot of conversations to get Nico on board, and I'm not sure that without him we could have told the story," Ned Parker said. "All three of these men are complex and interesting people, and we needed to hear the story from their perspectives."

Kenneth Foster was born disadvantaged: both his parents were drug addicts and met each other at a drug rehabilitation center. His mother worked as a prostitute to fund her habit, and she was jailed just a few months after Kenneth was born; his father went to prison two years later. They lived a chaotic lifestyle, sometimes together, sometimes apart, and the young Kenneth was dragged from home to home across Texas. On at least one occasion, he saw his mother perform a sexual act on a man for money to fund her habit. She eventually died from AIDS three years before her son's murder charge.

"The beginning of my childhood was real rough, you know, bouncing around from family to family. When I had time with my father, that was on his terms, watching him shoot drugs."

There was, though, a constant in his erratic young life: his grandparents on his father's side, Lawrence and Elise Foster. His grandfather was a schoolteacher for thirty years in San Antonio, a sprawling city in Texas, where prosperous suburbs nudge alongside violent areas, which had earned it the nickname "Drive-By City,' because it had the highest number of drive-by shootings in the States. Lawrence and his wife tried regularly to intervene to keep the young Kenneth safe. He lived with his grandparents for a few months when he was three, attending the local kindergarten, but then his mother insisted on taking him back to Austin with her.

"I had no legal papers to adopt him, so I gave him back to her," said Lawrence, talking to us from his neat home, the walls lined with family photographs, where there was a pile of albums full of pictures of the little boy whose memory he cherishes. "He moved in and out with her to Dallas and Austin, he did not attend school regular, and failed his early grades. They lived in her mother's house, and there was a number of individuals living there, and I would say ninety or ninety-five percent of them were drug users or doing something else not legal.

"I can't remember if it was because she got incarcerated, but I asked them to let him stay with me when he was about nine. I went to Dallas and picked him up. I got him doing really well in school; he was studying, doing his work. For some reason he wanted to be a policeman, would you believe."

Kenneth started to mix with the wrong crowd when he was a teenager, and his grandparents struggled to guide him away from those friends. There were run-ins with the law over marijuana. He finished high school but dropped out of college, and his girlfriend and baby daughter moved in with his grandfather (his grandmother had died). He wanted a career in rap music and was busy putting together a band at the time of the murder. When we talked to him inside the Mark W. Stiles Unit, a maximum-security prison in Texas, he did not try to use his background to explain his crime. Sitting in a sparse cubicle in an empty visits room, he was articulate, friendly, and very driven to present his own story: "For me to sit here and say I didn't have opportunities would be wrong. I'd be telling a lie if I said I didn't have opportunities... I've had to struggle with that, because you have individuals that grew up in the ghettoes, dirt poor, and my grandparents tried to rescue me from that and I didn't make good on it. They deserve better than what I did.

"My teenage years were probably better than a lot of people's. My grandparents did their best to get me through school and to provide for me. Unfortunately, on the other side of the coin, when I had time with my father, that time was spent on his terms, which was him going to the store stealing to support his habit, being in drug houses, watching him shoot drugs... Sometimes he'd try to teach me how to be a better criminal when I was just a child... Of course that's not good for a young boy coming up, because on the one hand I have my father setting a bad example, and then I have my grandparents that's trying to set a good example. So both sides influenced me.

"Other relatives had been in and out of prison; these things were influencing me, causing me to choose the wrong kind of friends, smoking marijuana or drinking, and of course those things lead you down a certain kind of path... I had the good side that was thriving, liked to go to school, liked learning, wanted to have a career, but I had other things that were digging at me.

"My grandparents were always upset if I got in trouble and there was something inside me that felt bad because I was letting them down."

But being upset for his grandparents was not enough to keep him out of trouble. He had drug convictions, he'd been a member of a street gang, and two years before the murder he shot a gun through the window of his car, seriously injuring two of the occupants of another vehicle, the crime for which he was put on deferred adjudication.

Kenneth said that it was his involvement with music that brought him into contact with the other three who were in the car on the night of the murder, and that they were helping him find new members for his band. He was driving a white Chevrolet Cavalier that his grandfather had rented for him when his own car was involved in a crash.

"The night in question we were hanging out, smoking, drinking, and kind of club-hopping, we wanted to see different clubs... So as we were driving, one of the occupants asked if maybe we wanted to pull a jack move, which is a kind of run-up on somebody and it's basically a robbery, under the law it's a robbery... I chose to participate, I said OK. I fell to peer pressure. So the night began with me stopping the car, and Julius and Mauriceo, on two different occasions, exited the car and hooked somebody up, grabbed their purse or their wallet."

Their first victim was a waitress going home after her shift in a coffee shop, who was pistol-whipped with the gun, a .357 Magnum, that was later used in the murder and which belonged to Dewayne Dillard. They took all her money.

Mike Ramos, the lead prosecutor in the case, drove us around the scenes of all three crimes the group committed that night. He described the waitress to us as "easy prey, a lone woman. She'd be very easy to rob at gunpoint. If they did not intend to go and use the gun, why was it loaded?"

The next victims were a group of three people, two women and a man, on their way to a cinema. Again, they were threatened at gunpoint and their handbags, credit cards, and money were taken.

Kenneth told us that he did not witness these robberies, as they took place out of sight of the car, but that he told Dewayne Dillard, who was also waiting in the car, that he wasn't comfortable with what was happening, and that after the second hit Dewayne told the others that they weren't doing any more holdups.

"There was an unsettling feeling in me, I knew it was wrong. We decided to stop," Kenneth said.

Mike Ramos disputes that Kenneth did not see the robberies and that they had stopped.

"The only way he could not see what was happening was if he wasn't there... He was a very big participant in this. He may not have pulled the trigger, but he facilitated the whole robbing spree. He pulled over; in fact, he was spotting them [the victims]. They were not going home, cutting it short."

After the two robberies, according to Kenneth, the group were driving aimlessly in the direction of a club that they had heard about. As they drove into the affluent north-central area of the city in the early hours of the morning, there was not much traffic on the roads, but there were two cars ahead of them, a white Toyota and a red Ford Mustang. As the two cars turned into a prosperous, tree-lined, semi-rural road with substantial detached houses fronted by driveways, Kenneth swung the steering wheel of the Chevrolet and followed them. The second car was driven by a young woman, and she turned into a drive, tailing the first car. The four men drove on, then did a U-turn and drove back past the driveway. The young woman walked to the end of the drive and flagged them down. When they stopped, according to the version Kenneth told us, she said:

"Hey, do I know you?"

"We said no, you don't know us," Kenneth told us. "She looked good, she was a beautiful woman. So one of the occupants in the car, I believe it was Mauriceo, who was a kind of class clown, a goofball, and liked to flirt with women, he said, 'Hey, you look good,' and she said, 'Well if you like what you see, take a picture. It will last longer.' So at that point Mauriceo jumped out of the car and approached the woman, whose name was Mary Patrick, and at the top of the drive Michael LaHood was there, and Mauriceo and Michael got into a dispute. What happened at this point is under a lot of controversy. The car was about seventy feet away at the bottom of the driveway, which went up a slope and into a carport. Michael's car was under the carport and Mary Patrick's car was on the driveway. So whatever took place up there is probably only known between Mauriceo, Michael, and Mary Patrick, because they were the only ones there.

"Nobody else exited the car; we didn't discuss robbing anybody... If it was a planned robbery, like what happened earlier in the night, there was always two people that left the car together. Why? Because you have one guy that's trying to make the grab and one that's watching his back. Right? So there was no plan to rob. He never said: 'Be prepared to take off.' He didn't say he had the gun."

But Kenneth was prepared to take off, and drove away when Mauriceo ran back down the drive after the sound of gunshots was heard.

When the police arrived, they found the body of twenty-five-year-old Michael LaHood lying face down, a stream of blood pouring from his head down the driveway. The murder happened just after 2:00 a.m., and the rest of the LaHood family were awoken by Mary Patrick frantically banging on their door and screaming that Mike had been shot.

Michael LaHood's background was very different from Kenneth Foster's. Michael was a member of a prominent legal family in San Antonio. His father ran a very successful legal practice and later became a judge. Michael was completing his own studies to become a lawyer in his father's practice, and his two younger brothers, Nico and Marc, would also later qualify as lawyers. At the time of the murder, all three brothers lived at home, although Michael had a separate house adjoining the main family home. He was taking Mary Patrick back there, after meeting up with her at the AllStars Gentleman's Sports Club, a strip club where she worked, and after stopping for a meal and drinks.

His brother Nico, a charismatic and driven person who, with persuasion, was generous with his time for us, showed us the outside of the family home where the murder happened. Although he was the only member of the LaHood family to speak to us, his parents knew he was participating with us, and he kept them informed all the way through. He described what happened after Mary banged on their door.

"My bedroom was on the other side of the house, I was just watching TV. I heard the alarm go off and got up and opened the door and saw my pop run by with a weapon, and I heard a female voice from down the hallway faintly saying 'Mike' and 'shot.' I grabbed the weapon and followed my pop. I walk out of the door and Mike's car was parked here. What I could see was literally a river of blood that was coming from under the car all the way down the driveway, so I walk around and the young lady was screaming at the top of her lungs, and then I saw my brother lying face down. And then my aunt said, 'Nico, he's gone.' When she said that, I looked at my pop and he went from being intense to like his spirit left his body. And he walked out to the front of the yard and cried by himself. I don't know whether to follow him, what to do. There was no CPR to do."

Later, Mary Patrick, who was crying, distraught, and visibly drunk, identified Dewayne Dillard as the killer, but at the police station Mauriceo Brown admitted shooting Michael after all three others in the car named him. Mary claimed in evidence that she was aware that her car was being followed and flashed her lights at the car ahead, driven by Michael, to warn him. When they parked, she went down the drive and accosted the men in the Cavalier.

"I was angry and said, 'Why in the hell are you following me?' Mike called to me and said I should get up to the house. Then a Black guy got out. He had a gun in his right hand. I ran to the house."

She heard the man say: "Give me your money, give me your wallet, give me your keys." Mike replied that Mary had the keys and would bring them.

"I turned round and looked at Mike and I saw the Black guy pointing the gun at Mike's head. Then I heard the gunshot and Mike fell. I ran and hid in some bushes for a moment, then I ran over to Mike and was telling him to get up. I saw blood coming from his head. I ran to the big house to get help."

We tried to involve Mary in telling her story for the film, but she didn't respond to our requests for help. We also spoke to the victims of the earlier robberies that night, but none of them wanted to be filmed.

Nico LaHood took up the story from his perspective: "I knew at that moment that life was going to be different. I knew there was a new normal in our lives. My mom was a mess, my pop was crying; I'd never seen him cry."

He remembers his older brother Michael as outgoing and being friends with everyone.

"He had a wide array of friends. He was a good guy, a great guy. He was in college and he'd always wanted to be a lawyer and practice with our pop."

Kenneth and the other three were arrested shortly afterward, when their car was spotted driving erratically. The policeman who pulled them over saw the gun on the floor at the back. They were all booked for capital murder.

In their statements, Kenneth, Julius, and Dewayne corroborated most of Mary's version of events, although Kenneth was the only one who said he did not know that Mauriceo had taken the gun with him when he went up the driveway. He also gave a second statement about the earlier robberies, saying that he had no idea they were going to happen, that he did not see them happen, and that afterwards, when he realized what they had done, he told them he would drop them back home.

Dewayne testified that the gun was on the back seat

between him and Mauriceo, who grabbed it when he got out of the car.

According to Kenneth: "Mauriceo never said anything, he never said he's taken the gun… We really thought he was going out to goof around with the female. And then he and Michael got into a confrontation. I wasn't there when it took place. According to Mauriceo's testimony, he said Michael brandished a weapon and he pulled his weapon and it went off. Mauriceo testified that we didn't plan a robbery, nobody encouraged him to rob, and he acted on his own accord… The jury didn't believe it. They convicted both of us for capital murder; they convicted me of being a conspirator to the crime; they convicted me mostly for being the driver. For driving the car they handed down the death sentence."

Dewayne was not charged with any offense for the night's activities (he was later sentenced to life imprisonment for killing the taxi driver two weeks before the murder of Michael LaHood). Prosecutor Mike Ramos said: "His role was very hard to prove. He never got out of the car, he never did anything else, but we tried to see if there was enough evidence to try him in this case. The case against him was dismissed."

The prominence of the LaHood family made it difficult for the young Black men in the car to get defense lawyers.

Talking to us, Kenneth was at pains not to criticize the LaHood family, and he stressed that Michael was a young man with a lot of potential.

"I say this without any bitterness, I don't say this with any cockiness: that family deserves every credit as a good family. But there was a lot of people my grandfather went to for advice, lawyers and judges, and they refused to talk to him.

Lawyers told him they wouldn't touch the case with a ten-foot pole or they'd never get another case in San Antonio."

Prosecutor Mike Ramos confirmed that a couple of lawyers did turn down the chance to defend Kenneth "out of respect to Mr. LaHood."

Kenneth also believes he faced the higher charge of capital murder because of the victim's prominent family. He cites other cases in which the drivers of cars used in robberies where a murder happened were given much lesser sentences than his. But he accepts his guilt.

"There's a lot of regret here. I was a part of this crime. Even though my crime may have been this much, and Mauriceo Brown's may have been this much," he gestured with his hands to demonstrate the difference. "I was there and I didn't have to be there and I didn't have to put myself in that position. There's a lot of sorrow about what happened to Michael... This shouldn't have happened to this man." Julius Steen's lawyers arranged a plea bargain for him, in which he gave evidence for the prosecution about the murder in return for a lesser sentence. He testified that he had "a pretty good idea" that Mauriceo was about to commit another gunpoint robbery and that he "thought" a robbery was "probably taking place." He went to prison for thirty years for aggravated robbery, leaving only Mauriceo and Kenneth in the dock for murder.

The five-day trial was a rowdy, distressing affair for the LaHood family. "It was intense. My friends were there, their friends were there, scuffles, fights, yelling. A lot of bailiffs," said Nico.

Mauriceo claimed the gun went off by accident after he drew it when he thought Michael LaHood had a weapon. There was no evidence that Michael LaHood had a weapon, and the prosecution claimed it was not possible to discharge the gun by accident. Mike Ramos told us:

"The trigger pull on a .357 automatic is much too hard for that. It's not an accident. It wasn't self-defense." If it was an accident or self-defense, why did the four men flee the scene and not try to get help, Ramos asked, and he also challenged the story that the men were looking for a club.

"A nightclub in this area? There's just no way. Then they changed the story to say they were looking for a friend's party, but they couldn't provide the name of the friend."

We asked Mike Ramos to explain why Mauriceo Brown faced a capital sentence. This is the definition he gave us: "The fact that he committed a murder in the commission of a felony makes it a capital murder, and the felony would be aggravated robbery."

Although the decision to prosecute for the death penalty was not made by him, Mike Ramos said he had no doubts about it being the right charge for Mauriceo, with nothing controversial about it.

We asked the same question about Kenneth:

"Kenneth never shot anyone, but according to the penal code, a person is criminally responsible for the conduct of another if acting with intent to promote, solicit, encourage, direct, or aid. And that's what we had here. He facilitated this whole spree. Without his vehicle and without him stopping, Mr. LaHood would probably be alive right now. I believe he was the brains behind all these robberies. He was smart enough to figure out 'I'm not going to get out, I've got these guys to do my dirty work.' I believe that Mary Patrick was a target because, first of all, she appeared to be alone and she was a woman. They thought she would be easy pickings.

"He knew they had weapons. To say he didn't know—I believe he is being untruthful... I was more convinced of [his guilt] even though Mauriceo Brown was the actual shooter. He may not have fired the weapon, but he facilitated that whole night. The fact that he drove away was used as evidence of guilt. I was very confident about this prosecution... I believe he was a very arrogant individual and would not accept his responsibility for what he had done.

"He manipulated the other individuals. The jury saw through that. I think he would say anything and he will say anything. I believe he'd still say to this day that he didn't anticipate Mr. LaHood getting murdered. Kenneth Foster's case was decided before Mauriceo Brown's, he was actually sentenced to death before Mauriceo Brown. That's how much they [the jury] believed he was involved in the case." Mike Ramos told us that another consideration for the death penalty is the future danger posed by the accused. If the jury says he is not likely to be a future danger, the automatic sentence is life imprisonment. If they believe he does pose a danger, the death penalty comes in.

"Kenneth Foster was no stranger to violence. The jury decided that he would have been a danger to society."

The defendants were shocked when the jury returned their verdicts, and Mike Ramos said Kenneth seemed most affected.

"When we were picking the jury, they were laughing and joking, like it was a kind of big joke. I don't think they thought they were going to be found guilty. When they were found guilty, they were a bit more concerned. Kenneth was the most in shock."

For Nico LaHood, the murder of his older brother marked a turning point. He himself had a previous conviction, from when he was caught selling ecstasy pills to an undercover policeman two years earlier, and at the time of the murder he was at college but not studying to be a lawyer. "I became a functioning angerholic. I was angry. I was angry and the world gave me no answers. You heard your mom cry as only a mom can cry; you helped load your dead brother's body on the gurney after they did the investigation and rigor mortis set in; and you helped your pop wash your brother's blood off the driveway.

"I didn't want to get help; I thought that was for weak people. I didn't celebrate birthdays. Christmas was, like, I stared at the empty chair. I felt guilty to laugh. I lived with regret that I wasn't there at the time of life that he needed me most. I used to sit outside my driveway with my weapon, challenging the devil to come back: 'Come back now, you son-of-a-bitch, when I'm ready for you, you coward!' I wanted justice and revenge on all of them, which absolutely affected my whole worldview."

He became determined to train as a lawyer.

"I needed to accomplish something, to make sure my family as a whole unit was taken care of." When he qualified, he practiced with his father for six years until his father became a judge. Nico was a defense lawyer, to the surprise of friends who thought his family's experience would make him want to prosecute criminals.

"But I purposely didn't take murder cases or child abuse cases."

Eventually he realized "brokenness creates more brokenness. And I just thought: 'I got to get my shit together.'"

His life changed when a friend introduced him to the church where Nico is now a stalwart of the congregation and speaks regularly at church gatherings, drawing on his experience of his brother's murder and expressing that he no longer feels anger and hate because of his Christian beliefs, which have brought him peace. He is a compelling speaker. He believes his faith has brought back joy into his life after the terrible events of the night his brother died. He has married and now has four children (his oldest boy is called Michael after his brother), and is very pleased that his parents have had the chance to meet their grandchildren.

He flew high in his legal career and was elected district attorney in 2015, which meant during his term of office, from 2015 to 2018, he had to make decisions over the death penalty system. He enjoyed the work of the DA's office, talking enthusiastically about making decisions that will help young offenders turn their lives around. He set up a special unit, the Convictions Integrity Unit, to examine whether past convictions are safe. He agreed to participate in our film because he said he could see it is an unusual situation.

"You have a situation where someone was murdered, there was a death sentence, one was executed, the other was commuted. Then the brother has this journey and ends up being district attorney in the same city where his brother was murdered... I understand that is something that is not normal, but it's normal to me.

"There's no way in hell I dreamed I would become the district attorney for Bexar County. A lot of people were curious; there was a group that thought I would seek the death penalty most of the time. I believe we are balanced, but we do seek the death penalty. Anybody that make a carte blanche statement that they're against the death penalty, I say, 'Have you tested your theory? Has your kid been shot in the face in

your driveway? You think you are against the death penalty—
you just don't know.'"

In the immediate aftermath of the case, while Nico struggled to adjust to "the new normal" of his life, Kenneth was
adjusting to life on Death Row.

"I can honestly say you don't understand Death Row until
you're there. I'm a twenty-year-old kid, and you don't know
anything about capital punishment, you don't know about the
execution chamber, you don't know if people are going to kill
you, fight you. It was scary. You're living every day knowing
that there is an execution hanging over your head... Some of
these guys became my friends and then they say, 'Hey, man, I
got an execution date,' and I'd know, that's going to be me. It's
a traumatic process."

A year before Kenneth was due to go to the death chamber, Mauriceo Brown was executed. Nico and Marc LaHood
watched the execution, Nico believing it was their responsibility to represent Mike's family.

"I was still very angry. When they ask why you are here,
I said, 'It's none of your fucking business why I am here. I'm
here because I want to follow this through. This individual
murdered my brother, and I need to see him go to the Lord.
I need to see him physically take his last breath,'" said Nico.

Before he died, Mauriceo turned to the LaHoods and
apologized: "I'm sorry you lost a brother, a loved one, and a
friend." He told his mother and siblings that he loved them.
"Keep your heads up and know that I will be in a better
place," he said, before turning to Nico and Marc again and
repeating his apology.

Nico said: "I remember feeling tremendous compassion for
his mother. I thought to myself: that [the murder] victimized

two families, my family and his own family. [The execution] was a justifiable death, not a murder. But I felt compassion for his mother and sister."

Kenneth's grandfather Lawrence has never wavered in his support for Kenneth, and it is impossible not to be impressed by his quiet dignity.

"He was charged with murder though he didn't do any murdering. Let's say a person is driving with another individual who says, 'Let's stop at the convenience store so I can get some cigarettes, candy.' And this individual goes in there and he robs or kills the cashier. The driver doesn't know anything about it, but under the law of parties he will be convicted of murder also," Lawrence said.

Lawrence got in touch with Lily Hughes, who was a member of an anti-death-penalty campaign group in Texas, and that's when the campaign to get Kenneth's sentence commuted began.

We talked to Lily in her cluttered office, carrier bags full of papers at her feet. She explained to us that the group is different from most of the mainstream abolition groups, who are fighting against the general principle of death as a punishment.

"We also wanted to bring in more political discussion about how the death penalty functions, shining a window on it by focusing on single cases. We wanted to humanize people on Death Row, because otherwise it's easy for people to think of Death Row prisoners as monsters who deserve to be there. We wanted to highlight how it could happen if you don't have a good lawyer. One of our slogans was 'Those without capital, get capital punishment.' Also, we wanted to highlight the statistic that if you are Black and the victim is White, that's much more likely to generate a capital case."

As she spoke to us, Lily held up a "Save Kenneth Foster" T-shirt. She showed us banners: "Don't let Kenneth Foster become another victim of a racially biased judiciary," a slogan she criticized for not being punchy enough, and another that she preferred for its directness: "Stop the Execution of Kenneth Foster."

"A big part of building around a single case was amplifying the voices that are not generally heard. In death penalty cases, the loudest voices were always the voices of the victim's family. Of course, they should be a loud voice. But we felt that the people on Death Row are also being victimized by the system. We felt by concentrating on his case we could humanize people on Death Row."

She explained that with limited resources, the campaign group had to be selective about the cases they backed.

"Kenneth's case was easy to understand because he didn't shoot anyone, that was understood by everyone. He wrote to us and presented his case in a really compelling way. And we were able to meet his family, especially his grandfather, and we felt like: here is something we can really work with." Showing us one of Kenneth's lengthy, typewritten letters, she said: "He always had a lot to say and he would always have a long list of things he needed me to do."

For Lily and her group, this was the first time they had worked on a case involving the law of parties. The slogan "Wrong time, wrong place" developed because they do not believe the murder was planned or premeditated. She invited Lawrence to speak at an event involving family members of Death Row prisoners, and she told us he was compelling when he spoke.

"It was just awesome! He spoke in a very loving way, he

just loved Kenneth so much. And he was very direct: 'He's innocent, he didn't mean this to happen.' And Kenneth himself did so much. He started writing to as many people as he could, lawyers, activists, politicians. He was talking about racism, class bias; we were really drawn to him."

Lawrence became a figurehead for the campaign, traveling all over the States to talk in universities and colleges, even going to Sweden with the campaigners.

The campaign started in earnest in 1999, before Mauriceo's execution, and it took time to gather steam. Leaflets were handed out, petitions organized, meetings held. Lawrence would read out Kenneth's statements. When Kenneth was given an execution date for August 2007, one year after Mauriceo's execution, the campaign gathered pace with only twelve months to go. Students and abolitionists from other states joined protest marches, waving placards and shouting slogans. A hip-hop music fundraiser drew a large crowd. Over ten thousand letters sent in support of Kenneth were printed off and held in a chain that surrounded the governor's mansion, and on another occasion protesters formed a human chain to block the driveway of the mansion. A month before the date of the execution, between two and three hundred people marched to a rally where former Death Row prisoners from all over the States spoke in Kenneth's support and the crowd chanted, "They say Death Row, we say hell no!"

At the same time, Kenneth now had a very dedicated death penalty lawyer working with the campaign.

Lily and her colleagues were thrilled by the commutation to life imprisonment, only the second commutation so close to an execution since the death penalty was resumed in Texas in 1982. She now considers Lawrence Foster to be a great friend.

She was proud of the way Kenneth lay down in protest when the prison officers moved him to Huntsville.

"He wanted to show that he wanted no part of the process."

She said, "Execution is premeditated murder." She hesitated and resumed talking with tears in her eyes and a catch in her voice. "I saw my long-time pen pal executed. Despite the sort of clinical veneer of the lethal injection process, it feels like witnessing a violent crime. You're watching your loved one be murdered right in front of your eyes, and you can't do anything."

Nico LaHood was very aware of the campaign. He said, "There was a lot of propaganda… Some of the groups I think were sincere, but I think they were ignorant, they just didn't know."

On the day before his scheduled execution, Kenneth was moved to Huntsville earlier than is standard. He said of the experience, "Because we had a reputation for being vocal and prepared to fight for our rights, they decided to move me a day early. I was scared to death. I didn't know why they were coming for me. I know I can't get executed before my date, but what do I know? So when they came to my cell, I went to ground. I laid down. I refused to walk. I made them carry me. They put me in the van and drove me to Huntsville."

We were able to include the film of the guards in riot gear lifting Kenneth onto a stretcher because the prison recorded it, to prove they did not use excessive force. He can be heard challenging the officers: "Where are you taking me, man? I'd walk with you if you tell me what you are doing with me, man. Am I going to see my family, yes or no? I'm not participating in this."

Outside the jail, crowds, many from other states, were

marching carrying placards: "Free Kenneth Foster," "Stop the Execution of Kenneth Foster," "Save Kenneth Foster."

Lawrence Foster told us that when he heard the death sentence had been commuted, "I cried. It was tears of joy, at the idea that he was free from the death penalty. I was there with his father, my son Ronnie, and I told him it was down to the power of prayer.

"Now the thing is to get him out of there. We still have work to do. I am ninety years old and I still say I am going to see him free. Even now. I do everything I possibly can to free him, and so I'm going to continue doing it and it's going to happen."

For Mike Ramos, the commutation was the wrong decision. "I was shocked Governor Perry did that. It was very poorly handled. Mr. Nico LaHood and the rest of us were on our way to Huntsville, and had he not been notified by a friend in the media we would have driven all the way up there. I agreed with the death penalty then and I agree with it today. I'll always agree with it."

Nico LaHood has accepted the governor's decision. "I've let it go. I'm OK with the Governor having that ultimate decision. There has to be checks and balances. But I think the governor should have talked to us, the victim's family."

The Foster family want the case to be reviewed by the Texas Board of Pardons and Paroles. The case has to be backed by two senior officials, one of whom is the district attorney. At the time we were filming, Nico LaHood was the DA.

Kenneth Foster would like to meet Nico LaHood.

"Over the years, we've wanted to build a bridge with the LaHood family. We want to show them the person that I have become. We want to discuss not only my sentence, but is rehabilitation and redemption possible? I want to show that my life is worth something."

He showed us a tattoo he had done after his sentence was commuted.

"It's a tombstone and the number 403. I was supposed to be the 403rd execution in Texas, and it has a small cross through it. It has my execution date, 30 August 2007, and a syringe with my death row number, 999232. I put that on my skin to remember what I went through, to remember how serious it is, to remember what happened to Michael LaHood."

He said that he wants to apologize to the LaHood family "from the depths of my heart... When you are seeking forgiveness, you have to be honest about what you did. You can't go into forgiveness lying about the mistakes you made. You have to be straight up and say, 'I did these things. I was a fool. I wasn't intelligent enough, I was immature.' When you hurt someone, they are going to have that hurt for the rest of their life, like a scar."

He told us he has been working with inmates, writing poetry.

"It's a daily walk. You have to walk it. I don't like being in prison, it's a horrible place, it's wretched, violent, vile, disgusting, and I hate being here. I put myself here, so I have to make it a reality, I have to make a world here, and I have to do that by re-educating myself.

"Every day for the last twenty-one years I've had to think: What can I do that's going to make a difference? It's hard to bring a triumph from a tragedy like this. This man shouldn't have lost his life, and even though I didn't kill him, I was there and I have to pay the price for that."

Kenneth Foster talks fluently and well; his responses were

prompt and erudite. But he cracked and cried at the hurt he had done to his family, particularly his grandfather.

"It's the worst feeling in the world to have someone treat you so good and for you to hurt them and disrespect them in the way I did."

Lawrence Foster misses being able to touch and hug the grandson he tried to rescue when he was a little boy.

"It's difficult, visiting and talking and there's a glass shield between you and you want to touch and you touch the glass and he touches from his side, and that's the extent of it."

He refuses to believe he will not see Kenneth freed in his lifetime.

"I'm going to see him free. My belief is that strong."

Kenneth sees a role for himself when he gets out of prison, and he and his supporters are hoping that he will be allowed parole before he has served the full forty years, which would not be until 2036. He wants to mentor and talk to young people about the risks they run when they get involved in drugs or crime.

But Nico LaHood has resisted meeting Kenneth because he does not believe he is sincere in his repentance. He wavered about it when we were talking with him, but was not prepared to commit to a meeting.

"The idea of meeting him does not enrage me anymore. It used to. But he has to be truthful. Even today, he's still saying that he didn't know what they were doing. There's no reconciliation without truth... Kenneth Foster made a lot of excuses for a long time... To say, 'I didn't know where I was going, and Mauriceo wanted me to go, we were just going to some party... and then I'm going to get killed for it on the death penalty.' We weren't dealing with a boy scout back then. He was on probation, community supervision, for shooting two guys. So I don't respect that.

"It would not benefit me, and I will not expend any resources to do something solely for him. He doesn't owe me anything, he can't pay me back. There's nothing he can do to pay me back.

"I'm willing to meet him if it honors God and it's under the right circumstances. But I have never heard that he acknowledges what they were doing... I wish him well and I hope his faith and this new work he has, influencing people in prison, is sincere. If he's changed his life, God bless him. But people want me to advocate for him to get out earlier than forty years. No! I want to make sure we are clear that I have no intention of advocating for Kenneth to get out sooner than he should. That's not going to happen. If I meet him, that's got nothing to do with his sentence. He's eligible for parole in forty years. If he's changed his life, God bless him. If he gets out after his time, I'm OK with that."

Nico spoke to us from his office during his term as district attorney. On his desk stood a large silver cross and a statue of Justice, the blindfolded Roman goddess with scales in one hand and a sword in the other, and the walls were lined with Nico's certificates of awards and qualifications. He explained the statue's blindfold, symbolizing impartiality: "She wears a blindfold for a reason. She doesn't know which [side] is which. You have to hold the system accountable."

Although he has resisted meeting Kenneth, Nico has met up with Lawrence Foster.

"I met with his grandfather and his daddy. I embraced them both. We talked about faith. I told them, 'You do not need my forgiveness, you did nothing to me.' But I understood they just felt responsible. I've met the grandfather more, and he's just a decent man. He's a good man, Mr. Foster. He reached out to me on that topic and I told him, very respectfully, that's not going to happen. A sentence is a sentence."

We were able to film Nico and Lawrence talking together in an outdoor cafe in San Antonio on a sunny Sunday morning, after they had both been to their respective churches. The two men greeted each other cordially, Lawrence, aged ninety-one at the time and smartly dressed in a suit, shaking hands warmly with Nico. Lawrence described Nico to us as "a square shooter."

"He's concerned about individuals and the law. He's just a fine man, I hold him in high esteem."

The purpose of the meeting was for Lawrence to apologize again for what his grandson did, but also to ask Nico if there was anything that could be done to reduce his sentence.

Lawrence said: "I'm really trying to find something that would be advantageous in our case, where Kenny may get another hearing and get something that may lead to him being released from prison."

Nico did not hold out any hope. Afterwards Nico told us: "He was kind of gently trying to touch on the fact that he believed Kenneth was being over-punished, or punished too harshly or unjustly. He's entitled to that opinion. Even if I wanted to advocate to get him out early, I have no authority. The law is the law. I mean, he's not eligible, regardless of who wants him out, until forty years."

Talking to us after we filmed him addressing the congregation at a church, we questioned Nico about his own criminal past. He accepts that "I'm a hypocrite if I don't believe that someone who is guilty of murder can't turn their life around.

"I sold drugs when I was young and foolish. And I was arrested for selling drugs. Well, I had to forgive myself. I was labeled a drug dealer, a criminal, because I made poor choices in my life. I didn't make a mistake—people talk about poor choices as mistakes. A mistake is an accident. I didn't make a mistake, I made a poor choice.

"I was pissed off at myself because I was dealing with these labels that I helped put on myself, so I've lived with it. I was disappointed and angry at myself. A lot of people have to forgive themselves, but first and foremost, you can't do it without truth. That's my point about Kenneth Foster. There's no reconciliation without truth. But that's why I believe in redemption. I'm praying about whether to meet with Kenneth Foster."

We re-interviewed Kenneth Foster three months after our first interview, again speaking through a screen in the whitewashed cubicle of the prison visits room, and we pressed him on points in his story, challenging him to clarify and reframe it.

He told us he could not remember the name of the club he and his three friends had been looking for when they became embroiled in the murder of Mike LaHood. Pressed, he told us that the club had already been shut down, and he reiterated that he cannot remember its name.

We asked why he followed Mary Patrick's car when she turned into the residential street.

"There's not even a good answer to that... The two cars, when they went into the residential area, we just followed. I know people are going to say we targeted them, but we just followed... We didn't know if they were going to a party or to a club, it was aimless."

Challenged about the robberies, he admitted they were dangerous.

"I guess I've always looked at my guilt as lesser, even though in the eyes of the law I'm the same. That night was the first time I had ever had a robbery-type situation. I've had aggravated assault charges, I've had a couple of drug charges, but I've never had a robbery situation before then." He told us he did not know that Dewayne had been involved in a murder case two weeks before the shooting of Michael LaHood.

"I was absolutely unaware of that until we were incarcerated."

He also denied knowing that, earlier in the evening, the victims had been pistol whipped, and that he must, therefore, have known that the men he was associating with were capable of violence.

"That was the first night that me and these guys had committed a crime together. I never saw him do it [the pistol-whipping]... When the first robbery happened I was parked behind a building. They ran round the front. They were never in visual eyesight... I'm not here to say that a crime wasn't committed."

He prevaricated when we asked him whether he still insisted that when he stopped the car outside the LaHood house, he did not know that the intention was to commit another robbery.

"I would definitely examine myself... Maybe I've convinced myself too that all these years... As far as knowing what my intent was versus Mauriceo's intent... that may be something of contention. But I know in my heart that what happened wasn't in our agreeance. But that's not to say I don't share the blame."

Then he told us:

"I want to say something, and it's something that Nico doesn't know, and it's something that some of my supporters don't know. But I want the world to know this. When we were in the car that night and Mary Patrick was here talking to us at the car and she said, 'Hey, are you guys following me or what?'...all this is in the trial record. But this part is not. When Michael LaHood was at the top of the driveway, I don't know if he got upset or maybe he was angry that she was talking to us so long but, regardless of whether anyone believes it or not, and I say this at the possibility of my own demise, he kind of gave us the bird." Kenneth raises his middle finger to illustrate the gesture. "And kind of in a joking manner I told Mauriceo, 'Man, you going to let that guy flick us off like that?' And it was really just a joke. It just didn't mean anything behind it, and that's when Mauriceo jumped out of the car and went up the driveway.

"I feel that if I hadn't said that, we would have just drove off. I'm accepting the guilt, the blame. If I have to do this life sentence because of something that my stupid mouth said, then I have to do it. What I said caused Mauriceo to get out of the car, trying to be a tough-guy man, and that's something I've had to live with.

"That's something I want to sit down in front of Nico and tell him we weren't trying to rob your brother, but perhaps what I went through, Death Row, was something to spank me on the butt, to warn me keep your mouth shut, pay attention, be humble in life.

"Why would you believe this? Because what I just said could hurt me, can be used against me possibly. So I've had to pray and think what I would want to say to Nico LaHood. My legal defense was always that we did not conspire to commit a crime. Me saying, 'Hey, man, you going to let the guy flick you off?' It's not a crime. But I accept a responsibility for what took place that night because of what I said. Mauriceo wasn't trying to kill that man, he was just trying to be a tough guy and he lost his life because of it, and I'm sorry for what I said.

I'm sorry for being a stiff-necked child that didn't know how to listen."

This admission from Kenneth, which could in law be interpreted as incitement to commit violence or even murder, was a major change in his story, and caused us problems.

We didn't know what this partial admission of guilt would mean for him, whether it could mean that the death penalty could be reinstated. We took legal advice, and the lawyers told us that Kenneth had, in fact, said something similar in one of his police interviews, so it was not entirely new and would not affect his sentence.

Immediately after making this partial confession to our team, Kenneth got in touch with his supporters at the campaign to tell them of the change to his story.

"They contacted us, asking us not to use the admission in our film," said Ned. "Kenneth is the poster boy for their challenge to the law of parties, and they were worried this weakened his case. I could see their point, but we felt the film should contain the whole truth.

"I think his motivation for telling us was to persuade Nico LaHood to visit him. He really wanted that meeting for reconciliation, because I think he felt that if they met in person he could persuade Nico to support his case."

Kenneth explained why he is so keen to meet Nico:

"I really want to talk to him about the power of a man to go through a situation like this and come through the other side a better man. Also to talk to an individual that maybe sometime in his life could have been where I'm at, sitting right here. I look at him as someone who was on the wrong course but got his life straight. I admire him for that, I admire him as a man, I admire what he does. Perhaps at some point we can have a legal discussion about was my case deserving of the death penalty? Have I done anything with my time to deserve a second chance?

"If you are really seeking forgiveness, you have to be honest about what you do. I would have to walk through, piece by piece, what happened that night. If anybody ever knows anything, and Nico and his family need to know, Mauriceo did not want that to happen. He was just being a show-off. There was no conspiracy to rob."

One of the questions we asked Kenneth in the second interview was whether, as well as reaching out to the LaHood family for reconciliation, he had ever reached out to other victims of his earlier violent life. The answer was no.

"Is that because he's not in prison for what he did to those people, or because they are not connected to the district attorney? We don't know," said Ned.

After the story of Kenneth Foster was broadcast, the public reaction was more divided than for any other episode in the *I Am A Killer* series, with much of the opinion dividing down racial lines.

"It exemplifies why we always want to take a rounded view of every case, allowing the viewers to make up their own minds," said Ned.

Nico LaHood did not secure a second term as district attorney, nor did he, at the time of our filming, agree to visit Kenneth Foster.

7

A SILENT ORDER

BRANDON HUTCHISON

"I can't believe I committed murder. I took away two men out of their lives. I'll never be able to give back. I'm truly sorry for what I did to them boys. I've never talked about this. I've never implicated anybody or myself in anything. I know what I did, and I'm taking full responsibility for that." When the gun was handed to Brandon Hutchison, he knew what he had to do. It was, he told us, "a silent order," a command that did not need any words. He implicitly knew that it was his job to carry out the cold-blooded killing of two brothers, Ronnie and Brian Yates, and he feared that if he did not go through with it, he would find himself on the wrong end of the gun barrel.

The murder of the Yates brothers happened in the early hours of New Year's Day, 1996, the culmination of a drink-and-drug-fueled New Year's Eve party in a garage in the small town of Verona, Missouri. Brandon Hutchison was there when the party ended with another man shooting and badly injuring Ronnie and Brian. It fell to Brandon to finish them off.

Brandon Hutchison talked to us from South Central Correctional Center in Licking, Missouri, a modern, mixed-security men's prison. Facing our cameras was a breakthrough moment for Brandon: he had never before talked about the crime, not at his trial or under interrogation. Even his ex-wife, with whom he remained close, had never heard him confess to it.

Brandon, a large, thickset man with a bushy, graying beard and shaved head, said he kept silent for twenty-three years in prison because "I thought that was what you were supposed to do. I thought a twenty-year-old kid was supposed to keep his mouth shut when he was involved in certain things. I could have started pointing fingers or trying to save myself but I just kept quiet."

Director Ingo Nyakairu said: "I was surprised how open he was being. In all the messages we had exchanged before we met, he had not fully talked about the crime. I genuinely felt when we interviewed him that he was being honest and that he was always truthful with us. He used his chance in front of us to get it all off his chest."

Ten days after we interviewed him for a second time, Brandon was diagnosed with liver and stomach cancer, and weeks later, in November 2019, he died in jail, nearly twenty-four years after the murders. All the interviews we conducted took place before his terminal diagnosis.

Brandon's childhood and teenage years were spent in Ventura, a small town on the coast of California between Los Angeles and Santa Barbara. He was the middle of three boys, and he described his as a close-knit family. His older brother Matt told us the area was full of orange trees, and they had freedom to run around as young children. But any happiness Brandon may have had as a child was overshadowed by sexual abuse by an older man, which began when he was a very young child and went on for years.

Matt said, "He would con him [Brandon] into doing things for him; 'I'll let you drive my truck if you do this for me.' It was straight up molestation. Then, when Brandon went to Iowa to my grandparents, he was molested there by another older man. Brandon was thirteen or fourteen then. It probably ate him up bad, you know. It was a big deal, maybe why he stayed on the drugs."

Brandon told us: "I'm not sure when it started, in kindergarten maybe. I was confused. It affected me emotionally and psychologically. I got help for my behavior problems my whole life. I was in special education classes. I was put to the side in school. I didn't like it. I didn't feel like I needed special help. I just had an anger problem and I was hyper. I never admitted the sexual abuse until I was eighteen."

He stressed that he was not looking for excuses for the crime he committed: "I don't believe being sexually abused made me murder someone, I really don't. There's no excuses for what I did."

Drugs and alcohol came into his life early.

"I was a drug addict, that's pretty much it. The methamphetamine use started heavy probably when I was about fifteen, but I smoked weed when I was younger, and drank. I used methamphetamines and alcohol to deal with the feelings I couldn't express."

Funding his drug habit led to petty crime, stealing and selling drugs. He stressed to us that he always had support from his family.

"My family always welcomed me back into their home, I always had a place to lay my head. They never gave up on me, they were always supportive."

He met his wife, Michelle, when he was fifteen, when he was selling weed to a friend of hers, and within nine months of their getting together Michelle was pregnant with their first son, Jared. It was, as Michelle described it, a "really tumultuous relationship," and they split before Jared's birth, but got back together, and their second son, Jacob, was born two and a half years later.

Michelle told us: "I was seventeen, not far from eighteen. And he was not quite sixteen. He told me he was older, and it slipped out how young he was. He was a big guy, pretty mature for his age, and a lot of fun to be with. His mom was pretty funny, the cool mom. Laurie and Bill [his parents] would open up their home. Even after we divorced, I've had his family take very good care of us."

From the start of their relationship, Michelle knew that Brandon had an addiction problem. After their second son was born, she realized he was using drugs a lot, and she broke off with him to protect her sons.

"I thought it was best, so the contact with the boys was removed. I didn't want that kind of life for them. I had my own struggles, drinking and struggling, working and trying to do the best I could."

Brandon told us: "I wish I could have taken the responsibility, but I was so wrapped up in methamphetamines. I had the opportunity to start a new life, my father got me a job with the carpenters' union, but I just continued to use drugs. The relationship with Michelle was on and off. I think it was just two teenage kids being crazy and partying, but I really quit seeing her when I was seventeen or eighteen years old."

At this stage, Brandon was living on the streets and sleeping on friends' couches; when his mother told him the family were moving to Missouri, he decided to join them.

"I wanted to get away from the life with the drugs, the gangs. Moving to Missouri was going to be a new start, a better chapter in my life. I was just trying to get my life together, become a citizen, do the right thing. It didn't work out."

His brother Matt remembered him joining the family about a year after they moved from California.

"He was strung, he was bad, the worst I'd ever seen him. He was pretty messed up, hard-core. He had a piece of rope holding up his britches."

Despite wanting a new start, Brandon soon fell back into the drug lifestyle. He knew Freddy Lopez, who also came from California and who was related to him by marriage. Freddy's wife, Kerry, (now his ex-wife) said: "We're not blood related but I've always seen Brandon as family. His grandpa was married to my dad's sister. I played with him since we were three to five years old. I love him very much."

Kerry had moved to Missouri from California, where her husband Freddy was part of a gang, the Party Boys. She was keen to get her children away from the gang culture their father was into, and left him to move to Verona, a small town with only six hundred inhabitants. But after a couple of weeks, Freddy, then twenty-eight, followed her, and their violent and dysfunctional marriage continued. After a few months living in a trailer, Kerry moved the family into a house owned by her grandmother when the old lady went into a nursing home.

Kerry traveled back to Verona to talk to us, and showed us round the outside of the house. "The rose bush I planted is still here. My flower beds are still there. The house was green back then," she told us.

"When we first arrived to film in Verona, the house was empty," Ingo said. "The town is such a small place, we just bumped into a guy one day and he told us he was the owner. By the time we went back with Kerry, he had tenants in there, but they were happy for us to film outside."

Kerry described her marriage: "Things were good when

Freddy was sober. When he was drinking he was gone for days at a time. I found out later that he was cheating on me throughout our whole relationship. I wanted a real life, where you work and come home."

Next door to the house was a large lock-up shop or garage, big enough for Freddy to make plans to turn it into a detail shop (a car workshop and car wash.) It seemed at first that Freddy really did intend to use the garage legitimately, and he bought all the equipment, but before long he was importing methamphetamine to the area.

"It was more of a front than anything, for the drug activity," Brandon said. "We were selling drugs. It just started going. [Freddy] was a marijuana dealer at the time; he'd bring back fifty to sixty pounds from California and sell it, go back, get some more."

Brandon said he introduced Freddy to selling methamphetamine, which sold for a much bigger profit margin.

"I was working with Freddy to build a clientele, but the drug use got the better of me again. I thought he was my friend. He was in charge of what was going on. I listened to Freddy Lopez."

Matt, Brandon's brother, remembered that time. "Freddy trapped the market. And Brandon, leaving California and trying to be clean, then having that right in his face, and then it was the snowball effect and downhill after that. Brandon could be easily manipulated, and when you're strung out and dependent on drugs and somebody's holding your drugs, you'd be pretty easily manipulated or scared. He was very fearful of Freddy. With Freddy, you wouldn't want to do him wrong or get on his back or be around when he was too drunk, Freddy was a bad, bad dude."

Michael Salazar was a teenager from California who had been in the same gang as Freddy and gravitated to Verona to work for him about a year after the Lopez family moved there.

"Michael was considered the dude to look out for Freddy," said Brandon. "They were from the same gang. They were tightening the ropes down on their organization. I didn't know Michael. I know him more now that we were in the Crossroads Correctional Center together than I ever did know Michael back then. He was manipulated, just like any other young Hispanic growing up in those areas. Michael was raised in a gang. I feel sorry for Michael because he never really got the chance to live."

Michael's childhood was tough, and he talked to us about it from Southeast Correctional Center in Charleston, Missouri.

"Michael was very open with us from the start," said Ingo. "When we were doing the initial research for the film, it was Michael who was emailing with all the details we needed. He wanted to put his story across. He is clearly intelligent, and his whole life has been blighted by something that happened when he was eighteen."

Michael described his early life as both "good and bad." "There were drugs in the house," he told us. "My mother and one of her associates, they did drugs. They did a lot of drugs. There were a lot of bad elements around, their friends were all people who had been in prison. There were instances where my mother's associate would take me to the department store to help him steal. We'd steal video games. We'd go to the grocery store and steal meat, cartons of cigarettes. My mom would be left alone with the other kids; the stress would mount up. She'd fall back into her drugs and I could do whatever I wanted, stay out all night with my friends, ditch school."

The good parts he remembered were learning to love movies with his mother, playing instruments, joining a marching band.

"I remember going to baseball games as a kid and everybody's got their family picking them up, but not me, I'm on my bike going through the neighborhood real fast cause I'm scared in the dark. But at the same time, men in and out of the house, drugs; it was the norm. I guess I was neglected to a degree, but I wasn't starving. Once I was a teenager, being around these kind of people was normal to me. I was hanging out, getting high.

"You know I was only arrested one time for committing a crime, a burglary when I was about sixteen. All the other times I was incarcerated was because my mother was deemed unfit by the court, so I couldn't stay with her. I was arrested because I was running around the streets and placed with my aunt in Arizona. I didn't like it there so I left her care and got arrested again in California. So I was absconding, or whatever you want to call it. So all the times I was locked up as a juvenile were because I wasn't living where I was supposed to be living, according to the courts. It wasn't like I committed crime after crime.

"My mom messed up a lot, made a lot of bad decisions. She died when she was young, thirty-six or thirty-eight. But that's not to put any blame on my family. I'm not here because of bad decisions they made."

He was in care and mentored for a couple of years until he was eighteen, and he was clean of drugs and doing well, holding down a job. But when all support stopped he found himself mixing with his old crowd of friends.

He said he moved to Missouri with the same aspirations that Brandon and Kerry both had, to get away from the drug lifestyle. Using exactly the same words, it was, he said, "for a new start." He knew Freddy Lopez's brother, and genuinely believed the car business was legitimate.

"They were doing a little bit of stuff on the side, selling dope, whatever, to fund the shop. In my mind, looking back, I was doing kind of good. We were doing good. It was just one night, one bad night."

He told us he met Brandon at the shop, where Brandon also helped out, although not every day.

"I would hang out with Brandon in the shop. We'd be having a beer, but we're working. You might occasionally do drugs. But we weren't running around together. Just in the shop. He was always trying to impress Freddy, and even me at times: 'Does that guy owe you money? I'll go get it for you,' things of that nature. To show he had his back, or whatever... I didn't think it was anything that was going to end up leading into any kind of trouble for me."

Kerry Lopez agreed about Brandon wanting to impress Freddy: "Brandon was like he had to prove something to Freddy. He seemed to want to please Freddy. Michael and Brandon were more like leeches, really. You know how a fly is attracted to shit. That's how it is when you're addicted to something; you're going to do anything for that person because they got the goods, they know where it's at."

When we interviewed Kerry, she walked with us around the outside of the semi-derelict lock-up shop where the first shootings happened. It was boarded up, the paint was peeling, and the wood was rotting. To Kerry's surprise, even after more than twenty years, the inside of the garage was the same as it was back then, painted in the colors that Freddy chose for the walls: red, white, and blue, for the American flag.

The events leading up to the murders began at a New Year's Eve party in the shop. Brandon gave us his account of the night:

"One of the first people that showed up was Timmy Yates, the victims' brother, but he left shortly afterwards. And we started drinking and partying, doing lines, and more people showed up. We were just partying and everybody seemed to be getting along. There were approximately twelve people there and we were all partying and doing lines of methamphetamines and drinking. Everybody was getting drunk and dancing. I met Ronnie and Brian that night."

At midnight, Michael told us, someone went into the house to get the two guns that Freddy kept hidden there, to shoot them in the air to celebrate the New Year. Freddy told Michael to only shoot the .22 pistol, because they did not have much ammunition for the .25, which belonged to Freddy's brother. Michael put the .25 in his pocket, and it wasn't put back after midnight with the other gun.

"I didn't do it intentionally, I just didn't put it away," said Michael. "I didn't want to go back to the house. At that young age, I was always thinking I was going to miss something."

By the early hours of New Year's Day, the party had thinned out. Brandon's brother Matt was there for a time but left when "the party was kind of getting dead." Brian and Ronnie Yates arrived at about 2:00 a.m., when most people had gone, looking for their brother Timmy. When they were told he had left earlier, they stayed on.

The Yates brothers were from a large family of six boys. Their brother Gary remembers them as the two who hung out together the most.

"They were pretty close to each other. Brian liked just getting drunk and partying and having fun, living like a kid."

He said both Brian and Ronnie were into motorbikes, and at the time of the murders they each had two small children. Brian was bringing his two children up alone, without their mother around.

Ingo said: "Gary was very touchy about [Brian and Ronnie] when I asked if they were into drugs. He said they did a bit of weed. But they were clearly not good boys."

"Brian and Ronnie Yates and me were sitting in the garage," said Brandon. "Freddy and Kerry were arguing and they went inside [the house]. There was me and the Yates brothers sat in the garage playing dominoes. For some reason they were talking about Michael and Freddy, referring to them as wetbacks, racial slurs, 'Them effing wetbacks.' They call Hispanics wetbacks because of the Rio Grande, I guess, swimming across the border. That's been a racial slur as long as I can remember. I went outside and met Michael and said, 'Man, you won't believe what these dudes are saying.'"

The accounts given by Brandon and Michael of what happened next are different. Brandon said Michael walked back into the shop and straightaway started shooting. According to Michael, he went back inside and one of the Yates brothers started following him about as he went for a beer, and when Michael asked, "Man, what's up?" he came in for abuse: "You think you're better than us," which he took as a reference to his Hispanic ethnicity.

Michael said that Ronnie Yates took a screwdriver from the tool rack and started to attack him, and that's when he pulled out the gun and started shooting. When Brian Yates got up, he shot him too.

"I remember Brandon was yelling at me, 'Man, what are you doing?'"

Brandon said that after shooting the brothers, it was Michael who grabbed the screwdriver and started stabbing Ronnie Yates, which Michael disputes.

"It was chaos," Brandon said. "I believe Ronald got paralyzed from the gunshot. He didn't fall at first, but then I see him hit the ground, he just dropped. He was crawling around on the floor. I was shocked. I've never seen somebody get shot like that in my life. I thought I was going to get shot too, just because I witnessed that. I went to the house and told Freddy something bad had happened, that he needed to come out to the garage."

Kerry Lopez told us that when Brandon knocked on their bedroom door, she told him to wait because she and Freddy were still arguing. Brandon knocked again and belligerently, according to Kerry, insisted Freddy come.

Brandon said: "And when he came out to the garage he's like, 'What the hell happened?' Ronald was trying to get out the back of the garage and Freddy said, 'Go get him!' I grabbed him back into the middle of the garage and I kicked him. I don't know what I was doing. I was in shock. I was scared. I was trying to figure out real quick what to do. Freddy was saying, 'What are we going to do?' Somebody said should we call an ambulance, and I'm like. 'They're dying,' and 'They're dead.' I thought Brian was dead because he was gurgling. They weren't moving. So Freddy said, 'Go get the car and pull it into the back of the shop.'"

Alarmed by the uproar, Kerry Lopez had gone to the back of the garage, where she crouched down and peered through a large crack at the bottom of the wooden doorframe, a crack that was still there when we filmed. She heard Freddy say, "We need to get them to hospital," and then Kerry ran round into the garage, and her first instinct, she told us, was to give CPR to Brian Yates.

"Brandon said, 'No, no, no.'" Kerry instead ran to a neighbor to get help.

"The neighbors were Spanish and didn't speak very much English. I'm not fluent in Spanish, but I tried my best. He finally did come over and Freddy came and told him to go home, that I was drunk," said Kerry.

Michael said he was waiting for Freddy to tell them what to do. "Freddy was the older man, he was the one I went to."

Acting under Freddy's orders, he went back into the house and collected the other gun and a set of scales used for weighing out drugs, which would have been incriminating evidence.

"I was a child, I was eighteen, even if I'd been around a bit," said Michael. "When it happened it was like I was a child again. From that point on it was all about Freddy's decisions. His decisions led me down this road. I wasn't in a frame of mind to be thinking logically. After I shot the two victims initially, I was in a haze. I went to Freddy to ask what to do. Whether it was Freddy or Brandon making the decisions for the rest of the night, every action I made I wasn't thinking, I was trusting in them."

Kerry said, "I don't think the murder was planned. I believe the Yates brothers owed Freddy some money, and it was quite a bit. But Brandon did get into an argument that night, got very aggressive, and he was throwing up signs to the Yates brothers. But I don't think he was planning on it. But after the shots, it was clear Brandon planned after that."

Michael and Brandon loaded the two victims into the boot of Freddy's white Honda Accord, and all three men got in, with Brandon driving. They drove out of Verona for seven or eight miles and turned onto a single dirt track leading to Freistatt, a small town largely inhabited by the descendants of German settlers. Noises from the boot told them that at least one of the Yates brothers was still alive. "Somebody started making noises in the trunk and Freddy told me to pull over and handed me the .22 pistol," said Brandon. "I guess I knew what I had to do. I guess I had to get out and shoot them. A silent order, I guess. I was just taking an order. I was afraid that if I didn't step up to the plate that I would have been out there with them.

"I pop the trunk and went back there and lift the lid. I don't know if it was Ronald or Brian. I grabbed one of their heads and shot them. Two shots... whoever it was, I put them outside the car and I did the same thing to the other body... I wasn't worrying about them, I was worrying about staying alive... I was convicted of murder but I'm not a murderer in my heart."

The autopsy report showed that Ronald had been shot through both eyes from close range and in the back of his head, and Brian had a gunshot below his right eye and another to his right ear. They also had earlier wounds inflicted by Michael, in Brian's case to his stomach and chest, and for Ronald, a gunshot which left a bullet lodged in his spine. The murders were initially assumed by the police to be cold-blooded gangland executions, which Brandon denied.

"It was pitch dark," said Brandon. "I've never been involved in any type of murdering, so for me to know how to do an execution-style murder or anything like that... Me and Michael got out of the car; we were grabbing the first body that was in the trunk and shooting. I wasn't aiming. There was no calculation in it, there really wasn't."

Michael admitted he helped get the bodies out of the car. The blood-stained carpet from the trunk was dumped close to the bodies. As the three drove away, one of the men remembered that the brothers had left a car at Freddy's house, so they turned back and Michael searched the bodies for the keys.

When we interviewed Brandon, we asked him how a racial slur could have escalated into the deaths of two men and if there had possibly been more to it, because the Yates brothers owed Freddy money, and Brandon and Michael were his enforcers.

Brandon said: "I asked Michael multiple times if there was a drug or bigger picture to this event, and he's telling me no. It was just over a racial slur. I've always thought there was a bigger picture. There's statements that they owed money, I don't know about that.

"The reason I killed the Yates brothers was to keep myself alive. I thought that since I witnessed all that stuff that went on in the shop, that if I put myself in the middle of this, that everything would be all right. It was wrong, the wrong way to look at it. I was involved with some pretty shady characters and it just came to my mind that's how I would stay alive.

"We made our way to Hoberg and Michael got out and hid the guns. We went to a friend of ours, Troy Evans, where I took a shower and Freddy got on the phone, and we made our way back to Verona. I wanted to tell Troy so bad, but Freddy kept yelling at me and telling me don't be talking.

"It was a bad feeling, an empty feeling. I should have stood up for them, should have stood up for the Yates brothers instead of making them victims. I could have called an ambulance. I could have not gone out there and told Michael that they was making racial slurs."

Troy Evans became another casualty in the case, because when he later found out what they had done, and how he had unknowingly helped them, he committed suicide before having to give evidence in court.

The three men drove back to Verona, where Freddy gave Brandon and Michael money to leave the area. Michael collected all his belongings, and at 7:00 a.m. the two of them drove off in the victims' car and dumped it, and then they got a lift to a Greyhound bus station where they boarded a bus to Michael's girlfriend's home in Yuma, Arizona.

"Freddy knew the cops were going to come for him, he was scared," said Kerry. "We laid a blanket down in front of the Christmas tree and he just held me. He knew what was going to come."

It was very early on New Year's Day that the bodies were found, by a man out hunting coyotes. He drove home to Freistatt, told his wife, and because they did not have a phone, they drove to a nearby town, Monett, to report it to the police.

Deputy sheriff Walter Metevier, from the Lawrence County police, recalled getting the call at about 6:00 a.m. and driving to the scene. He took us to the narrow road where the bodies were found, one in the grass verge, the other in the road.

"It was not a very pretty scene. In my life, I had never been to a double homicide; it was scary. I knew this was an execution because they were shot in the eyes at close range. We turned the bodies over and found wounds in their backs, so they were incapacitated and brought out here, then assassinated. Detectives determined it might be gang affiliated. Somebody was sending a message."

The bodies were identified from a pair of false teeth found near the scene. Inside the dental plate was etched a prison number and the name Brian Yates. Because the dirt road was muddy, they were able to get good casts of two sets of footprints and the tire tracks.

"Once we identified the bodies, it didn't take long to bring it back to Freddy Lopez. Investigations zeroed in on Freddy Lopez's house and the little detail shop next to it," said Deputy Metevier.

Gary Yates was at his mother's house when the sheriff arrived.

"He informed us that they believed they had found Ronnie and Brian dead on Farm Road outside Freistatt. From there on it was just a tragedy. Everybody was in shock. Me and my stepdad went to the funeral home and confirmed it was them. It was just horrifying seeing my brothers laying there on a steel table, lifeless, with bruises and scrapes all over their faces where they'd been dragged across a floor, and bullet holes in their eyes and the side of their heads. It's just unhuman. That was the last day I ever seen my brothers, and I'll remember that for the rest of my life. It's an image I can't get out of my head, and for two years after that I had nightmares. I just don't understand how anybody can do that to another human being. I just hope the guys that did this feel remorse and they really regret what they did to my brothers, because they took away two loving fathers... That's what drugs do to people, they take lives."

Brandon and Michael stayed for a couple of days with Michael's aunt and uncle, and went to church with them.

"Freddy Lopez's family showed up, his brother and father and a few of his cousins, out of the blue," said Brandon. "They took us five or six hours to Desert Hot Springs in California, to his dad's house."

Michael naively felt safe, because he was "with my homies. They are who I grew up with; this is who I can trust."

They heard that Freddy had already been arrested back in Verona, and his family turned on the two men, accusing them of getting Freddy into trouble, and insisting that they turn themselves in. When they got into a car, Michael believed they were going out to eat, but instead Freddy's family took them to a police station, where the police were waiting for them.

"They took us to the sheriff's office and we turned ourselves in," said Brandon. "We told the deputy. I talked to the police for ten minutes and that was it. I've never talked again until now. I never implicated anybody or myself.

"There's a rumor Michael Salazar told me years ago that they were going to kill me in Desert Hot Springs and put a suicide note on me with a confession to the murders. The people that were involved were not good people."

At first Michael also remained silent, but when he heard that Freddy had confessed and was helping the police, he also started talking.

"I was crying, I was in pieces, but it was all coming out," he said. "I see now that they [the police] was just playing on my emotions, they want me to talk so they're telling me, 'Oh, you did good, man, the judges are going to believe you. The judge is going to hear you and see that you are remorseful and that you were scared and only did what you were told, you only look about fifteen.' I confessed everything."

Back in jail in Missouri, waiting for trial, Brandon's girlfriend Michelle, the mother of his two sons, got in touch. She said: "I ran into his cousin's girlfriend, and she gave me the number for his parents. They told me he was in jail. We were in California, so we packed our stuff and moved to Missouri. I fully believed everything was going to work out. I wanted him to be part of the boys' lives. I'm grateful that [while he waited for trial] the boys were able to have contact visits; they know what their dad feels like, they know what it's like to hug him and touch him. Even though it was a very difficult time, I'm grateful the boys had the time they did. I fully believed that he was innocent, but I wasn't surprised that he was in a situation like that because of his drug use. He said he loved me, and I loved him, and he was the one I wanted to spend the rest of my life with. I didn't ask details, I just didn't want to know. I was fully confident that he was innocent, not capable of doing anything like that."

She shrugged ruefully, and tears came to her eyes when she told us that she had faith in the justice system.

"I was very young, idealistic, I thought everyone's part in the events would be revealed."

Brandon and Michelle got married in the Lawrence County jail while he was waiting for his trial.

"I asked her to marry me, and I told her I loved her, and I just wanted to take that step," Brandon explained. "She was one of my only serious girlfriends. She said she would marry me, and we got married in the county jail. I remember I broke down and started crying, just knowing that I was going to prison, Death Row. That I will never be able to touch her or have more kids with her and it was sad. But it was a good day, too."

Michelle told us that she wanted to marry him because "I had this idea in my head that we were going to have a home and a life, similar to [his parents] Laurie and Bill and my mom and dad. A family that loves each other no matter what. On the day we married, I was very excited. I knew at core he was a good person. We were allowed to hug and kiss, and then the next time I saw him it was behind glass, when he'd been sentenced."

In 2001, Michelle and Brandon divorced, but she remained in his life.

Brandon, Michael, and Freddy were tried separately, and Brandon's case came up first. Freddy Lopez took a deal, agreeing to give evidence against the other two in return for a lesser charge of second-degree murder, which carried a sentence tariff of thirty to forty years and meant he avoided both life without parole and the death sentence.

"Freddy whistled like a bird," said his ex-wife, Kerry. "He told everything, showed where the guns were and where they buried or burnt the clothes. Just, you know, to get thirty years to life. I believe he was responsible, because if it wasn't for Freddy transporting the drugs, and if he'd listened to me, his wife, and got a normal job, none of this would have happened."

Matt Selby is the lawyer who prosecuted the case, and he told us he remembered it as unusual.

"What was shocking was the manner in which they had been shot, in the eyes or between the eyes, in the head. So it was an execution-style killing, and that was definitely unusual. We made the decision to seek the death penalty in the first two cases [Brandon and Michael's] because it was a multiple homicide, two people killed, and secondly, the heinous nature of the crime. It was the first death penalty case I had been involved in.

"Throughout the investigation, we found there had been a lot of drugs moving through that house. And people had gone there that night for drugs, knowing that there would likely be drugs and alcohol. Brandon was a larger guy, a good-sized kid, and I think we had some information that he could be violent. It was a very fast-moving investigation; there was a lot of people involved."

In Freddy's initial statement, he denied being in the car that took the Yates brothers from his shop, but he later admitted he was there.

"His attorneys approached us about him helping us," said Matt Selby. "We didn't actually reach a deal, but I think there was an expectation, let me put it that way, that he would probably not end up [charged] with first-degree murder. I don't think there was a deal reached other than definitely the death penalty was taken off the table."

He said the prosecutors felt that the case against Freddy was not as strong as that against the other two. "There was no evidence he was in the garage. To what degree he may have directed the others, we don't know. We may not even have got a conviction at all... The only information that we had, other than what we could piece together through physical evidence and statements from people who had been there before and things that came afterwards, came from Freddy. So there was a decision to offer him something, some sort of leniency, if he cooperated. There was an agreement that he would testify in both cases, Brandon and Michael, and he testified in Brandon's."

Matt Selby told us that when the prosecutors assessed the case, they concluded that the strongest case was against Brandon and that Freddy's evidence was crucial.

"There was deliberation when you get out of the car and open the trunk, that's obviously a thought-out act. Our strongest death penalty argument was on him. Without Freddy, I'm not sure we would have been able to say which one of Michael or Brandon did the shooting at the back of the car."

Brandon's legal team did not have much evidence to present in defense.

"My family hired an attorney but there wasn't much I could say," Brandon said. "I didn't want to talk about it. There was no witnesses for me. I was in fear for my family's life. I just kept my mouth shut."

Matt Selby confirmed that there was very little mitigation heard in court about Brandon's background.

"They [the defense] didn't check out his background and bring in psychologists and psychiatrists and everybody as witnesses. He was twenty-one, but from looking at him you could easily have thought he was twenty-eight or thirty. We didn't have much background information on him. Michael Salazar, on the other hand, was smaller and could have passed for fifteen, and our case for getting first-degree murder on him was less strong."

Brandon wasn't expecting the death penalty.

"It seemed like it hit me at one time and I broke down and hugged Michelle and started crying."

Michelle recalled it vividly: "When he heard the sentence, he went over to the wall. I remember him just going over by the wall, turning round, and sliding down the wall, in tears. It was devastating. They gave him a minute with me."

For Michelle, the trial was unfair because it focused a lot of attention on Brandon being angry and threatening to punch someone earlier on the night of the party.

"How that implicates someone in a murder is beyond me. They focused on a lot of smaller things, to sway the jury. His family did not have the money to get him the representation he needed."

Brandon's brother Matt told us that he believes "Brandon

was a fall guy. He was put in a bad spot where he would have been killed, too. Freddy was the kingpin. Brandon was very fearful of Freddy."

Michael Salazar went to trial next, and Freddy had originally agreed to testify against him too. But Freddy's circumstances changed dramatically when his cousin's wife in California, Dolores Trejo, won the $34 million jackpot on the state lottery in January 1997. The family were able to pay for different lawyers for Freddy. They chose Dee Wampler, a high-profile lawyer who, among many other clients, had defended the Mafia boss John Gotti. His services did not come cheap. Because of his cooperation with the prosecution, Freddy's original lawyers had negotiated a second-degree murder charge with the likelihood of a life sentence with a thirty-year tariff before he could get parole. But the new legal team overturned it and told prosecutors he would not be testifying against Michael.

Michael was charged with first-degree murder under the law of common purpose.

"It means I was responsible for my conduct and the conduct of another person if I aid and assist. If I helped put them in the car, helped take them out, then I'm just as guilty. But I didn't have that common purpose to take them to the side of the road and kill them. I thought we'd take them into the country and throw them out and someone will help them; that's what's in my mind.

"I wasn't ready for all this, not expecting all this. I just wanted to go home. I grew up in California around gangs and drugs and I'd never been involved in anything close to this. I'm only in the county for a couple of months and I'm seeing two people getting killed."

His defense in court was that he acted in self-defense in the initial shootings because one of the Yates brothers was attacking him with a screwdriver. Evidence showed that there were puncture wounds on Brian's body consistent with their being inflicted by a screwdriver, but there was no physical evidence of an attack on Michael. Michael himself didn't testify, and regrets it because he believes the prosecution made him look callous and cold hearted.

Matt Selby explained that the initial shooting of the Yates brothers, carried out by Michael, would "more likely be second-degree murder. But what happened next—there's no question, and it's the argument to the jury—was done intentionally with deliberation. Our trial strategy was that, even though Brandon Hutchison is the one that shot them in the head and finished them off… something set Michael off and he pulled a gun. There was zero evidence that the Yates brothers had a gun. And for him to fire multiple shots into them both, that's what started this whole series of events. So regardless of whether he's the one that finished it or not, what started everything, but particularly the death process for Ronald and Brian Yates, was the actions of Michael Salazar.

"If it wasn't the intention to kill them, why didn't they take them to hospital? If it wasn't the intention to kill, why did they run? If it wasn't the intention to murder them, not just kill them, why did they clean up the blood? Why did they hide the screwdrivers? Why did they get rid of the drugs and the scales? Those are what would have been on the list of things I would have argued were consciousness of guilt and of their intent to cause the deaths of Ronald and Brian Yates."

Gary Yates told us he does not believe that Michael was attacked by Brian.

"Brian's the one that got stabbed with a screwdriver, and Brian was a pretty good-sized guy, a hunky fellow. Salazar wasn't as big as Brian, so how did Salazar get the screwdriver off him? I believe he is lying about that."

Michael was found guilty of both murders. He was given a life sentence without parole, and is still in prison.

Finally, Freddy came before the court almost two years after the murders, and under the direction of his new attorneys, Dee Wampler and his colleague Shawn Askinosie, he pleaded guilty, so there was no jury trial.

"The new attorneys came in and then you start negotiating all over again," said Matt Selby. "Then there was an additional factor came into play. Ronald and Brian Yates both had young children. Then there were discussions not with us but between the attorneys and the Yates brothers' parents, and there was something worked out with trust funds set up for the children and to help the grandparents raise them. I wasn't party to it, but we ended up with an agreement on a ten-year sentence for second-degree murder."

The trust fund set up for the children of the Yates brothers was $230,000.

The prosecution accepted the reduction of first-degree murder to second-degree murder on both counts. They also agreed that the maximum sentence should be ten years on each count, to be served concurrently.

"The state recognizes his cooperation, and appreciated his testimony in the case of Brandon Hutchison. He cooperated and helped us find the weapons," the lead prosecuting attorney, Robert George, told the court. "We've made a recommendation of ten years at the request of the victims in this case."

Crucially, Joyce Kellum, the mother of Brian and Ronnie Yates, gave evidence.

"I feel like this man was more involved and could have done more than what he did, and some of my family will not be happy with this sentence. But I think we need to get on with our lives. The four grandchildren need to be able to go on with their lives. And I just want to let all this rest now. I don't want to go through any more. I've been through the other trials. I think we just need to let it rest. My boys need to rest, my grandchildren need to rest.

"I have two grandchildren down in Columbus that know what went on. The two little ones live with me; they do not understand why their father is not with them. I cannot tell them why. I just don't think I could go through another trial. Like I said, I think he was more involved, but I appreciate the fact that he came forward."

The court also heard a letter from a lawyer acting on behalf of the families of Brian and Ronnie Yates.

"Although my clients firmly believe that Mr. Lopez did play a role in the deaths, his subsequent acts to assist the police have not gone unnoticed. Thus, after much consideration and prayer, it is the desire of these family members to request this court not to sentence Mr. Lopez to more than a ten-year term of imprisonment."

Freddy addressed the court and said, "I know I am going to prison. But before I go, I want to apologize to the families who have suffered because of this nightmare. I have no offering of excuses for you today. We were all wrong in how we handled ourselves that early morning. I can offer my sincere apologies to the victims' families and to my very own family. I pray for all who have suffered through this never-ending tragedy."

Freddy did not take part in our film.

"We would have liked to talk to him, but he never responded when we tried to contact him," said Ingo. "Kerry Lopez was able to pass a message to him through their son, letting him know what we were doing and telling him he could put the record straight from his side, but he didn't want to do it."

Since his release, after serving eight years, Freddy has been in jail again, for drugs offenses.

Ingo said that, even after more than twenty years in prison, both Brandon and Michael were at first reluctant to talk about Freddy.

"He still seems to have power and influence, and it took a lot to get them to say anything about him," said Ingo.

Gary Yates did not agree with the plea bargain that got Freddy Lopez a reduced sentence for his involvement in the deaths of his brothers.

"I know Freddy made a deal with the district attorney and with my mom, his family paid my mom. They put money in a trust fund to help raise the kids. But at the time I did not know that he only gets a short sentence because of that. I wouldn't have agreed to it. I don't believe someone should plea bargain and pay his way out of a horrendous crime like that. I think the reason my mom settled is because she's old. I don't think she should have taken the money. Her and my stepdad was in their sixties, it's just too hard on them."

Kerry Lopez, who divorced Freddy in 2009, also told us that she felt her ex-husband got off too lightly because he was able to buy the services of good lawyers.

"Paying to get a certain amount of time, I don't think that was right," she said. "You know, it's all over money."

Michael Salazar was at first diffident when we spoke to him, but he opened up and was articulate and thoughtful.

"I'm the first to admit my participating that night was messed up. But I didn't shoot these guys in the head and I didn't kill them. I want to be held accountable for my actions, based on the truth. I was being told what to do by this big guy and this old guy. I was an eighteen-year-old kid being misled and manipulated by these older and bigger men. I don't agree that I should spend the rest of my life in prison. But I'm biased!" He laughed as he told us this.

He said he has prayed for the Yates family, and he understood why they might feel anger toward him, even after all these years.

"I pray for Freddy, I pray for Brandon. I don't sit here and resent and blame them. I made a lot of bad decisions that night."

He also doesn't blame his fractured, dysfunctional childhood for the crime he committed. He reminisced to us about good things from his early years, the aunt and uncle who taught him religious faith, and the uncle who ignited his passion for sport.

"Sport is big in prison. Everybody's into sport, you know, watching it, playing it, gambling. That's one of the biggest pastimes... The passion for sport that I have right now is because of him."

Brandon spent fifteen years on Death Row.

"I didn't really think about death every day. They kept me pretty medicated. I knew I was going to be in prison until I was executed or for the rest of my life. There's only one ending to it."

In 2011, Brandon's appeal against his sentence succeeded,

based on the fact that his trial did not hear about Freddy's plea deal and that his defense lawyers had not presented any mitigation at his trial, not telling the jury about his limited learning abilities. Tests carried out showed that his IQ was in the bottom 8 per cent of the population. His sentence was commuted to life without parole.

"There was a relief, for me and my family. But then there comes a whole different set of emotions. I know that one of these institutions in Missouri is where I'm going to pass away. So I have to come to terms with it."

Brandon agreed to be interviewed by us because, "I want people to be able to see me, not as that dope-fiend monster that I was, drug addict, a young punk. There is still a person in here, there's still good in me. I hope people can forgive me because I feel for the Yates family and the community that was terrified over what happened. I caused so much pain to a lot of people. You commit a crime and it can spread out and impact a lot more people than you believe."

Matt, his brother, confirmed the effect on Brandon's own family.

"My mom had a nervous breakdown and my dad stressed out. Me, I just ran to drugs and alcohol for a little while."

When we met Michael, we played him Brandon's confession, and apart from disagreeing with some details, he was genuinely surprised that after all the many years of silence, Brandon had finally talked about the murders.

"He's never admitted it. Hopefully he feels better. I've always known what happened, but just to hear him say it... Even though I know the truth, it made me feel better. I'm glad he finally admitted that he did shoot them. I've always been willing to accept responsibility for what I've done. I'm not sitting here saying I'm only 30 percent responsible and he's 80 percent and Freddy's 90 percent—I'm not sitting here blaming them. I'm responsible for my actions and the decisions I made, whether I was intoxicated or not.

"I forgave Brandon a long time ago for doing what he did. I've forgiven Freddy, you know, for telling on us at the beginning. Getting his family to turn us in the way they did. And I've forgiven myself. It didn't happen overnight, it took a long time. I'm not going to sit here and hold on to any anger toward them, that's not going to help me none. That's not going to help me live today, tomorrow. I'm at peace in here. I don't want to be in here, but I live every day trying to make it the best I can. Brandon, I love you, man, and I will continue praying for you and your family."

Michelle also confronted the truth when we played her Brandon's confession, and she cried as she listened to his voice. She had already accepted Brandon's part in the disposal of the bodies and his being present when the murders happened. Through stifled sobs she still offered Brandon support.

"I had a hard time believing he pulled the trigger. But I believe he was given an ultimatum. He didn't make the right choice, but I can't imagine what it would be like. I am not in a position to judge. Listening to this [Brandon's confession] just gives me a lot more questions than answers."

For Gary Yates, hearing Brandon's confession after so many years "gives me a little bit of comfort. I feel he does kind of feel some remorse, but I don't feel he deserves to live. He took two lives away. Why should he still be living? Brandon Hutchison was the executioner, Michael Salazar initiated it, and I feel that Freddy Lopez is the one that organized it, the ringleader. All three are guilty. I believe they should all get the same sentence, they should all get the death penalty, and they should not be living now, in my eyes."

When we revisited Brandon in jail for the second interview, three months after the first, he had no regrets about speaking to us and owning up for the first time to his part in the murders.

"The truth can't hurt nothing. And to be changed as a man inside your heart, I think you have to go with the truth and admit my guilt. Hopefully the healing process can help on both sides, the victims' families and the victims in my family. I never admitted it to anybody. I have never told anything until right now."

Ingo said, "When we met him again, I asked him a tricky question: Why had he let Michelle believe in his innocence all these years, not telling her the truth even when marrying her? He was straightforward in all his dealings with us, and he was straightforward in his answer."

"I never gave Michelle or anybody else any details of the murders," Brandon said. "Maybe I should have done, instead of taking four years from her life. I just thought it was the right thing to do. I kept my silence for fear for my family and my own safety."

We played him the tape of parts of our interview with Michael.

"Michael was a teenager when he caught this case. If I got any hard feelings toward anybody it would be Freddy. Michael's a good person. He was just manipulated by the wrong people. I don't think nobody deserves life without parole. I believe if you can be rehabilitated you should be given that chance.

"There was a lot of injustice. To get a conviction, the prosecution made a deal with the devil. They didn't make the deal

with the man that pulled the trigger. They wanted a conviction. Mr. Lopez had millions of dollars to give back to the
situation. And I think he used his manipulation and his criminal way of thinking to get what was best for him. There was
a lot of crookedness going on doing that. There was a lot of
money transferring from hand to hand with Mr. Lopez and his
lawyers. Freddy paid for a ten-year sentence.

"Freddy is not a good person. I've heard stories about
Freddy for a long time. I knew what Freddy was capable of. I
knew that they were going to murder me in the desert and put
a suicide note on me. I knew this stuff, my father knew this
stuff. When you're talking about Freddy Lopez, you're not
just talking about an ordinary person. You're talking about
a very manipulative criminal person. I kept my silence out of
fear for my family and my own safety."

Brandon also told us how he had reached the decision to
tell the truth for the first time, in front of our camera.

"I don't think any of this has hit me until the last four
or five years of my life. I never really felt that remorse for
what I had done. People say, 'I got remorse.' I've never felt the
pain of remorse. I was watching a program on TV and this
grandmother or mother was talking about her daughter being
murdered, and I literally felt what she was feeling. And all I
could think about was the Yates' mother.

"The next morning, I woke up and there was a message from
you guys wanting to do a story on my case. It was the right time
to tell the truth, admit to what I did. There's a weight lifted. I
feel better, I feel a relief. I don't want to gain anything from telling the truth, except I wish the victims' families would understand the grief I go through for what I put them through... The
brothers' kids, I'm sorry that I put them through a life without

a father. I hope they understand I'm not a monster. I wasn't out tracking down people to hurt. Something bad happened that night, it went bad. I regret not saving their lives instead of taking it. I'm sorry to take these two people out of your lives, people that meant so much to you."

He told us he was pleased to have talked so openly. "I feel great for what I talked to you guys about."

At this second interview, Brandon told us that he had not been feeling well, and was struggling to keep food down, and was going to have tests.

"When he got the diagnosis of cancer, he contacted me to tell me," said Ingo. "But at that stage he hoped there was something that could be done. It is very, very sad that so soon after finally coming to terms with his part in the crime, he passed away. Michelle got in touch after his death, but she was very upset, especially as her mother also died soon afterward.

"After we met Michael, he made contact with Brandon, and the two of them exchanged good messages. They both realized they did not blame each other. Brandon died at peace with himself, and I'm glad we were able to be part of that."

8

A FAMILY AFFAIR

DEANDRA BUCHANAN

"Whenever certain things happen to certain people that they love, they're going to do everything they can to make you out to be a monster, to make sure you get what they believe you deserve, which meant, at the time, a lot of them wanted me to die."

Deandra Buchanan was talking to us from a bare room at Jefferson City Correctional Center, a modern maximum-security prison on No More Victims Road, twelve miles from the city center of Jefferson, Missouri. He had been incarcerated there for most of the eighteen years he had spent in prison, sentenced to life without parole for the brutal murder of three people, one of them the mother of his children, on 7 November 2000.

Filming in the empty visits room, where prisoners meet their families and friends, was problematic for director Jeremy Turner, who found the room was lined with a bank of noisy vending machines.

"They were like fridges, making humming noise for a while and then going quiet. There was no way to switch them off—we tried," he said.

In the end, both the crew and Deandra developed a rhythm for the recording: questions were asked during the quiet phase of the cycle, then he answered during the next quiet phase.

Deandra sat back confidently on a plastic chair, and the first impression the crew got was of a man with charisma and charm. He summed himself up for us at that first meeting: "I'm just considering myself a down-to-earth normal person who tries to help others and better myself at the same time. More like a people person. I try to look out for people. I have a caring heart."

Deandra, known to friends and family as Dre, was a drug dealer who cooked and sold crack cocaine and marijuana from a home in Columbia that belonged to his stepfather, William Jefferson. He was living there because he was on probation for physically assaulting his girlfriend Angie, the mother of his two little daughters. Despite having gotten a court order to keep him away, she had moved back to live with him and brought their two little girls, one only five months old. On the night of 7 November 2000, several emergency calls were made, and the first police officers to get to the house found Angie outside on the sidewalk, shot through the neck, bleeding profusely, her two little children still clinging to her.

Lieutenant Geoff Jones recalled the night for us, retracing the same route he followed as he sped to the scene, his dash-cam video recording it.

"The whole time the radio is just full of the dispatcher giving information. There were people shot. They were trying to give a suspect description, one piece of information right after the next. When I turned the corner, I saw someone lying on the ground. When I got out I could see a woman lying there, and there were children on top of her. One of them was trying to get out from under her arm. There was blood pooling around her neck. She had no idea we were there. She was not conscious, she was barely breathing. She was bleeding out. She didn't respond to us at all. We knew that it was bad for her.

"She was obviously holding those children when she got shot, and it appeared to me by the way she was lying there that she had opened her arms up so that her children would avoid the blast."

Inside the house they found two more victims. William Jefferson was dead at the scene, having been blasted at close range in the chest. Juanita Hoffman, Deandra's aunt, who had helped bring him up, was also bleeding from chest wounds. Although she was able to walk from the house, and told police who had shot her, she died several hours after arriving at the hospital.

The fourth victim, Jerry Key, who was found when Dre was arrested a few streets away, spent two weeks in hospital and is permanently disabled.

Deandra Buchanan never denied committing the shocking murders: his defense centered on his being under the influence of drugs which caused paranoid, psychotic behavior, claiming that therefore he was not responsible for his actions.

"He presented himself as a victim," said Jeremy. "And that was the version of himself he stuck to."

Deandra Buchanan's life started out in Centreville, Illinois. He was the child of a fifteen-year-old mother and sixteen-year-old father, whose grandparents were largely responsible for bringing him up. His mother was not always around, but he remembers his father being very involved.

"He kept me on the narrow path, exposed me to religion, made sure I brought home good grades, and pretty much exposed me to all different types of instruments, sports, science, you name it.

"I lost my father in a motorcycle accident. I was ten or eleven at the time. I was supposed to go riding with him but he wouldn't let me go. I displayed my frustration and anger, but knowing my father, I knew not to get out of hand because I didn't want to get a whupping." He smiled and chuckled at the memory of himself as a small boy.

"I stormed off, so my grandmother sent me outside to play in the yard. My cousin's father pulled up in a truck and told me, 'I think your dad was just in an accident.' So he put me in his truck and took me to this area. And when we got there it was a wreck, and they took the sheet off and I saw my father's body. It was a gruesome sight."

Deandra dates his going off the rails to that day.

"I believe that was a turning point in my life, it caused me to stray onto another path. I started acting out at school, fighting, getting into stuff like that, fighting in the neighborhood."

By the time he was twelve he was hanging out in gambling clubs.

"That was the beginning of me being fascinated with the life of crime. I saw the money on the table, and the older men were dressed nice and had smart cars. I was fourteen when I ended up getting into the drug trade. It was the early eighties and it was a serious epidemic in the inner cities with this cocaine thing. I was taught how to sell it. It wasn't no work, just taking a piece of drugs and giving it to somebody else. I was intelligent enough to see it was more money, but I wasn't intelligent enough to know exactly where I was going. And it was like a beginning and no end. We would run up on these cars and stick our hands in the cars, and one time this guy hit my hand and took off with the product. So a load of guys who was teaching us how to do all this stuff put a gun in my hand. I was fourteen when I got my first illegal gun. And it was in my mind that [being robbed] would never happen again, so I made sure I kept a weapon on me at all times."

He was fourteen when he had his first serious brush with the law and was put on probation. It was at the same age that he started smoking marijuana, and by sixteen he was expelled from high school for selling drugs in school. He was earning so much that his grandfather gave him the nickname "Easy Money." When one of his uncles offered him a legal job in his cleaning service, Deandra told him: "Man, why would I come and work for you for all those hours and only make twenty dollars when I can sell this right here and make twenty dollars in two minutes?" His uncle warned him about the chances he was taking. Money became a driving force.

"I end up buying a car, a little jewelry, stuff like that. Money influences things. It makes things happen. I said, 'Fuck school.' I fit the lifestyle of a criminal man. And I made a vow to try to become what I saw on TV. I made my mind up that I wanted to be a gangster. The women never knew all my business. When I met women they didn't really know how deep I was into the criminal lifestyle. They only saw the clothes, the car, and my demeanor, because I was raised to be very respectful."

He told us he was numb to violence from an early age, not just after the death of his father but after seeing beatings with weapons and even gunshots in school.

"Being in that kind of world, you have to have a somewhat cold heart to be able to carry out violence if somebody did something to you, because you didn't want to be viewed as being weak. If you disrespect me, I'm going to disrespect you. I think the glamour of that lifestyle kind of captivated me. And unfortunately, what's in the dark comes to the light."

As he grew into his twenties, Deandra started setting up legitimate companies to help launder his money and give him a respectable front. He moved from Illinois to Columbia to avoid the law, choosing Columbia because his aunt Juanita lived there.

Juanita had been close to her sister Lydia, Deandra's mother, and Juanita's three daughters, Toni, Shontai, and Mija, remember him as a child, as they grew up alongside him.

"He was spoiled," Toni told us, her sisters nodding in agreement as they sat around Toni's table recalling for us their mother and the cousin who killed her. For director Jeremy Turner, they were "a powerful collection of personalities. They had tough lives, made tougher by the loss of their mother. I think they, and the others who talked to us, wanted a platform to put their side forward and speak on behalf of the victims. They wanted us to know that this was not a horrible accident but the end of a journey Deandra was on."

Toni told us more about their childhood with Deandra: "Me and my sisters, we were girls, but we went to Grandmama's house to play with his toys because he had everything. But he was cool. He was somebody I looked up to. Our family's close knit, so we just always been close and we grew a bond. It was more of a sister–brother bond with all of us."

Her sister Shontai said, "He was never mistreated; we all had a good life."

Toni told us the death of his father impacted him.

"I remember when Uncle Jim-Jim passed away. I know it affected him. I don't think he even cried like a normal child would losing a parent. But you know, over the years he found different ways to deal with it. As he got a little older, he started smoking marijuana. I think that kind of took the edge off."

By the time he was twenty, according to Deandra, his life had descended into drug-related violence. He couldn't count the number of murders he had seen. He had been robbed at gunpoint when he was carrying out a drug deal, escaped an attempt on his life when he was living in California, and he was expecting retaliation from another drug dealer whom he had shot in the leg in East St. Louis, Illinois.

"I was involved in all kinds of violence where I have seen people lose their life. I mean, it's nothing to be proud of now I think back on it. But back then, we thought that was the thing to do."

When he was twenty-three he was introduced to fifteen-year-old Angela Brown by her cousin.

"Aw, man, she was the type of girl I sought after. She was the type of girl I had dated in the past. From first sight, when we saw each other it was just one of them moments. She liked how I looked, I liked how she look, and we just began to talk. And we went out on a date and it never stopped. She was a very beautiful, intelligent girl. By the time I met her, I was a fully fledged criminal, but she didn't know it though. I decided I was going to stay here [Columbia] for a while, get off into drugs activities, but I needed a front, so I started a moving company. When she met me, that's what I had."

Angie was an attractive girl, described by her mother, Valeria, as quiet and bookish. She was still at school when they met, and Deandra wooed her respectfully and attentively.

"She was a goofball," her mother said. "Everybody that came in contact with her, she just filled their heart with joy because she was a lovely person... She didn't see no bad on nobody. She talked well. She read, she didn't go to bars—she hated that. She always went to school, she was a bookworm. Everybody she came in contact with said she's mature for her age.

"When she turned sixteen she came to me and said, 'Momma, I want to go out on a date with this guy.' I said OK, we need to talk to him. He was a total gentleman and everything. He was nice, polite, spoke polite, brought her back on time, called her on the phone like normal girlfriend and boyfriend. I liked him at first. You wouldn't think he was a wolf in sheep's clothing.

"Angie fell in love with him. I found out he was too old. She said, 'No he isn't, he is my school friend.' I think she just said that because that's what he wanted her to say because if I found out he was older he would never have dated her."

Angie was still only sixteen when her mother saw bruises on her arm and she knew Deandra was abusing her.

"So I told Angie that's not love, that's not love at all, you need to do better."

She said Angie stayed with him because he was her first love "and he bought her rings, jewelry, clothes, and all that stuff."

Soon after she started going out with Deandra, Angie moved out of Valeria's home, and he prevented her from going to visit her mother, who for a time did not know where they were living. The rift between mother and daughter lasted until Angie's first child, Dreisha (known as Esha), was born, when Angie was eighteen. Deandra was there when she gave birth.

"I'll never forget the day," he told us. "I was right in the delivery room when she came out of her mom's womb... I'm looking at my daughter like I'm going to do everything I can to make sure she OK... It's unconditional! Knowing that's your daughter! Man, I was like, I did never put my hands on her! I'm serious! I would never whup my daughters."

Valeria saw her daughter and new granddaughter at the hospital. But the breach was not completely healed, and when Valeria saw Angie a few months later, she noticed bruises again. When Angie's brother tried to persuade her to leave Deandra, her reply was: "I love him. I love him so much."

After other domestic bust-ups, Valeria said, "I knew deep down in my soul that he's the one who's going to take Angie's life."

Deandra told us how Angie found out the true nature of his business.

"I really didn't expose her to too much of my criminal behavior in the beginning. But eventually I had to explain my lifestyle. An incident occurred. Somebody broke into one of our houses that we were renting and ransacked the place, and I had to sit down and tell her what was going on. I said, 'Look, I don't live the way you think I live. I'm into a lot of criminality, and they came here looking for drugs and money.' And that's when we started going to the shooting range together, taught her how to use weapons, things of that nature, then also taught her how not to come straight home whenever she's out working, never come directly home. She accepted it. I said, 'Look, we can't let nobody know where we live at.' This was before we even had a child. I think she just wanted to be with me. I cared a lot about her. We were talking about getting married, but I didn't want to move too fast, so we got engaged."

He told us, with no outward recognition of his role in her death, "I still miss her."

Devon McTye, Angie's best friend, godmother to her two

children, and the granddaughter of William Jefferson, who died in the carnage that night, talked to us with an array of family photographs spread on the table in front of her. She showed us photographs of the day her grandfather married Deandra's mother, a proud lineup including Deandra, who was the groomsman.

Angie knew Deandra had three other children, one of whom was born when he was fifteen. Devon showed us a photograph of Angie playing with two of these children.

"By other women! So, you see, she was pretty involved in their lives and trying to be a good role model. She's pretty tolerant of Deandra," Devon said.

Devon knew Angie from the age of thirteen, when they met at school. Like Angie's mother, Valeria, she described her friend as quiet, studious, never getting in trouble at school.

"She was very, very beautiful. She didn't think of herself as a pretty girl, but when you saw her, she was strikingly beautiful. She was pretty timid. It took a lot to get her to be talkative. I think that was because of the relationship she was in with Deandra."

Devon knew Deandra before she knew Angie, having met him when she was eleven and her grandfather was in a relationship with Lydia, his mother. At that age, she thought he was great, "a cool dude."

"Dre had a personality that would capture folks. He seemed a cool person that would help you out. But then, the longer I knew him, the more I got to see the other side. Which is the abuser, the monster. Seeing him interact with Angie, and with other women...that negative side, how he would treat Angie. He was like Dr. Jekyll and Mr. Hyde, two different personalities."

She understood the initial attraction for Angie.

"When you are sixteen, you want to date somebody in their twenties, spoiling you, like he's got a car, a house, gives you money. That's kind of how he pulled Angie in. That was his way of building up control over her. She was pretty much mentally controlled by him, like she just couldn't leave him though he'd been physically violent to her. Once I started talking to Angie, that's when I knew what was really going on between them, the abuse. He took the natural path of an abuser. He started out with the gifts and the spoiling and taking her on trips and driving her around, nice cars, showing her off. He got from that to 'You've got to live with me,' then to 'You can't leave the house unless I say so,' to 'You can't hang out with your family, be around your friends,' to killing her, just step by step. The drugs were part of it, but they weren't the reason for it."

Shontai Hoffman, Juanita's daughter, corroborated what Devon said about physical abuse.

"Angela showed me where Deandra had beaten her with a wire hanger, and she showed me welts from the top of her neck to her knees where he whupped her and whupped her." Deandra and Devon gave us two different accounts of the events that led to him being put on probation, a few months before the murders, when he assaulted Angie during her second pregnancy. Deandra said: "Our second daughter was born the year this crime happened, my crime. I was only able to spend a little time with her cause me and Angie had split up. It was something that transpired in one of our houses, when she broke a code that I live by. We had a security system and all this. My little brother was staying with me and he said, 'Do you know that Angie's cousin just left from over here?' And I was like, 'No! How does she even know where we live at?' I'm already fucked up from hearing this information, literally blown away because we already had a talk with her about security measures. But what really ticked me off, a lot, was some guys was in the car on the driveway and my little brother said they never got out. She just allowed them to invade this so-called privacy we thought we had. So this got me really hot. I didn't really know who I can trust now, because when she'd done that after we already had an understanding, it was like a barrier broke. The trust factor was broke. And that's when we kind of fell out and there was a little domestic abuse. I end up shaking her up a little bit. I grab her and shake her because she wouldn't tell me exactly what I thought I should hear! And she was like, 'Oh, it was only my cousin,' and I was like, 'Who the fuck was in the fuckin' car? Who was these dudes? I'm hot. So she called the police. They came, they arrested me. They took her, locked me up.

"I came back, got my clothes, because I didn't even trust being in this house no more, because the security was just infiltrated. Having those experiences, with certain family members, it caused me not to trust certain people."

When we played Devon the tape of Deandra telling us this, she was keen to counter his assertion that he was "shaking her up a little bit."

"It wasn't just a shake. I think he chooses to describe it like that because he doesn't want to seem like the bad guy, when clearly he is the bad guy. He ran out into the street after her and was hitting her with a baseball bat. Somebody broke it up and Angie went into a violence shelter. And she was so afraid of him that even after he did all that to her, she still came back. He had that much control over her. She was only twenty when she died. He got to her right at the time of her life that she was totally vulnerable to somebody like him, because he's a classic batterer... He was a classic narcissist. He said whatever he needed to say to get whatever he needed."

Deandra was put on six months' probation, one condition of which was that he had no contact with Angie. His stepfather, William Jefferson, put his house up as a bail bond for him, even though he was no longer married to Deandra's mother, and the court ordered that he should live there. Another condition was that he took an anger management course, but he pulled out before he completed it and moved to California for three months. For a short time, Angie's life was peaceful.

"She was living with me. She had her own apartment but she was staying with me," said her mother. "She started getting her color back, started getting healthy looking. But when she didn't come home from work, I knew he was back, I knew that was going to be bad, him being back. He'd take the kids and use them as a pawn to get her back. She loved her kids to death."

It was after his daughter Drejanay's birth that Deandra returned to Columbia, where he had more drug deals set up. According to him, he decided to see his daughters. After staying with him in different hotels and then briefly back at her apartment, Angie and the two little girls moved to be with him at William Jefferson's house.

"She was so afraid of him that even though he did all that to her and the police separated them, she still came back! She still went back after he did that," said Devon.

Deandra put a different spin on it: "She and I were together with our daughters. We were hanging out and stuff like that, and that's when some stuff transpired. Love is strange; you love a person but your trust is not there and you don't ever really want to turn your back on them. I want to be a father to my daughters, and I'm trying to let her know I'm not one of them deadbeat guys that isn't going to be there for his kids, and I still cared for her. I still love her. But the trust is not like it used to be."

At the time of the shootings, the police had a warrant out for his arrest after urine tests showed cocaine and marijuana in his blood, and he had gone to great lengths to avoid detection, having his fingerprints "stripped" to prevent identification, obtaining a false birth certificate under another name, and changing his hairstyle. He regularly carried a .45-caliber pistol and a twelve-gauge shotgun.

On the day of the murders, Devon went with her grandfather to vote; it was the first time she had voted, and it was the last time she saw her grandfather. She had rowed with Deandra about the way he treated Angie, so that night, although she and her mother called at the house, she stayed in the car while her mother chatted with him on the doorstep.

"I will never know why it was that particular night, but I always knew he would try to kill Angie," said Devon. "I always knew in my head. The other people that were there that night were really collateral damage. There was literally no excuse or reason for him to have shot my grandfather or shot Juanita. Those are two people that had his back. My grandfather died a hero that night. He was not going to let Dre do nothing to nobody else because that's his house, his domain. My grandfather treated him like a son, and Dre returned the favor by putting a bullet in his heart."

The details of what happened that night came out at the trial.

Deandra kept the back door of the house barricaded because it opened into the bedroom he was sharing with Angie and his daughters, and he was constantly afraid the police or other drug dealers would burst in. He kept his money and supplies of drugs in the room.

He told us again how careful he was about security. "When I had my own house, I had a weapon in every room. A friend of mine was killed. Somebody knocked on the door, he answered the door, and they shot him and killed him. So from that point on, I don't open doors. I pay a guy fifty bucks a day literally to answer doors for me. My security was just beyond normal. But for us who lived that lifestyle, it's normal. I thought everything was under control because I surrounded myself with people who believed in violence, people who believed in selling drugs. I was always a paranoid individual because I lived a paranoid lifestyle."

The day had not gone well for Angie. She and Deandra had been arguing, and according to witnesses at his trial, he was "upset with her all day." Early in the evening he was heard saying, "I'm going to kill me a bunch of motherfuckers tonight," and he threatened to kill Angie. The people who heard him did not take him seriously: they had heard Dre raging before.

That evening there was a party at William Jefferson's house. The old man was a dapper figure, much loved in the community, and always very hospitable. Juanita Hoffman was also living there but had just found herself a new apartment and was due to move out, so the celebration was a farewell party for her. As well as Angie and her two children, two-year-old Dreisha and five-month-old Drejanay, there were also Linda Dawson, a friend of Juanita's, Linda's boyfriend Jeffrey

Stemmons, and two small grandchildren of Juanita's in the house. The group drank alcohol and some of them smoked marijuana.

According to Deandra, he contacted a friend of his to bring some marijuana, and he claimed he had no idea that the joints he then smoked were spiked with another drug. Other witnesses reported that he was smoking "primos," marijuana cigarettes laced with cocaine. His behavior became more agitated and paranoid.

While the others sat around watching a movie, he paced the house with his shotgun. When another relative knocked at the door, he checked through the window before allowing anyone to open it. Later, as his mood escalated, he accused Angela of infidelity and said the others in the house were trying to kill him or put him in jail. They took little notice of his threats. He even claimed later to have dialed the 911 emergency service and told the operator he needed help because people were plotting to kill him.

In his interview with us, he said his first suspicion of a plot was when the friend who brought the marijuana did not stay around to smoke it with him. He stuck to this story that there really was a plot against him and that his suspicions were not entirely the product of drug-induced paranoia.

"I say to my door guy, 'I thought he was going to hang out and smoke some with us?' And I notice that the bedroom door was open and the light was on."

He said he heard a door open.

"So I say, 'Who just came in here?' and everybody was like, 'Nobody came in here.' But I noticed that the bathroom light was off and the bedroom door was closed... I say, 'Well, if there is nobody in here, go open up the bedroom door.'

And my door guy say, 'Man, you tripping, there isn't nobody in there.' But he never went open up the door. So I grab a weapon. I say, 'Man, go open up the fucking door.' And in the midst of this, I don't know how, my mind was just not right, what was going on within me; all of a sudden I get to feeling strange as a motherfucker. Like whatever I was smoking was beyond what I've smoked before. And I'm like, 'Man, I am not feeling right. I'm serious. Something's wrong with me. Open up the fucking door.' And fuck, that's all I really remember. I don't even know what took place, what the fuck happened."

Sensing that things were getting out of control, Juanita tried to leave the house with her two small grandchildren. Deandra blocked her way and forbade her to open the outside door. At this point, William Jefferson asked Linda Dawson to call the police. She and some of the others managed to remove the barricade and flee from the house. Jeffrey Stemmons hid in a bedroom cupboard.

Then a gunshot was heard. According to Deandra's statement to the police, his aunt Juanita asked him to go outside with her, but he claimed she then tried to shut the door. He forced it open and dropped the shotgun, which went off—although he claimed he believed it was someone shooting at him.

Juanita retreated toward the back of the living room, and Jeffrey (hiding in the cupboard) heard her shout: "Deandra, stop this. I love you." Deandra said she tried to grab the shotgun, and he pulled it out of her grasp and shot her in the chest. As she lay bleeding, he became aware the other partygoers were escaping from the back of the house and began walking toward them. In the kitchen, his stepfather, William, was hiding next to the refrigerator. As Deandra approached,

William put his hands up. Deandra pumped the shotgun and fired at close range into the old man's chest, the slug hitting his heart and liver, killing him instantly.

Deandra chased after the people who were running away outside and fired two shots randomly toward them, then reloaded the shotgun with shells from his pocket. Seeing Angie among those running away, he ran after her and called, "Come here." Holding the baby and clutching the hand of two-year-old Dreisha, Angie stopped running. He said he told her he needed help, but then he put the muzzle of the shotgun against her neck and pulled the trigger. The shot hit her spinal cord and she collapsed in a pool of blood, still holding the children. She survived but was brain dead, and after three days in hospital she died.

Deandra later told the police he deliberately shot her at close range in the neck to avoid hitting the children. Of the other partygoers, he said, "If I could have caught them all, I think I'd have got [killed] them all."

Hiding the shotgun inside his clothes, he ran from the scene. Jerry Key, an acquaintance of his, was driving past and, knowing nothing of the murders, stopped to offer him a lift. Deandra checked there was nobody else in the car and climbed in, immediately pulling out the shotgun and ordering Jerry Key to drive. When Jerry asked where to, Deandra replied that he didn't know, and said he had just shot his girlfriend (Jerry knew Angie). As he was driving, Jerry later told the police, he saw the muzzle of the shotgun was slowly being turned in his direction, and he pushed it away. Seeing an approaching police car, Jerry slowed down and was then shot in the chest after Deandra said, "I don't need you no more."

Jerry was able to jump out of the window of the car while

it was still moving, and the vehicle rolled off the street and stopped in a garden. Deandra got out and ran to the back of the house but surrendered quickly to police. It was lieutenant Krista Jones (wife of Geoff Jones, who had found the bodies) who arrested him. She was driving toward the scene of the murders when she saw the car crash and followed him into the backyard of the house.

"I started yelling at him to show me his hands, keep his hands where I could see them," she said. "And he was doing what I was asking but he seemed worked up. He was yelling really fast to the point that I really couldn't understand a lot of what he was saying. I remember being kind of surprised that even though he was acting so agitated, he was doing the things that I was telling him to do. So I knew that he was at least understanding my commands."

Lieutenant Jones told us that she believed he was obeying her orders because he was in control of himself enough to know that he didn't want "suicide by cop": the act of deliberately getting oneself killed by the police.

Deandra told us: "According to what I seen in the [police] paperwork, they said I was slamming my head all up against the police door and windows. I don't remember none of this stuff and I said that somebody was trying to kill me. It was either them or me and they said I was belligerent, sweating, and mucus coming out of my nose, and at one point they said I told them, 'You can't protect me!' So they put me in a suicide cell, observation."

When he first arrived at the police station, he confessed to the murders, and his confession was recorded and videotaped. He was agitated, talking rapidly, and giving a garbled account of what he had done.

"When you got a funny feeling in your fucking soul about something that is going to happen to you, that's when I grabbed the gun. I pointed the gun. I didn't point the gun to shoot anybody. I didn't want anybody to encircle me. I tried to build a circle around, then they backed up. Then they are going to say, 'No, we got the kids'... What the fuck is that about? If you aren't up to nothing? My fucking kids and my little cousins!"

Responding to a question from the police interviewer, he answered coherently and confirmed that the gun was loaded.

"At least seven and one in the chamber. That was like house protection... I didn't snap on nobody right there."

He described how he believed his aunt was trying to push him out of the house: "I'm begging my auntie to explain what the fuck is happening and asking her why she won't go outside with me. And why can't I go outside with her. 'I'm your fucking nephew, why you treating me like this? What, am I going to die or something?' So I get over there...she opened the door. I aren't pointing the gun at no motherfucking body. And she pushes me out. I came, 'Why the fuck did you try to lock me out? What's outside that you don't want me to be out there with you?' Everybody looking crazy, moving away from me, moving to the back of the house. That's when I called you guys [the police]. Cause I needed help because there is nobody in this house who was trying to help me, not even my auntie... She came at me, to take the fucking gun from me. 'Why you trying to take my gun?' I yanked it back and then, oh man, I lost it. I just lost love, lost everybody I love."

He described seeing his stepfather against the refrigerator and saying, "Yo, Pops."

"I looked at him. He looked at me. And I was like, man, I

want to fuck with you all for trying to fuck with me... And I pulled the trigger and I ran out of the house. All of a sudden I see someone I knew, to the right, and I see my kids' mother."

The detective prompted him to continue.

"The gun was out of bullets. I went to my back pockets and I loaded the gun back up."

He ran after Angie.

"She had my kids! She was running for real. I said, 'Come on, Angie,' and she stopped. I'm asking her why all of a sudden, you know, why the fuck are you all trying to take my life? She got these kids! All of a sudden I just lost it for her. The simple fact that she tried to set me up, several times."

Asked whether he shot her in the head, he said, "I don't know. It was away from my daughter, that's all I know. I saw to it that my daughter was safe... I just took off running because I knew it wasn't safe for me to be there."

He talked about encountering Jerry Key and being suspicious of him because in the past, Jerry had dated Angie. He was questioned again about working the pump on the shotgun and reloading. The detective asked him, "Did you have to jack the action to get the tube into the chamber?"

"Yeah, yeah, you have to," Deandra replied. This statement, on the police video, became a key component at his trial, demonstrating that he deliberated on each of his victims.

He was asked by the police interviewer how many people he had shot that night, and he answered clearly, "Four. But I admit I did it."

When he relived the story for us, he said that he fell asleep in his cell after this interview and slept for two or three days. When he woke, he could not remember what had happened and was told by a police officer what he had done.

"When she told me, a tear came down my eye and I was like, 'You bullshit,' and she was like, 'No.' I actually gave up. I said, 'Fuck it, if they kill me, they kill me. Shit, after what I realized I had done, I was like, man, shit, they are going to execute me; fuck it, let them execute me. I mean because I felt why should I live based on what I just done? Even though I didn't intentionally do it, but knowing that I'm responsible for it, I didn't even want to live no more."

To this day, despite the statement he gave to the police after his arrest, Deandra insists he has no recollection of the shootings.

"I felt like shit knowing that I was responsible for those that I love dying and being killed. It took a lot of therapy to get me where I am today."

Devon McTye, who saw Deandra on the doorstep not long before the killings, challenged his claim that he was high.

"It was not drugs that night. I don't care what he says about him being high off any drug that night. I saw Dre with my own eyes ten minutes before this happened. He was not high. I know he was not induced into some type of psychosis because of drug use. That's a false, patented lie that he likes to tell... The thing that gets me about that night is Angie could have escaped. But because Dre called her back, that's how Angie died that night. Because he was calling her name, she just froze up and went to him. That's when he shot her in the neck, while she was holding the kids. She's holding a five-month-old baby and you shoot her in the neck like she's a piece of trash."

While Angie's killer was being held in police custody, her mother's own life was collapsing around her.

"Someone knocked at my door and told me that Angie gotten hurt really bad. They said Deandra shot three people."

Valeria rushed to the hospital, where Angie was undergoing emergency treatment. Soon afterward, the policeman who found Angie, Geoff Jones, brought Drejanay and Dreisha to her, and they have lived with her ever since.

"At first I didn't know how to be a mom anymore. I had to learn all over again, changing diapers, paying for the babysitter, buying little kids' clothes. My life revolved around them. The holidays are tough. When Angie first died, I couldn't do Christmas; I sent the girls to my mom's house, where my sister lived, and they had Christmas there, and it took about three years for me to cope with Christmas.

"My last word to Angie, I promised they would go to college before they took her off the breathing machine. And I'm going to make sure when they start dating that we look them up and make sure they are proper for them."

The stress of losing her daughter and having two little children to care for made Valeria start drinking heavily.

"I was trying to numb the pain. You know, it's a dark, dark place. You're trying to get back but it's hard to get back. So I stayed drunk all the time. And it was always dark in here, I always had dark curtains up. And I wouldn't let the girls go outside and play."

It was with the help of an outreach program run by her local church that she managed to stop drinking. She has also faced dealing with cancer and heart problems.

In their emotional interview, Juanita's three daughters told us about their mother and the night she died.

"She was awesome!" said Toni, her sisters both nodding. "Nobody's perfect, but when you speak of Juanita Hoffman, she was the closest thing to being perfect.

"My housephone rang and it was my big sister, Shontai,

very upset and screaming on the phone: 'Toni, you need to come into town because Deandra, he shot her.' And at that point I just started screaming. At the hospital I looked at the doctor and I grabbed him and said, 'Please, doctor, please don't tell me that I have lost my mom.' That's when the reality hit me. She was gone forever. Oh, man... Then you sit there and I could feel her pain, you know, the shots, and I'm sitting here wondering what, you know, when he pointed the gun at her, was she thinking? Was she scared?" Toni sobbed as she spoke, her sister Shontai buried her head in her hands, and Mija lowered her head to the table. The trial of Deandra Buchanan was another ordeal for Angie's family and the families of the other victims. We talked to Kevin Crane, who is now a judge at the Boone County Courthouse, an impressive building fronted by four thirty-foot columns. Kevin was the main prosecution lawyer when Deandra faced the court. He set out to prove that Deandra acted with deliberation when carrying out the killings: "Buchanan was charged by me with three counts of murder. Murder One is the only thing that in Missouri has the potential for life without eligibility for probation parole. It's also the only crime for which the death penalty is possible.

"The family and friends that were at the residence that night of the homicides, they had fun together. William Jefferson was kind of the patriarchal guy. He owned this place and he was very welcoming to everybody, and everybody felt very comfortable there.

"I don't question that Deandra was under the influence of a controlled substance. But there's never any suggestion that he was ingesting it involuntarily. He was ingesting the cocaine himself. You can't go, 'I drank a fifth of whisky and I don't remember killing people.' It's not a defense, so that was off the table. There's got to be some responsibility on the individual here, you know. I mean, it starts with the individual. You don't blame the drug, you don't blame the gun; you blame the individual.

"So I'm trying to charge this case, and what I'm looking at...is there deliberation prior to killing somebody? Cool reflection on the matter of killing another person, however brief, is deliberation. Well, in this case we had three victims. In this case we had each of the victims shot by the defendant with a pump shotgun. Not only do you have to load and reload the weapon to accomplish these three murders and then commit the final assault, he had to rack the weapon every time he fired a shot... You're not spontaneously doing that. I demonstrated to the jury that he deliberated on each of the three victims that he killed."

An important part of the prosecution case was the video-taped recording of Deandra's police interview only hours after he committed the murders.

"He said he had no memory of the events. The video showed he had," said Kevin Crane.

He recalled the impact in the courtroom when the police officer who found Angie's body and tried to revive her, Geoff Jones, broke down as he described the scene.

"Without any theatrics," Kevin said. "It just goes to show the impact these situations have... He'll never forget that. It will be with him for the rest of his life."

In the first phase of the trial, the jury quickly found Deandra guilty. The second phase required the jury to decide the right level of punishment, and this was when Deandra's legal team mounted their defense that he was high on drugs at the time and had mental health issues.

The jury voted by ten votes to two for the death penalty, a decision that was confirmed by the judge. Deandra was sentenced to death on 22 April 2002. Angie's mother, Valeria, was pleased.

"I had a deep hate and I want him to hurt just like he hurt everybody else. I want them to put him to death because he deserve it. I mean, he killed the people you say you love. He didn't love them that much if he took their lives.

"It made me feel good. But then I realized the girls only got one parent left and that's him, and he's got to answer for what he did to them when they're ready to see him."

However, after a year and a half on Death Row, the sentence was reduced to life without the possibility of parole because the jury had not been unanimous and it was ruled that the judge should not have handed down the death penalty without the full backing of the jury.

Since then, Deandra has continued to work on his own case. He told us that he used friends to find out what drug he had taken that night, and according to them the cannabis he smoked was laced with PCP, which is known to cause hallucinations and violent behavior.

But he accepted that whatever drug he had ingested, it was "my lifestyle that caused all this."

Ten years after her daughter was murdered, Valeria visited Deandra in jail. She was supported by two women from her church. She was very nervous.

"So he sat across the table from me. We couldn't talk about the girls, that was off the table. He's got no contact with them. I asked him why he did what he did, and all he did was talk about himself... So then he talked about hisself some more and I said, 'God, if he talks about himself one

more time I'm going to walk out this place and call it a day.'
And he talked about hisself... So I gave him a hug...and I
walked out that door.

"He didn't take responsibility. I wanted him to take all of
it, from the time he was abusing her and everything to the
time of the shooting. I want him to take it all, not just the
murder, from the time he kept beating on her, and how I tried
to save her from him. I wanted him to admit it, to say yes, I
was abusing Angela, which I should not have been doing...
Because I knew he was a monster. He's like a leopard; it never
changes its spots."

She told him she forgave him, "Because it was keeping me
in that time zone. When something tragic happens, you stay
there. You don't move on. I was stuck in that year. That's the
one piece that I need to close the door... I came back and got
on with being a momma. I did forgive him. And then I forgave
myself."

Although what happened to their mother was not kept from
Angie's little girls, it wasn't an everyday subject of conversation until one day when Drejanay was thirteen or fourteen
and was in the same class at school as Deandra's son, her
half-brother. The girls did not know about their father's other
children, and it opened up a conversation. Valeria got out the
newspaper clippings of the murders and the trial.

"They didn't mention it anymore. They were kind of quiet."

Valeria said that one day the girls may want to see him.
"He's the only biological parent they have left. When they're
ready, and up to it emotionally and physically, they can see
him anytime they want to. He didn't give me a good answer
[as to why he did it] and I don't think he will give them a good
answer, but he just needs to take responsibility for his actions."

According to Deandra, he has already apologized to his daughters for taking their mother from them in letters sent on by members of his family.

"Whenever my daughters are ready to come and visit with me, I'm physically here. Man, the most important thing I can tell them is I'm sorry. Seriously! I'm sorry. And I continue to do what I need to do, to better myself so that I will never be that person again. Regardless of if they ever know that, regardless of who knows that, I know that I am not that same person, for a fact."

We went with Valeria and her two granddaughters to visit Angie's well-kept grave, where Drejanay read out the verse on the heart-shaped headstone:

> *"So if tomorrow starts without me,*
> *don't think we're far apart,*
> *For every time you think of me, I'm*
> *right here in your heart."*

Valeria explained that she and the girls were happy because "I know she is in a better place. She don't have to deal with the pain that cost her her life. And she know that her girls are taken care of, so I think she can finally rest. And I can rest a bit, knowing that the girls are achieving their goals." At our second interview with Deandra, he knew we had talked to members of the victims' families and to others involved in his case.

"I still struggle trying to figure out why this happened. Over these years, I wrestle: How the fuck did I allow myself to do this? How did I allow myself to shoot my aunt, my girl, my stepfather? Shoot my girl while she holding my daughter?"

Deandra told us that the only reason he agreed to see Valeria was because "she's entitled to whatever I need to do to help. That's the only reason. It wasn't about me. They said I don't have to do it. I said, 'Well, if this is what she wants, I'll do it for her. I don't mind. I'm getting nothing out of it. I'm doing it for her because of what I took from her. I could never give it back.'"

He told us, with a look of puzzlement on his face, that he doesn't know what Valeria wants to hear from him.

"I've already told her, I've apologized and am sorry for what I've done. I know I was a piece of shit. I knew that I wasn't right. 'I know that you told me to get some help. I know I didn't listen to you.' At the time I thought it was all under control."

We played him Kevin Crane's definition of deliberation, the "cool reflection on the matter of killing another person" necessary for a first-degree murder charge. He became slightly agitated as he forcefully argued that there was no reflection or premeditation.

"This wasn't a planned situation. I didn't say, 'OK, this is what I am going to do.' I didn't set off to go kill my girlfriend, my auntie, my stepfather. Not one time did I sit back and say, 'OK, this is what I am going to do today.' Hell no! According to everything and everybody that was there that night, I just flipped out. That wasn't no premeditated, planned-out situation."

Jeremy Turner said: "He did not like these questions. He sat back and stared at me, then insisted he could not remember the interview he gave to the police after his arrest. He continually came back to the claim that he smoked a bad joint."

Deandra listened to tapes of the assertions made by Valeria,

Devon, and Shontai about the level of violence he inflicted on Angie. He refuted Devon's allegation that he always intended to kill Angie.

"If that was the case, I could have been done that. Shit, if I wanted to kill her I could have killed her. And the only thing I keep concluding is this chemical that I got my hands on that I wasn't aware of caused me to react like this. And when you compile that with my lifestyle, way before I even met Angie, I been involved in all kind of violence where I have seen people lose their life. I mean, it's nothing to be proud of now I think back on it. But back then we thought that was the thing to do. I'm going to react a certain way based on the way I've been living and conditioned."

As he heard Shontai speaking about Angie being beaten with a wire hanger, he frowned and looked puzzled, and then his composure shattered and he became agitated.

"He became increasingly shirty," said Jeremy. "He didn't like what people were saying. His attitude all the way through was that he was the victim, and he didn't like the fact that not everyone was buying that."

Deandra spoke forcibly: "Whoa, stop that for a minute... Let me tell you something, I never whupped her with no clothes hanger. This is what really, really kind of frustrates me, enough to say fuck them all. That kind of stuff there is the type of shit that's kind of getting me upset, because even to this day, you still would put that out there like I used a clothes hanger to whup her. Like I'm some kind of guerrilla pimp or some shit.

"You see this is the thing that be kind of getting me a little, I'm not going to say upset, cause I understand what I done. But it gets...I'm serious...it gets real struggling because usually I'm like...eighteen years I've been doing everything I can to make amends, and then, when you hear stuff like that...that's what really be getting me kind of disturbed.

"When you add some falsehood to tell your side of the story, to try to continue to put me in a negative light. And I'm being honest with you. It kind of frustrates me that, regardless to what they say or how they say it or how they believe or what they feel, I'm going to attack this case and a lot of them going to be upset.

"They can bombard the courthouse, they can contact the prosecutors. I wouldn't even care. For that type of stuff, that lets me know that, after eighteen years, who's to say I could ever trust them? I'm serious. And this is how I have to think. Based on what I just hear, who's to say that when I get out of here I can honestly say I can be safe in an environment where they at?

"Nah, I can't do it. Because *I am* going to get out of here."

He nodded his head to emphasize this and continued to stare defiantly into the camera.

At the time we interviewed him, he had an appeal pending, but in 2018, Deandra Buchanan's appeal was rejected. He continues to campaign for his release, and now has a fiancée from London who has moved to live near him and fight for his release. She is Kaye Vassell, who has two children with N-Dubz rapper Dappy; she first heard of Deandra when she watched our Netflix film.

9

CROSSING THE LINE

CAVONA FLENOY

"I feel like I need to tell my story because I don't feel like a killer. I was just a hurt little girl that had a lot of pain. I'm not a bad person. I just made a mistake. It could have been different. I could have just walked away, because it's not right to take somebody's life, and if I can I would take it back, because it was wrong."

Cavona Flenoy was eighteen when she shot dead thirty-year-old Hassan Abbas in his apartment in the quiet, small town of Riverside in Platte County, Missouri, in March 2010. She is now serving a twenty-five-year prison sentence, and we talked to her at Chillicothe Correctional Center, one of two women's prisons in Missouri.

Cavona is one of only seven hundred women who commit murder in the United States every year, accounting for less than 10 percent of the murder total. The area where she committed the murder has low crime rates, and murder is extremely rare there: there were no murders for more than five years before Hassan's death, or for nine years afterwards.

"The citizens of Platte County have decided that they believe in strict law enforcement. We likely have higher sentences for murder than many other counties in Missouri. Platte County has a desire for safety, and it's not uncommon to have defendants say that 'if I'd known I was committing this crime in Platte County, I never would have done it.' That to me is exactly what I want criminals to think when they cross the line into Platte County: 'This is not a place to commit a crime, because if I do I'm going to prison for a long time.'"

These were the words of Eric Zahnd, the prosecuting attorney in Platte County, when he talked to us about prosecuting Cavona's case.

The murder happened nine months before Cavona faced Eric Zahnd across the courtroom.

Hassan had picked Cavona up earlier in the evening, near her home in Kansas City, Kansas. When Hassan drove Cavona back to his apartment, they crossed not only the county line but also the state line, and drove six miles from the city to Riverside.

When she was arrested for his killing, Cavona pleaded guilty to second-degree murder in a plea bargain with the prosecution. Had she decided to go to trial, she would have been charged with first-degree murder and could have been sentenced to life without any possibility of parole or even faced the death penalty. But by agreeing to a second-degree plea, she gave up the chance to argue that she acted in self-defense when she shot Hassan, whose body was found naked apart from a T-shirt and a condom. She accepted the plea bargain because, she says, her lawyer assured her she would get a ten-year sentence and be eligible for release after eight and half years. Being sentenced to twenty-five years came as a shock to her and her family, and means that her baby son, a year old at the time of the murder, will be a grown man before she is released.

"When we first approached her to tell her story to us, she wasn't too keen," said director Ingo Nyakairu. "But she and her family feel strongly it was unfair for her to have such a long sentence, and they wanted to highlight what they see as the injustice of it."

Cavona was ten years into her sentence when she outlined to us the events leading up to the murder and the story of her earlier life. She had a troubled and difficult childhood. "I didn't feel poor, I never went without anything; my mother worked two jobs. But I felt I was between heaven and hell, because my mother was a minister and my daddy was a hustler. He was not always bad. He woke me up, gave me snacks, cooked my favorite breakfast, and told me every day I am the most beautiful girl in the world."

She is part of a big, extended family, and has one sister, three half-brothers, and one half-sister. Her mother, Stacey Lewis, who is now separated from Cavona's father, described them as "a very close family." Cavona was the youngest, and her mother reminisced about her early years: "She was very unique, even as a baby. She had these big, bright, bubble eyes, and stuff like that. Her main thing was dancing. Cavona was a dancer. She could dance you under the table."

Stacey's eyes glistened with pride as she showed us pictures of young Cavona dressed in dance costumes.

Problems with Cavona's father started when her uncle, his brother, was shot by his own son.

"After that, my daddy started drinking a lot. Alcohol is a drug and it can change you," Cavona said. "He didn't trust his kids. He felt like one of his kids was going to hurt him too. He felt like he was next; the paranoia of alcohol. One day our house burnt down and we had to live in a hotel because he was trying to cook something on the stove. There was cussing and verbal abuse; he would call us bitches and hoes and say we were never going to be nothing. There were times when he would turn off the lights and we won't have lights. My mother used to be on her knees praying. Then, at like 2:30 in the morning, she would take us out to get ice cream to make us feel better."

Cavona's own desperate narrative began when she was raped for the first time at twelve years old. She was captain of her school drill team. She was walking home from a practice when an older teenager she knew attacked her.

"He grabbed me and put me in the basement and raped me and took my virginity. I went home and told my mother, and we went to the house and my mother called the police. He [the attacker] said I had never been in the house, but I gave the police a description so they took him to the jail."

Her mother, Stacey, gave us more details about the rape. "He allowed his dog to come out, and she picked up the dog and took it back to the house. He had two friends there. They held her in the house and allowed him to take her downstairs. I was so angry with him. I gave the police her clothing."

Her attacker was charged and went to court, where he was given a probation sentence.

"I just kept thinking probation wasn't enough. I lost. I lost the best part of me. I lost my virginity. I lost hope. I lost my self-esteem. It made me angry, bitter, and I started to feel nasty about myself and ugly," Cavona told us. When we interviewed her she was wearing a beige prison top, a white T-shirt, and her hair was in cornrows; her big eyes welled with tears as she relived her early life.

Her mother pinpointed the rape as when her daughter's behavior began to change.

"She started acting out, taking lots of baths, tearing up paper. Later she said to me, 'Momma, do you know how it feels to be twelve years old and blood running down your leg?' That hurt me so bad, because I saw the terror in her eyes."

When she was fourteen, Cavona was walking home from school with a boy.

"He pushed me down, and he lift my shirt and he started licking my breast."

She escaped and ran back to school. The police were called. When the case went to court, it was thrown out.

"I didn't feel like he got justice for what he did, so I was bitter and angry inside. I feel like they got away with it. They just got slap on the wrist, easy. No justice for me. Just probation, no jail time. That's when I started being the little girl that was bitter and angry."

"Once that happened, it's like I totally lost my daughter," said Stacey. "She laid out in the street and wanted the cars to run over her and stuff like that."

She was referred for help with her mental health problems, but she didn't find talking over the events of the past was a solution.

"They got me a counselor. So when I started talking about it I get angry because it's just, like, bringing up past issues. They put me on medication so that I just stayed asleep. How is that dealing with my problems? I started using drugs and alcohol to numb my mind, numb my heart, and I just feel like I'm living in hell. I felt like the walking dead, and when you get real drunk, real high, you get out of it. And I would sing pop songs and gospel songs or I danced to take away the pain."

There were two more rapes, one by a stranger who put a gun to her head, and one by a friend of her father's. Neither case was reported to the police, and she did not tell her family about her father's friend, who continued to visit the home. When she was fifteen, her mother found her with one of her father's guns, about to shoot herself.

Stacey describes her daughter's life as "going spiraling down the hill. She didn't want to listen to me because she was so hurt."

For a time, according to Stacey, Cavona ran wild, got herself involved in bad relationships, and clocked up a minor police record. She ran away from home frequently.

At this stage, Cavona decided that if she had a boyfriend she would have someone to protect her. Soon she moved in with one. That boyfriend was a drug user and abusive, on one occasion beating her so badly that she was rushed to hospital. When the police asked her if she wanted to report the attack, she said no.

"What was he just going to get—probation? I just felt, why go through all that paperwork and pain, going back and forth to court, when you know nothing happens. It made me feel not worthy. I was never going to be loved; this is what I deserve. This is my life, I've got to accept my life." When she was seventeen, Cavona gave birth to her son, after a brief liaison with a friend.

"My baby daddy...we weren't a real couple. I just wanted a child and I asked God for a boy that was going to love me unconditionally. That was the most beautiful thing, because I felt my son was going to be the only man that probably wouldn't hurt me."

It was after her son was born, Cavona told us, that she decided she would not let anyone abuse or hurt her again. "I have somebody to protect now, and if I don't start protecting myself, how can I protect my son? So I just felt a whole shield that I had to start saying no, no harm, no hurt, no more pain."

Stacey told us that although she didn't want her daughter to get pregnant at seventeen, "I thought this will slow her down. This will change her. She was a wonderful mom. She took her baby everywhere with her. She always kept him [well] dressed."

At the time of the murder of Hassan Abbas, Cavona had moved into an apartment on her own with her son and was trying to carve out a life for them both.

"I was working and going to church and helping my mother, cleaning up her house and stuff."

She was still using alcohol and drugs as an escape route, and she had run up a large total of traffic violations, owing $3,000 in fines. She found the letters demanding the fines so overwhelming that she threw them away. Despite her resolution to avoid pain, she had another relationship with an unsuitable man, which she later broke off.

"He was mad at me and he gave his new girlfriend my address. So four girls with bats in their hand was knocking at my door, and I had my son there. So I called the police and said that somebody is trying to knock down my door and the police came."

The girls left as soon as they heard the police sirens, but because the police had a traffic warrant for Cavona, they handcuffed her and took her to the police station. She said it confirmed in her mind that the police were never going to help her.

"I was crying because my son was in the apartment and people were telling me they were about to hurt me and my baby. But all you think about is a traffic warrant.

"I called my cousin and told him what was going on, and I told him I could not be here with these girls about to beat down my door. He told me I needed some protection, and he said there was a gun for sale and it was a hundred dollars, and at first I was no, no, no.' But he said, 'You probably going to need some protection,' so I got the gun. That was about a week before the murder. I had the gun with me all the time in my purse. For protection. I even took it to work, to my mom's house."

Near to her apartment was a liquor store where she regularly bought alcohol. In March 2010, she drove to the store, and the man serving her said he knew she was using fake ID.

"He said I can have the liquor if I go on a date with his cousin Hassan, because he is looking for a friend. So I agreed to go on a date."

Hassan Abbas came from Sudan and was studying at a local college. Most of his close family lived in the United Arab Emirates. According to the evidence, Hassan approached her at the liquor store and asked for her phone number. Cavona later said that he gave her thirty dollars and bought food and diapers for the baby, and she went back with him to his apartment, where Hassan's roommate pinched her bottom, which she didn't like. She told Hassan she wanted to go home, but he refused to take her and she ended up spending the night, but Cavona says nothing sexual happened. When he took her home the next morning, he promised he would take her out for a meal. As it was going to be at an all-you-can-eat buffet at a local restaurant called Golden Corral, she was very keen to go, and she rang him three times the following day to try to arrange it. He was away, but when he returned he rang her back, and picked her up four days after their first meeting in his dark-blue Honda.

In her first interview with us, Cavona said that at their initial meeting she gave Hassan her phone number, and that a couple of days later Hassan called her for a date. She did not talk about meeting him four days earlier, but evidence shows that she did, and she herself admitted it at the time, both in her first police interview and when she was talking to a psychologist before her sentencing.

She said that on the day of Tuesday, 9 March, "I dropped my son off at my mother's house. My mother didn't want me to go anywhere. She was telling me that she could feel something bad is about to happen. She don't want to get a call to say I'm dead anywhere. She wants me to stay at her house for a couple of days. I said it's OK, everything will be fine.

"Hassan picked me up. He said he was taking me to the Golden Corral. As we were going on the highway, we're driving a long time, and he said he wanted to go to his house and take a shower. So I'm thinking that when I get in from working I would want to take a shower myself, so I understood."

They drove across the state line into Missouri, and then six miles out of Kansas City into Riverside. Hassan lived in the El Chaparral Apartments, a modern, well-appointed block on landscaped grounds in a quiet, wooded area.

"He said he had some type of religion that meant I had to take my shoes off. Then he asked me if I wanted some Hennessy, so I had some, then he gave me something that I didn't know what it was. He said it was PCP, and so I tried it, smoked it. Then he got in the shower, and when he came out he was butt naked with the condom on. He told me that I owed him for the liquor and everything.

"He told me that I had to suck his dick or fuck him or I wasn't going anywhere and he wanted to keep me here for his sex slave. I told him, 'Please, no. I can pay for the liquor, just please let me go home. Let me go back to my son.' He said no, you're staying with me.

"I felt like he was going to keep me there. This man is like six feet, seven inches and two hundred pounds; I'm 105 pounds and four feet, ten inches tall. So in my mind it's no way I can run and get away from this man. But I guess I could have tried to run away. I just felt like it was going to be me or him.

"Then he lay down and I tried to go the other way and he said no. So at the first instant I grabbed the gun out my purse and I close my eyes and I shot and hit him. And after I shot, he ran toward me and told me to give him the gun. I'm like, me as a kid looking at the movies, when someone gets shot, they cannot move anywhere and they cannot run after you and hurt you. He said come here, and I tried to shut the door, and he was pushing on the door. We were wrestling back and forth, and I'm grabbing the door back, so I started shooting again; I'm shooting through the door and I'm like, 'Please stop, please stop, just let me go home to my son.' So then after that I ran, and he still opened up the door and ran after me. So his books and everything was on the table, so I swished the books to try to hit him and stop him running at me. His car keys was on the side so I grabbed them and he's still chasing me out. That's when he fell over and I heard a big boom."

Hassan Abbas had been shot four times: once in the face, once in the side, once in the shoulder, and once in the chest. "I ran down and got in his car and I didn't know where I was going, so I got on the highway and I just kept going straight to see if I see something familiar. I didn't know where I was. I was lost for a long time. At that point I was thinking he wasn't dead and he was going to come and hurt me, he was going to come back because he knew where my house was. So I was just praying, and I see the sign for West 70 and hopefully that is the one to get back to Kansas City. I kept going and finally saw a familiar place.

"I wasn't going to call the police. What would they do to help me? At that time I wasn't thinking about going to authority for help. I felt like he was in the wrong. I'm tired of people abusing me. Tired of people taking advantage of me. Of people hurting me. I've been hurt all my life.

"I was young, I was going through my own thing at that time, mental illness. If I could change everything, I would walk away."

Shortly after she fled, Hassan's roommate arrived home and found him dying. He was rushed to hospital, still with a faint pulse, but died a short time later. The first police officer on the scene found his body in the doorway, a trail of blood from the bedroom through the living room to the door. Pictures of the crime scene show Cavona's sneakers, which she left behind.

Cavona told us she found Hassan's wallet in the glove box of the car, and she and a male friend tried to use his credit card to buy fuel. It was declined. She claimed the same friend changed the license plates on the car but then threatened to kill her if she did not have sex with him. Once again, she fled.

Cavona was arrested two days later at a family assistance office where she had applied for benefits for her son and where she wanted to register for a course to help her prepare for job interviews. She knew the arrest was coming because the man at the liquor store knew the apartment block where she lived as well as her first name.

"We were able to identify Miss Flenoy pretty quickly with information from the roommate," said detective sergeant Dennis Jones, one of the detectives assigned to the case. "We were able to get her name from the clerk at the liquor store. She had his car, so we knew what vehicle we were looking for."

Cavona was taken to the police station at Riverside, where she was interviewed by two female detectives.

"The detective said I looked young. I started crying very, very heavily."

She was left alone with a couple of sheets of paper and told to write down anything she felt like writing. On the police video the detective is heard saying: "Write a letter to yourself, God, to your mother. I mean, whatever you want to do, that is totally up to you. Doodle, draw, whatever helps you relax, OK."

Cavona scribbled all over the sheet. Two sentences out of many were highlighted at her trial:

"I push him down like I was about to fuck him. I got the gun and I just pull the trigger."

There were many other scribbles. She wrote that Abbas said, "Will you do it for money?" and she wrote, "I don't suck dick." Most of her scribbles were prayers and apologies: "I'm sorry, I'm sorry," "sorry Mom."

"I was just writing stuff down," Cavona told us. "But it came out the wrong way, like pushing him down so that I can fuck him. But in my mind was 'Keep him down, not up, so that I can run.' A lot of things I wrote about was on that paper, I was pleading to God for protection of my son, and I don't want to get hurt no more, just pleading, begging."

When the detectives returned, the scribblings were taken away to be used later by the prosecution.

"After, she [the detective] came back in, and that's when I told her I was the female that shot Hassan. They let me call my mother and I cried and said, 'Big Momma, they called me a murderer and I wish I could take it back.' And she said, 'Baby, you got to stay strong.' I was ashamed to say murderer. I tried to block it. I said, 'Momma, hold my baby tight.'"

We were able to include parts of her videotaped police interview, during which she sobs continually and wails in distress: "I got raped my whole life. I don't trust nobody. The people that raped me so many times, none of them got in trouble, none of them." She was convulsed in sobs, and her comments became unintelligible, mingled with groans of desperation.

In another section of the video, the detective asked her if she was at Hassan's apartment on the Sunday before the day of the murder.

"No, I wasn't over there Sunday. I was just down there Friday and Tuesday."

She was asked if she spent the night there on Friday, and she answered, "Yeah, and he took me home on Saturday morning."

Asked how long she had the gun she replied, "I just got it on Saturday."

"We discovered that she knew he had just recently received $2,400 in tax return money," said Detective Jones. "That was the real motive, some type of robbery or some way of getting some cash or some monetary value from Mr. Abbas. That's the reason she was there, that's the reason she bought a gun."

Cavona agreed to plead guilty to second-degree murder along with more charges associated with stealing the car and attempting to use Hassan's cards. The alternative was to be charged with first-degree murder and to go to trial.

We tried to contact Hassan's family, and through the intermediary of a cousin in Chicago, we offered them the chance to take part in the film, putting forward Hassan's side of the story, but they declined our offer.

Eric Zahnd, the prosecutor, told us when we interviewed him in his office that the offer of a second-degree guilty plea was "a fairly generous plea agreement given the facts of the case.

"We did believe that if we charged her with first-degree murder, if she went to trial, we had a reasonable chance of convicting her of first-degree murder. The difference between first- and second-degree murder is what we call deliberation or, commonly, premeditation. We believed we had strong evidence of premeditation starting with the note she wrote. In the words of the Missouri law, she coolly reflected upon the matter for some period of time, no matter how brief, and decided that she was going to shoot Mr. Abbas, ultimately resulting in his death.

"Cavona Flenoy looked like an innocent little girl. Her actions demonstrated her to be a dangerous and violent, murderous person. I believe that we could have proven a first-degree murder case, and Miss Flenoy would have spent the rest of her life in prison without any possibility of parole.

"Given some of the mitigating circumstances in this case, Miss Flenoy was a very young woman—her age and some of the things she recounted having been through as a young person—we believed that the chance of parole was a just outcome. And so we offered her the chance to plead guilty to second-degree murder, which she did.

"That means she'll be eligible for parole by the time she's about forty and will certainly be released by the time she's forty-five, so she'll have a chance to re-enter society to, I assume, reconnect with her son, who was quite young.

"We wrote a letter to her attorney making the offer to plead guilty as charged, and also explained that if she decided not to, we would charge first-degree murder, and that we believed the evidence was strong to convict her of first degree.

"Miss Flenoy had a choice to make, whether she wanted to plead guilty to second-degree murder, when she had admitted what she had done, or whether she wanted to take the case to trial and risk life in prison without the possibility of parole."

By accepting the plea bargain, Cavona gave up the chance to argue that she acted in self-defense, fearing a rape. She maintained to us that she accepted the plea on the advice of her attorney: "My lawyer said the judge would have sympathy for me because of how young you are and what you have been going through."

Cavona claimed her lawyer said that "because I was only eighteen and taking responsibility for what you did, the judge will give you a ten-year sentence, 85 percent [of the total sentence]. So I asked her and she said I would likely do eight and a half years. I was thinking OK, my son will be nine.

"So I talked to my mother and grandmother, because that's who paid for my lawyer, and I said I did do it, I did hurt somebody, and I will be a hypocrite if I say I don't want to do time for it, so I'm going to take this time and do it because I hurt somebody.

"So it wasn't a real plea offer. They mainly told me if I don't take the second-degree murder, they're going to make sure I never see my son again and I will live in the penitentiary for the rest of my life. So of course I took it, but I didn't think my lawyer really had my back. I was young and didn't know much about the law, and of course I love my son. So I got what they wanted.

"She [my lawyer] said I didn't get physically hurt by him, so she said I would never get self-defense. I didn't know nothing about nothing, I was nothing but a child. So I went to court... in my mind I'm thinking I'm going to do eight and half years."

Stacey corroborated her daughter's story.

"I don't believe that my daughter wanted to hurt this man. He tried to make her do something that she didn't want to do. Cavona told the lawyer that she wanted to claim self-defense. Self-defense is like a sentence between five and ten years, but the lawyer advised Cavona to plead guilty to a second-degree murder because she was going to lose in trial. I knew she was going to go to prison, but the lawyer had told me that it was up to the judge how much time she got. I thought the most my daughter would have was ten. I thought she would do most on probation."

Eric Zahnd never accepted that she acted in self-defense. "I don't believe there was a viable self-defense claim. Her attorney came to the same conclusion, the correct conclusion, because she did not need self-defense when Mr. Abbas was naked from the waist down. He was in no condition to chase after her, and she could have been completely safe. The evidence shows she was the only person with a gun. She did not have to pull the trigger."

His opinion was underpinned by Detective Sergeant Jones: "During the investigation, we found out she planned this whole event, so she wasn't a victim."

The prosecution case was that Cavona had gone to the apartment with the gun with the intention of robbing Hassan.

"The evidence points to it likely being a robbery gone bad, that ended very sadly in a murder," said Eric Zahnd. "After Mr. Abbas was dead, she stole his car, she stole his wallet, she tried to use his credit card. Those are the actions of somebody who wanted to steal from another person and was willing to use force up to murder to accomplish that act. After Hassan and Miss Flenoy [first] met, they went back to his apartment and she had her son, her young son, and they all spent that evening not only with Mr. Abbas but with his roommate. Miss Flenoy later told folks that she didn't like the roommate because allegedly he had touched her on the buttocks. But at any event, she stayed that night and Mr. Abbas took her back home.

"The next day Cavona Flenoy bought a handgun for one hundred dollars. We also know that in the intervening time between that weekend and the Tuesday when Hassan died, Cavona Flenoy called Mr. Abbas multiple times trying to set up a meeting.

"We know that Miss Flenoy was in somewhat desperate financial straits. We know she bought a gun right before returning to that apartment. We know that after Mr. Abbas was killed, she not only stole his car but tried to use his credit card and changed the license plates on his car. That's all evidence of flight. And to me as a prosecutor, that's evidence of guilt, that she knew she had done something terrible and wanted to get away with it.

"She later talked about perhaps this was self-defense, that Mr. Abbas had come after her and maybe she was afraid she would be sexually assaulted. What she did does not seem to me to be the actions of somebody who thought they were going to be assaulted and had to act in self-defense. Instead of calling the police and saying that somebody just tried to hurt me and I didn't have a choice, she left Mr. Abbas there to die.

"If this young woman really believed she would be raped, why not just flee the apartment while Mr. Abbas was naked from the waist down? She was in an apartment complex where there would have been other people and she could have cried for help, and I certainly think help would have been on the way for her. So, to me, her explanation of what happened never made sense, and the alternate explanation that this was a robbery gone bad makes a lot more sense.

"In my opinion, she didn't give a full account of the murder until she was left alone in the interview room with a couple of sheets of paper. Among the things she wrote down was 'I pushed him down like I was about to fuck him. I got the gun and I just pulled the trigger.' That to me is the most forthright admission by Miss Flenoy as to what really happened.

"She did show considerable remorse. The question for us is always whether this is remorse about what she's done or remorse about having been caught."

According to Eric, Hassan's family wanted her to face the death penalty.

"Not only were his family overseas but none of them spoke English, so it made our efforts to communicate with them difficult. We were able to communicate through a cousin who was living in Chicago. But you can imagine how traumatic this was for them. They didn't understand the American system of justice.

"This case is like many others where the prosecutor has to stand up for the victim because his family is a continent away. Growing up in a tough neighborhood and having bad things happen to you as a child certainly does not give you the right to shoot somebody down in cold blood. I have no doubt Miss Flenoy faced many challenges as a young child and a young woman. But none of these challenges permit her to gun down somebody who, by independent evidence, was not a real threat to her.

"I don't know what happened to Miss Flenoy. I will tell you that in some instances there is a very powerful incentive for people, once they've gotten caught for a serious crime like murder, to exaggerate things that happened to them in the past. I don't know whether Ms Flenoy is being completely truthful or exaggerating. I do know that during the police interview, she repeatedly lied to present herself in a better light. And so that makes it difficult, when she's talking to her psychologist or today telling us about things from her life, to know whether those things happened or not. I didn't contest the fact that she had a difficult childhood."

Before the sentencing hearing, Cavona was twice interviewed by Dr. Marilyn Hutchinson, a psychologist, who presented a report about her to the court. We interviewed Dr. Hutchinson about Cavona's mental state when she saw her. She remembered the case well.

"Most of the cases that I do have some sort of inherent tragedy in them. People who were abused in childhood. People who had long suffered in domestic violence situations. This particular case was true to that. In the DVD that was made of the police interrogation, I was struck by the fact that she had multiple instances of sexual assaults at a young age.

"I gave her a number of psychological diagnoses. Her primary diagnosis was post-traumatic stress disorder. I found her to be an anxious, depressed, slightly suicidal woman who was really scared. I diagnosed her with depression and with a generalized anxiety disorder. She seemed pretty overwhelmed with the situation she was in. She didn't really understand much of that situation.

"I also diagnosed her with a personality disorder, which comes from both early childhood experiences and genetic loadings. These are the things that make us who we are across all situations. She had many areas of her thinking and her thoughtfulness that didn't function very well. She would have had the personality strengths of someone who was much, much younger—and she was only nineteen.

"Her childhood was quite difficult. Home was not a safe space. She told me that she would intentionally get suspended from school because she would get to go home and sleep, because she would have been up all night. She reported rape and assault to the police and nothing happened. She clearly would have learned: I'm not a person who matters; people can do to me what they want; people who are in authority aren't really going to help and I'm on my own.

"The post-traumatic stress disorder is the result of the sexual trauma and physical abuse that she had. PTSD is something happens to you from the outside and internally you don't have the capacity to integrate it with the emotions that come from that experience. For some people it can be a car wreck, war, a dog bite. Two people having the same experience, one might get it and one might not. But if you have it, it causes you to be extremely reactive to any situation that mirrors it. So if it's a dog bite, you are likely to be afraid of dogs in the future.

"If you are raped you are likely to be afraid of a situation in which you were previously sexually assaulted. When that happens, all the emotions of the previous instances flood into the current experience. It's like a snowball that she had all these previous sexual assaults. The emotions of those would be compounded into that single moment. It never goes to the executive center of the brain that says, 'What shall I do here? What would be a good choice?' There is an immediate freeze, fight or flight, that is completely outside of conscious control and is just an impulse in the moment. What she did was fight.

It was conditioned by PTSD. She would have been in a highly emotional state, flooded with adrenaline.

"She told me that. Without any prompting, she said she could remember all those times. She said she was overwhelmed with all the feelings of when it has happened before and she was committed to not letting it happen again."

Dr. Hutchinson challenged the prosecution case that Cavona was carrying out a planned robbery.

"There's nothing in her history or her psychological presentation that says she would be very good at planning. And it certainly isn't a very good plan. You don't leave your shoes if you plan to rob somebody. I have no belief that it was a robbery."

The psychologist told us that in her opinion it was unfair of the police to leave her with sheets of paper and then produce one line out of all her scribblings to build a prosecution case.

"She was left with paper and a pencil at a time when she was extremely emotionally distraught. She wasn't asked to write a statement. She was left alone to try and manage her own emotions. She was not informed of the purpose or how it would be used.

"In those pages of writing she was talking about how upset she was, how guilty she was, how she never intended to be sexual with him, how she had responded to what he said. There is one line that the prosecutors used as a way to say that she somehow was planning or intended this. They used that [to mean] that she had an intention of distracting him so she could shoot him and steal his car. When what she wanted was dinner."

In her opinion, there was a "really strong case of self-defense."

"Cavona's plea to second-degree murder was a mistake. The fact that she pled to second-degree said that she was guilty of things that were not true. She didn't have that intention to kill him. She was trying to defend herself. So that should have been presented to a jury and I think would have led to a different outcome for her.

"I don't think she was a person that it was appropriate necessarily for a long-term sentence...she was not a person who was going to be violent in the future, she was not a risk to society. I know that she killed a man. I believe wholeheartedly that she did it in self-defense. I believe that she was treated unfairly and that it was not just."

Asked when she was in the witness box to recommend an appropriate sentence, Dr. Hutchinson told the court that she felt a sentence of three to five years, in a prison where she could get psychological support and vocational training, would be appropriate for Cavona, with a similar period of probation supervision when she was released.

Cavona and her family were very hopeful they would get a good outcome after Dr. Hutchinson's evidence.

Stacey said, "Marilyn Hutchinson was my voice. She told everything like I tell it. I thought, 'Wow, they got to listen to this.'"

But in his summing up, prior to handing down the sentence, the judge said, "I don't doubt that Ms Flenoy had a tumultuous and, if you will, tragic life. And I don't doubt that her family is suffering. I also don't doubt that Mr. Abbas's family feel the tragedy of this incident.

"It's disturbing to the court that on the Saturday before the Tuesday of the murder, that a hundred dollars was spent for a weapon, when apparently Ms Flenoy needed food. And it's disturbing that the weapon was bought the day after she met Mr. Abbas, and a couple of days before that weapon was used on Mr. Abbas."

When the judge pronounced a twenty-five-year sentence, Cavona collapsed in hysterics.

"I just couldn't believe it. I didn't have the understanding," she said. "I felt like my lawyer was supposed to be good for me, so she told me what to say yes and no to."

Her mother and the rest of her family and friends, who were in court to support her, were aghast.

"She cried out of control," said Stacey. "They darn near had to pick her up and carry her. I could accept my daughter getting something, because a life was taken. It wasn't like I wanted her to walk out like she did nothing. The bottom line is they didn't care. They didn't care what my daughter's past was. The only thing they cared about was this girl came into Platte County and she was black of color. She killed someone in their county. They paint that picture: if you come in Platte County, this is what you're going to get. She never should have pleaded guilty to second-degree murder. I feel like they forced a statement out of her. They forced her to take second degree, and I will live with that."

Stacey told us she believes Platte Count is a racist area. "When I first came up there [to Platte County] this man, a White Caucasian wearing overalls, literally spat on the ground as we were walking. We were scared. I was scared for my daughter. They treated us cruel. They literally wanted to throw us out after the verdict. They got four or five guards for us, their hands on their gun, like they are ready for us to make a big disturbance after the sentence. They told us to take the stairs, but my brother said we would take the elevator. They treated us pretty badly."

Eric Zahnd, the prosecutor, believes the sentence was justified.

"I do not believe a short prison sentence would have been appropriate in this case. Hassan Abbas paid for Cavona Flenoy's crimes with his life. I believe that a long prison sentence was absolutely justified. I didn't believe she should spend the rest of her life behind bars without parole, I believe she deserved an opportunity to prove to the parole board that she would be the sort of person who could be returned to society. I did owe it to Hassan Abbas to see that justice was done, and he was killed for no other reason than he met the wrong woman.

"I'm a representative of the people of Platte County, and it's my great honor and my solemn responsibility to represent them and the state of Missouri in criminal cases. And when someone is murdered we're going to ask for a sentence that we believe responds to that crime with not only justice in mind but the interests of the victim and the family in mind."

Cavona told us she regretted taking a plea bargain that, she claims, she did not fully understand. She is adamant that if she had the chance again, she would have taken her case to a full trial.

"I am older now and more mature and I know more about the law. I would take everything to trial and I would explain everything that was taken wrongly, like when I said I pushed him down. I was of a conscious mind that if I act like I was going to [shoot], I will be able to run. A lot of things that was on that paper they never said [in court]."

After the sentence, she felt she no longer wanted to live. "I just feel, why am I here? Why am I even living? How am I going to do twenty-five years? How is that going to make me better? It is going to make me worse. I feel like this is a dream and one day I am going to wake up. I was going through my own thing at that time, my own mental illness."

Cavona appealed, and two and a half years after the sentence the case again came before the court, which ruled that she had received appropriate legal representation at the time of her original trial. The court also declined Cavona's attempt to withdraw her guilty plea, and her twenty-five-year sentence was upheld.

She then appealed to overturn the decision to now allow her to withdraw her guilty plea, but four and half years after the murder she again lost the case. Kate Webber, a senior Missouri public defender, was the lawyer who handled this bid.

"Once Cavona pled guilty to murder, it was going to be extremely difficult to convince a judge to vacate that guilty plea. I filed a brief, arguing that basically the court should have allowed her to withdraw her plea."

When we interviewed her in her office, Kate explained that the legal system in Missouri is a "guilty-plea mill."

"Only about 3 percent of people charged with crimes actually go to trial, and that's because there is unbelievable pressure from start to finish to plead guilty. If the 97 percent of people who plead guilty actually demanded a trial, the system would grind to a halt. We don't have the resources for that.

"In Platte County, a plea offer is sort of a carrot and stick: here's the good thing we'll do, we'll recommend second-degree murder. But if you don't accept this offer by this date, we will recharge with first-degree murder.

"What choice did Miss Flenoy have at this point? Roll the dice and maybe never see my two-year-old son again outside the walls of a prison, or just go ahead and take this sentence and hope that the judge sees through it and gives me some decent time? What kind of choice is that?

"It's just very unfortunate that this happened in Platte County, because I think a young White woman with the same circumstances and background, there probably would have been a different outcome. I think that plays a factor. After all, the prosecutor is an elected official, elected by the people around him. And the people around him are largely White.

"The larger cities tend to understand the realities of what Miss Flenoy's life was like, and Platte County doesn't. I don't see how the world is safer because Cavona Flenoy is in prison for twenty-five years. She took a life, but she is not a killer. If the state's theory was this was a planned robbery, a planned murder, with deliberation, she planned to kill somebody, take his car, his credit cards, other property, it doesn't fit with the dozens of cases I've seen where that's happened. She did take his car, because he had driven her over there. She had no way to get home. She tried to use the card because the car was on empty. These are the actions of someone who felt threatened, panicked, and then really panicked when she realized what had happened. You don't leave your shoes at a crime scene. You don't run out.

"The police utilized all the familiar tactics to encourage her to talk to them, which she had no obligation to do whatsoever. Now, they interrupt the interrogation and leave her with a pad of paper and a pen. This is a common tactic for getting people to make incriminating statements or statements that could be twisted into incriminating statements. One little line could be interpreted as incriminating, but I think it's a very ambiguous statement, and there were many, many other statements in that doodling that directly contradict the inference that the state was trying to portray.

"For example, those notes included a comment that there was just no way she was going to have sex with this guy. But Mr. Zahnd didn't bring that part out. He brought out the one thing that she said that could be twisted to look incriminating."

Life in prison was tough for Cavona at first.

"My first few days were very scary. It's mainly my son. You know, I didn't even get to see my baby walk until he walked through these doors. He just grew up. I couldn't help with his homework, help him get dressed. Or be with my big momma. When I first came in and people asked me what I was there for, I used to lie and say it was probation violation. I was ashamed to say second-degree murder.

"I still get flashbacks and still have visions of that day and the only thing I can do is pray and ask that God forgive me. At night, the whole little scene comes back to my mind and I don't want to go back to sleep because I feel if I close my eyes that whole scene will come back up. Every night I figure that I hurt somebody's son, and so I fear if somebody's going to hurt my little baby, the joy of my life.

"People say I am funny, I got a good sense of humor, [they say] I have a beautiful smile, and they love to be around me, and they say, 'Girl, you are not supposed to be in here.' I hear that almost every day."

Cavona's family have visited her faithfully while she has been in prison. Even though she had been in prison for ten years when we met her, Cavona had a close bond with her son.

"He is like my best friend, he loves me unconditionally and he thinks I'm the best mom ever. And so I love him. He's the one that I get up for every morning, he's my pride and joy."

Her grandmother was now too old and infirm, but her mother came regularly, bringing her son, and in between their visits she saw other members of the family. At first her mother and grandmother told the little boy that she was at college. It was Cavona who told him the truth.

"When he was about five I told him his mother is in the penitentiary. And I said I got a bit more time to do but I promise when I get out I will never ever leave you again."

For Stacey, her daughter's imprisonment was also hard at first.

"My life was based around her. I had a full-time job and my grandson was one year old when she left. The days off I had, I would come and see her. If anybody knows anything about a child being in prison, it's like your child has died. But when you believe in your child, nothing can keep you from them. And my grandson knows my daughter because I have taken him to see her since she left. I want him to know his mother. He loves his mother, and I've trained him up to love his mother.

"I stayed up late at night with him, because he knew that she was gone. I would lay her coat on his bed, so that he [could] smell her scent. I walked the floor with him at night and I still got up at 5:00 a.m. to go to my job."

Meeting Cavona for a second time, ninety days after her first interview, after more facts about the murder had emerged, Ingo challenged her about aspects of what she originally told us.

"I asked her how long she had had the gun and why did she take it with her. She was very sketchy about it: the police said she got it three days before the murder, but she said she'd had it a week and a half. The main thing we wanted to know about was the discrepancy about how many times she had been to that apartment before. We knew she had been there before the day of the murder, and I wanted to give her the chance to give that information up." But she stuck to her story that she had not been there until the day of the murder, and when we played her our interview with Detective Sergeant Jones, who outlined how she went there four days earlier, she looked confused, her big eyes widened even more. and she paused for a few seconds before she said: "Some stuff I don't, like, umm, know. Like, in that time I was on drugs and alcohol, so I cannot literally say every single part of every single thing. Like, I don't remember everything. It's not like I'm one of the persons that got up in the morning and said today I'm going to shoot somebody. No. No. I didn't even remember I had the gun in my purse until I was in the room. Like it was in my purse a week and a half before I even met Hassan."

We played her an excerpt from Eric Zahnd's interview in which he referenced her writing "I pushed him down like I was going to fuck him. I got the gun and I just pulled the trigger." Eric said that in his opinion this was when she gave a full account of the murder.

"I mean, at the time I guess I was just writing stuff down, you know, a little stuff that happened but it came out the wrong way," Cavona said. "Pushing down so I could fuck him—I literally was trying to have in my mind what is a faster way that can keep him down and not up so I could run. But through my mind I felt like after that I don't have no chance. I felt like the option was to shoot."

Ingo was surprised that she didn't correct the original story she told us, particularly about whether or not she had been to the apartment before the day of the murder.

"She knew, because we told her, that we were going to look at the evidence. I think she analyzed and felt it made her look worse if she admitted going there before. Maybe she just didn't want to put herself in such a bad light, as she maybe saw it. She's grown up in prison, she's a lot more religious now. She wanted us to think she'd come to terms with what she's done, but deep down she's stored parts of it at the back of her mind.

"I was hoping she would tell the truth. If she had, I think people would have been able to understand her more. It's quite sad, because she faces a tough life, and she's not going to see her son properly for many years."

Before we left, Cavona said, "That person that was there that night was not me. It was that scared little girl at the age of twelve that was going through all the emotions that really didn't get healed, and really didn't forgive all those times that I was hurt. I am not that girl that was in that room that day, but I'm so glad that girl is buried away because that was an ugly, ugly, ugly side.

"Now I have twenty-five years. Like, is this really my life? Is this really what I deserve? I wish I could take it back...I wish I could take it back...but I can't."

She was crying bitterly as she said this.

Ingo has not heard from Cavona or her mother since the film aired, and he has no idea how they felt about it.

"I suspect they hoped it would change something for Cavona. But, ultimately, that's not what the program is about."

10

OWNING IT

CHARLES ARMENTROUT

"I think it's fair to say that I destroyed my family a long time ago. When I shot my father, and even before that. Then I think I hurt my family again, soul-wrenching pain. People always want to say I'm sorry. That doesn't work. When you ring a bell, the bell doesn't un-ring, you can't unravel time and go back."

Charles "Billy" Armentrout committed two horrific crimes. When he was eighteen years old, he shot his father six times, narrowly avoiding killing him. Ten years later he beat his eighty-one-year-old grandmother to death in a brutal, sustained, drug-crazed attack. During fifteen years in prison, the first eight spent on Death Row, he claimed he was innocent of the murder, and he named the man who he alleged did it.

Then everything changed.

In 2010, Charles finally owned his crime, confessing the truth to an astonished group of other inmates at Potosi Correctional Center during a session in the prison's Impact of Crime on Victims (ICV) program. It was a revelation to those around him, and to Charles himself.

When we met him, he had lived with the truth for nine years, and had come to terms with his sentence—which means he will almost certainly never be released—and has found a way to live a different and more fulfilling life within the prison, a complete turn-around that brought tears to the eyes of some of his family and an old friend when they heard the recording of him talking to us.

"When I first shook his hand I knew he was someone quite exceptional," said Gareth Morrow, the director of the film. "He was composed in a very natural way, and was the same off camera as he was on. He seemed calm, peaceful, and one of the prison staff commented to us, 'He's like a monk.' For someone with such a violent past, it was a revelation."

Charles was known as Billy all his early life, until he went into prison after killing his grandmother. He is now known as Charles, or to other prisoners by the nickname "Trout."

He had what he described as a "turbulent" start in life, growing up in St. Louis, Missouri, about fifty-five miles from the jail that is now his home.

"My mom and dad got divorced when I was four or five. My mom got custody. It was a pretty bad divorce, a lot of animosity on both sides. I took it pretty hard at that young age. It seemed like my dad and my mother both used me as a ploy, a tool, to aggravate the other one. I guess that's like so many divorce cases where, maybe not intentionally, parents end up involving a kid in the dynamics of it. In the custody battle, my father wanted me because he knew it would bother my mother, and my mother wanted me because she knew it would bother him. I was in the middle. She would tell me that my father did not love me, did not want me. When parents argue in the presence of a child, they can't process it. It affects them deeply. I believe the seed of anger I carried for my father came from that."

He remembered one time when his father kicked in the door and took him from his mother. Although his mother did not drink or take drugs and was, in his words, "a typical mother," his father, he said, abused both alcohol and drugs. "My mother remarried, and I didn't like my stepfather so I rebelled. I had no self-worth. I didn't apply myself at school and got into a lot of behavioral problems."

Altogether, Billy went to eight different schools.

"My stepfather didn't have a very good way of interacting with me, so I don't have a very good way of interacting with him. When you've got an adult who is all the time telling you you're stupid, you're dumb, that plays a factor in your development. And it escalated to the point where I tried everything I could to get a response from him. I was just a mean kid. He didn't physically abuse me as much as mentally and verbally, and I think over time that took a toll on me. Got me to where I didn't think I could do anything. I think that's where all the negative behavior started coming from."

His father, Bill, also remarried, and Billy would spend weekends with his dad, his new stepmother, Mary, and his stepsister, Wendy, Mary's daughter, who was two years younger than him. When we met Mary and Wendy they remembered those weekends with young Billy with smiles wreathing their faces.

"I first met Billy when he was five," said Mary. "Wendy was three. He was such a sweet little boy, precocious and always smiling."

They had good family times, and Wendy and Mary showed us photographs of trips to the beach, to Disney World. Wendy looked forward to the weekends with her older brother.

"I was an only child. Billy was funny, always laughing and trying to make people laugh. He was my big brother, and we would get into mischief, going further into the woods than we were supposed to. It was fun, I enjoyed Billy," she said.

Billy also remembered those times with great pleasure. "It was the highlight of my life to visit my dad on weekends and

spend time with my sister. Those childhood memories are
some of the best I've got."

But Billy's relationship with his father was almost as difficult as with his stepfather.

"He did get into trouble a bit, and his father would spank
him and degrade him, at such an early age," said Mary. "I felt
sorry for him, but I only saw him at weekends, and I was only
married to his dad for a few years. Billy's mom and dad had
a very bad relationship, and Billy was caught in the middle,
being tossed back and forth. All Billy wanted was to be with
his father, and he suffered a lot from the way he was treated."

Mary thinks his relationship with his mother deteriorated
when she had more children with his stepfather.

"I think all her attention went to this new man and their
children and her life and Billy was kind of set aside. So he
couldn't wait until he was old enough to show up on his
dad's doorstep. And his dad was not a welcoming person."
His father would mete out harsh physical punishment if Billy
transgressed in even small ways. Wendy remembered a fishing
trip when the two children were told to be completely silent
while Bill was fly-fishing; when Billy started giggling, his
father took the rowing boat oar and hit him across the head
with it, yelling at him not to cry with the pain.

She also recalled being able to tie her shoelaces before Billy,
even though she was two years younger, because her mother
had taught her.

"His dad just threw a fit. He would get furious about little
things. He never took the time to show him how to tie his
laces, but he would throw a fit that he couldn't do it."

She saw Billy being hit so often that when Billy accidentally let off a little firework at the Fourth of July celebrations

that struck his father's back, and his father turned round in a
fury demanding to know who did it, she whispered under her
breath, "Don't say a word, don't say a word."

"I knew what would happen. I'd seen so much of Bill
hitting Billy for trivial things, I knew he would just beat Billy
to death. Bill was a vicious man. He didn't think twice about
hurting anybody. Not just my mom, because she's a woman
and not as strong as him. I think Bill would have attacked
anybody who crossed him."

Billy told us that it was when he got into high school that
he got involved with drugs and hanging around with friends.

"I grew up in a neighborhood where there was a lot of
violence. I think I was maybe eleven when I first used marijuana. I was hanging around with the wrong people, wanted
to be the life of the party, the big shot. I didn't do anything
outside of petty thieving, nothing violent. To get money for
marijuana or just to be able to have money, be the guy."

Escaping the abuse her husband meted out to her, Mary left
her marriage when Billy was seven, and she and Wendy did
not see him again until he was thirteen, when he knocked at
the door of the apartment where they were living.

"He stuck his head round the door and said, 'Hi' with a
real big smile. He stayed for a while, ate with us, then Wendy
had school in the morning and I had work so I said, 'Why
don't I take you home?' He wanted to sleep on the couch but
I said no, because we had school and work. He said he didn't
have to go home. I gave him a pair of jeans and a T-shirt. I
took him home but he asked to be dropped off a block or two
away," said Mary.

"After that visit, we just noticed little things going missing.
He was breaking in. Once I had some money from a school

fundraiser on top of the refrigerator, and that was one of the things that went missing."

At first they did not realize it was Billy, but after one break-in all the posters in Wendy's bedroom were torn off the wall, and she remembered telling Billy about hiding her birthday money behind a poster. Then Mary was called about her credit cards being used, and that's when they knew for certain it was Billy.

"I just remembered Billy as my big brother," said Wendy. "And then when he came back into our lives it wasn't the same boy. He wasn't the same big brother I felt comfortable around."

Mary rang Billy's father. "I said I didn't want to call the police, but Bill or his mother had to talk to him," she told us. "Bill must have told him that he couldn't go over to us anymore, and that's when the big one happened. The door was off its hinges. The apartment was completely vandalized. He had cut up my mom's clothing. It wasn't just a burglary. It was anger lashed out," said Wendy.

Mary and her daughter had to move home after an even more frightening incident.

"I was at home," said Wendy, who was a young teenager at the time. "Someone in the hallway called out, 'Package for Eberhardt' like it was the postman. So I went to look and there weren't any boxes by the mailboxes."

As she returned to the apartment, Billy appeared from behind the door and produced a gun.

"He put it on my face so that I could feel it was cold, it was a real gun. It was intimidation when I wouldn't invite him in. He was showing he was capable of violence."

After this, Mary and Wendy changed address.

For Billy, his reason for choosing to rob and terrorize two people with whom he had an affectionate relationship is still a mystery.

"I burglarized their home just because I was there. I guess I was being rebellious and wanting to cause some harm, but I don't think at that age I was comprehending what I was doing. Man, I was a monster. I didn't care. I cared about me," he said.

Mary understands why Billy sought out the wrong crowd of friends: "Billy didn't have any kind of a life. I never saw Billy get any compassion or nurturing or guidance. And I imagine that if you don't have it, you look for somebody to accept you. I think he found other people who accepted him and welcomed him into their lives and maybe weren't the best role models. Maybe they weren't the ones to go to for guidance, a path. I don't think he was given a chance to see things any other way, to be taught basic things. Maybe that just hardens you."

Relations with his stepfather had deteriorated even more, and when he was seventeen a U.S. Marine recruitment officer visited his school and said they would accept him into the marines if he had a General Educational Development certificate.

"I got the paperwork and went home, and my mother contacted my father and they were both on board with it. My mother set up for me to take the GED, but I had a lot of reservations because over the course of time my stepfather had called me stupid, dumb, and other adjectives so I was really scared that if I failed he would have more ammunition. So I didn't take it. Two years later, in prison, I took the GED and scored the highest of the inmate class. I regret to this day because so many things could have been different...

It was because I was intimidated and scared and worried that I would look stupid.

"My dad called me on my eighteenth birthday and said, 'Well, you're eighteen now, you can come and live with me and there's nothing your mother can do about it.' At that time I and my stepfather were really at odds, to the point of almost physical blows between the two of us, and I'd moved in with a neighbor across the road for a time because it was just so tenuous with my stepfather. So I said, 'OK, I'm moving.' My mom wasn't happy, but she couldn't do anything about it.

"At first it was fine, but I was not making the right choices. I started involving myself with old friends. My dad got me a good job, but I couldn't get up in the mornings and I ended up getting fired after four or five warnings. So I robbed a gas station, then another one and another one. By the time I was done I robbed six gas stations. I robbed the one where my mother and stepfather worked two times. I was armed with my father's .32 Colt semi-automatic.

"I didn't have no intention of hurting anyone. But now I reflect back, the gun was loaded. I enjoyed it, the thrill was intense. I was a loose cannon. Then I took some money out of my father's account and he eventually found out about it.

He was mad, said he could see why my mother had so much trouble with me. I thought he was going to kick me out of the house and ship me back to my mother and stepfather. I couldn't deal with the failure, having my stepdad be condescending toward me. I felt like I was in a corner, and I didn't have no way out. I had some kind of insanity at that point in time. I waited for him to come home; we have a door up the stairs and I was on the other side of the door. When he reached the doorknob I started firing. I ambushed him. So I shot him. I shot at him eight or nine times, hit him six times, three in the chest; just missed his heart.

"He didn't do anything wrong, he really didn't. I didn't care, I cared about me. I think maybe the animosity between my parents through the years led me to believe he was less than a really loving father. But I don't want to deflect from the choices I have made. It was my choice, I did it. In the grand scheme of things, people have grown up with a lot worse parents than me and been just fine. I was motivated by self-interest and greed. Could the abuse I suffered from him be why I shot him? It probably is in there, but it's not one solitary thing. It's a combination of things, and I believe it was more based on my fear of going back."

Billy's father did not die from the bullet wounds, and he was rushed to hospital. The next time Mary and Wendy heard of Billy was when Bill called Mary from the hospital, where he was recovering.

"He knew Billy was the one who shot him but he told the police he didn't know who it was. The police found Billy running down the road not far away and Billy told them that someone had broken in and he got away. Just made up some sort of story. He thought he'd killed his dad, and when he saw him in the ambulance and Bill opened his eyes, Billy screamed. Bill told me this. He said, 'You know that little bastard thought he'd killed me.'"

Director Gareth Morrow was puzzled as to why Billy shot his father, not his stepfather, but Mary said she could understand it:

"I felt sorry for Billy because his dad treated him like a slave, made him clean up after him, and just didn't want him to be part of his life, basically. Billy wanted to be with his dad, but when he got to be with his dad it was bad, bad. He wasn't a father thinking for Billy. Knowing how Bill treated him, I wasn't surprised that Billy was going to react like this someday."

Despite the fact that his father refused to identify him, the police took Billy into custody for the armed robberies of the petrol stations.

"He didn't want to prosecute me. He thought I was insane. During the hours after he was shot, the police department realized I had robbed gas stations," Billy told us. A few months later, while he was in the county jail awaiting sentencing for the gas station robberies, his grandmother rang to say his father had died.

"We don't know whether he committed suicide or whether it was accidental, because he was found in his truck inside of his garage and he had been drinking. So I don't know," said Bill's ex-wife Mary.

"It happened about four months after Billy had shot him. He just went downhill from that. He just drank and drank and drank and probably popped some pills. But whether he did it intentionally nobody will ever know. I would never think of his dad doing that because of who he was. I think he more or less felt he deserved to be shot after the way he treated him."

Billy told us he believed his father committed suicide "because of me. I believe the pain of his own son shooting him broke him."

At the age of eighteen, Billy was sentenced to nineteen years in prison for the armed robberies, and he served ten, during which time he took some vocational courses and even did a paralegal course. But he admits he associated with the wrong prison crowd.

"I guess you would call them the bad element. They smuggled dope in, did drugs, made hooch. I smoked weed all the way through, but I never touched cocaine or heroin, even though it was all there."

After he was released, one of the terms of his parole was that he had to live at an approved address.

"My grandmother was the only one who agreed to accept me on parole. My grandmother, my father's mother, Inez Notter, was a real firecracker. She was small in stature. She had a big heart. And ultimately she forgave me for shooting her son. Absolutely incredible. She's the only one that sent me money regularly in prison. The relationship with my mother was just broken. You hear everywhere about unconditional love, but I truly don't believe a man or a woman can have unconditional love, because there comes a point where they're crushed by pain caused by a family member, to the point that they lose the love. I think that's what happened in my mother's case.

"My aunt Joanne argued with my grandmother about it, but my grandmother overrode her and let me stay there."

It started well, with Billy holding down two jobs and buying himself a car while living with his eighty-one-year-old grandmother. But a new girlfriend, Bridget, introduced him to her group of friends, including Anna, Kim, another girl also called Bridget (Anna's sister), Rick Lacey, and on the fringe of the group, Roger Brannan. With the exception of Roger, they all had serious drug habits.

"Rick Lacey was a good dude, a guy's guy. He grew up in the neighborhood. He was a dope fiend, a petty criminal. I don't think he ever hurt anybody. I knew him through Bridget, Anna, and Kim. We got along so I started hanging out with that crew. We'd do dope, and then they'd go out to get money and come back with a credit card they'd stolen and we'd go and use it," Billy told us.

He had less contact with Roger: "Roger was a character that I associated with due to the fact that my girlfriend Bridget knew him and stayed in his house, as a crash pad, basically. We'd hang out at his house and smoke weed and watch MTV," Billy said.

We tracked down and talked to two of the women, sisters Anna and Bridget (not Billy's girlfriend). They have both escaped their previous lives and are living away from St. Louis.

"When we first met Billy he wasn't into the drugs scene. He knew my best friend, Bridget," said Anna. "He met her a week before. He said he had just come out of prison. I thought it might be for credit card fraud or carjacking or something like that."

Bridget added, "I just thought it was one of the stories he told. And I thought if he did shoot his dad, maybe he had been molested or something like that. He was only eighteen when he did it. I didn't think he was a psycho or anything. So we kind of shrugged it off."

Anna said, "He used to give my friend Bridget and me money to do drugs and he would never do any. He came up with five hundred dollars a day, rolling with money. When I asked him where he got it, he said he had a trust fund and his grandmother was the overseer of it. He said it was from his father, which seemed kind of weird because he said he had shot his dad six times. I didn't question it too much. His habit started with us blowing smoke in his face. Then one day he said, 'Can I try a little bit?' So he snorted and after that he wanted more and more. He got a pretty bad drug habit."

When we played them the tape of Billy talking about his crime, both women cried and hugged each other with relief at having escaped the life they once led.

Billy told us that his addiction to crack cocaine was instantaneous.

"It just bit me and I couldn't shake it. We were all into drugs, doing whatever we could to get the money. At that time I maybe slept at my grandmother's house once or twice a week; most of the times, I was staying at their houses and we just hung out.

"I don't want to water down accountability. It's my choice to take the drugs. Whether or not the drug had an addictive quality, I should have been man enough to say no. It's a choice. I vividly remember driving to my grandmother's house to get money and I was talking to myself. I said, 'If you keep doing this, going down this road, you're going to end up dying.' And I said to myself, 'Screw it.' And from that point on it just got worse."

Billy explained to us how he funded his drug habit, which required up to three hundred dollars a day.

"I would ask my grandmother for money and she would give me money, and then she started not giving me money, so I stole checks and wrote them on her account. She confronted me and I said I was sorry, and I said I would pay it back. There came a point when the bank was flagging it and she was having trouble with her account."

Anna met Billy's grandmother when he took her to Inez's house. The old lady made them both a sandwich, and she wrapped a sweater round Anna because she knew that Billy's car had no heating.

"She was a beautiful person. She would have done anything

for anybody. Billy got a check from her, so I thought it was all legit and it was from his trust fund. We went to a bank and cashed it."

Anna went to the bank a few times with Billy.

"We would cash the checks, buy a bunch of drugs, and go to a hotel room and party. One day we went to cash a check and the bank stopped us while they called his grandmother, and this particular time she said OK. When we go in three or four days later to cash a check at a drive-in teller, and we waited a long time, then the cops came running over to the window and the first thing is Billy screams, 'She signed my grandma's name.' So they put us both in a police car, I was fingerprinted, and they did a handwriting analysis and they let me go and they kept him. I didn't hear from him for a couple of days after that. His grandmother made his bail. After that incident I didn't hang with him as much."

We also talked to Roger Brannan, and he confirmed he was on the edge of the group, never doing hard drugs.

"I only knew Billy for about two months; I met him through the girls. I would give the girls food or a place to sleep. When you are doing crack rock, there are people that stay up for days and then they need to get some sleep. Bridget would come to my house and sleep, and when she woke up I had food for her. She was my friend and I wanted to help her out. I guess you would call it my wild younger days. It was mostly partying, and I did my drug, which was weed. I never done the other stuff, crack or heroin, but they all did.

"Some of the stuff that was going on I knew, but there's a lot I didn't because I slept every night, like a normal person would. They would be up for days, trying to figure out ways to get money for their habit. The guys would rob people and break into homes and sell whatever they stole to buy drugs. They call it being on a mission, and when they are on a mission they do whatever it takes to get money for drugs. I wasn't no part of that. And I thank God that I've never done the drugs they did. It was a bad time in my life." On the day of the murder, 18 March 1995, Billy had been up for two days on a crack high without sleeping. Throughout our interview with him, he was at pains to stress that he does not blame drugs, or his need for drugs, for what he did. On that day, Anna had taken his car to go and buy fifteen dollars of crack when she was pulled over by the police. She was taken to jail and the car was impounded.

Billy described what happened next: "My car was impounded and I didn't have no money. I went to my grandmother's house and asked her for some more money. She said no. I couldn't figure out how to get money. I asked her a couple more times and she got upset. She told me I needed to leave and I told her I was not leaving. Only way I thought I could get some money was to rob her, beat her up. We argued and I went to my room and grabbed a miniature baseball bat and I followed her into her bedroom and I beat her to death. Viciously.

"When I first swung the bat, I knew I had to kill her. I could have walked out of the house, that's what I should have done, and that will haunt me for the rest of my life. I made the wrong choice yet again. I beat her until she was unconscious, tied her up. I rifled the drawers, found some money, and left. Yeah, I killed her. It was bad. My thoughts revolved around me and nobody else. I didn't care. I had no feelings. I came back the next day and cleaned up and tried to hide the body. I took the body down to the basement and hid it in a trunk.

I don't think I felt anything, I was numb. In my messed-up mindset, I was trying to figure a way out of it. It was self-survival, as harsh as that may sound.

"Roger Brannan and Bridget came over to pick me up, and I tried to have Roger cash a check, but the bank wouldn't cash it. Roger had no idea, and Bridget had no idea, that my grandmother was dead."

Bridget recalled that day and shivered with horror at the memory.

"He was behaving like nothing happened. I don't understand how someone can do something so horrific and then just go about their business. I was in her house, not knowing she was in the basement, dead. I said, 'Billy, where's your grandma?' and he said, 'Oh, she's at the beauty parlor with my aunt, she's getting her hair done.' Wow, I was literally in the house and the poor woman was in the basement."

Bridget was at Rick Lacey's house when the police came for Billy, three days after the murder.

"We told Billy earlier that day that he was all over the news, about his grandma. He said he had no idea where she was. Later that night he showed up again and we all panicked. We told him, 'You can't stay here, you have to leave.' We basically made him leave, and he went out the back window and the police were at the front door."

We talked to the two detectives who arrested Billy and who interviewed him at the police station. Detective Bill McDonough and detective Rubin Haman, now both retired, were at the house when Inez's body was discovered in the basement while her daughter Joanne, who had reported her missing, waited upstairs. The body, wrapped in a blanket and bedspread, had been bent double in the trunk. Medical examination showed blunt trauma injuries to the front and back of her head. Her lower jaw was fractured, she had eight fractured ribs, and her right leg was broken in two places. Her leg was broken after death, when the body was dragged to the basement.

The two detectives were quickly assigned to the manhunt for the obvious suspect, Billy.

"We had the word out on the street. Everybody involved had informants that were familiar with the streets, and they put it out there that we were looking for him, and we got a call at the homicide office with a lead," said detective Bill McDonough. "It was an address, and I believe it was Rick Lacey's house. We jumped in our cars and drove down there."

They went to the back of the house.

"The bad guy always goes out the back. Homicide knocked on the front door and out the back window came Billy Armentrout, like a gift from God dropped right at my feet. There was a slight tussle, I wrestled with him briefly, and we got him under control and put handcuffs on him," said Detective McDonough.

In the car on the way back to the police station, the two detectives talked to their suspect. Bill McDonough told us, "He gave me an idea of how bad that crack monster really had him when he said, 'Is this about my grandma?' We said yeah, and he goes, 'If you let me smoke crack one more time I'll tell you anything you want to know.' I was floored at that, offended, and I just said, 'Billy, it's going to hit you eventually what happened here. You killed your grandma over this thing that you want one more hit of. That's not happening. When you come to the realization that you did this to your grandma, we're here to talk to you.' And that was the end of the conversation."

The two detectives conducted a videotaped interview with Billy at the police station, parts of which we showed in our film. Although Billy, in a checked shirt, jeans, and with long, unkempt hair, looked spaced out, he talked coherently, presenting the story he would stick to for many years to come, claiming that Rick Lacey carried out the murder of Inez Notter while he was in another room of the house.

Billy explained his decision to throw the blame on Rick: "I hadn't thought of implicating Rick or anybody else. I was just ignoring it. Then I went to Rick's house and all of a sudden the cops were there. And in my criminal mind, he set me up. So I was being handcuffed after jumping through a window and I looked toward the house and I saw Rick Lacey talking to a police officer, and that's when I said, 'I didn't do it. Rick Lacey did it.' And when they interviewed me on tape that's what I said. I fabricated a nice little story to convince them he was involved, because of my displeasure that he called the cops. I felt betrayed.

"At that point I was probably at the lowest point I've ever been in my life. I remember not caring. I didn't care. I was done. I had caused so much pain to so many people that I just blocked it out. I didn't want to deal with it."

Rick Lacey and several of Billy's group of drug addict friends were brought in for questioning, but the police quickly released Rick.

"We were quite confident that Rick Lacey had nothing to do with it," said Detective Haman. "There was no physical evidence of Rick Lacey at Inez Notter's house, no fingerprints. He didn't even know where the house was. And while Armentrout was trying to hide, Rick was sitting in his house, smoking crack, not trying to hide."

The detectives had experience dealing with murders during the crack wars in St. Louis in the 1990s.

"You have a guy that is smoking crack," said Detective McDonough. "He is just a tsunami walking through the neighborhood, and anything he sees he is going to take either by deception or by violence. Billy crossed into a whole different realm when he murdered his grandma."

His colleague Detective Haman added: "He beat an eighty-one-year-old woman who didn't weigh one hundred pounds. He'll try to do this again, but he's going to pick on the most vulnerable. I think he's evil, but he's a coward too."

Roger Brannan first heard about the murder was when he was arrested for trying to cash the check for Billy. "I was sleeping and they knocked on the door. They arrested me. It scared the hell out of me. They took me to the police station. And then they started talking about murder. I was shocked. I told them what I knew, because I wasn't going to jail for something somebody else did. I was just shocked that something like this happened, and I wanted the cops to know that I didn't have nothing to do with it. I always thought it was Billy. He was trying to blame someone else, and he picked on Rick."

Mary and Wendy heard about the murder of Inez when her daughter, Billy's aunt Joanne, rang to tell them.

"I didn't know that he was out of prison," said Wendy. "I knew he was going down the road in a bad direction, and I knew what he had attempted to do to his father. So I wasn't shocked that he killed somebody. I was surprised it was his grandmother. I thought it might have been some deal that had gone wrong or something like that."

At the trial, Billy elected to defend himself, a very unusual decision.

"I knew that if I let the public defenders represent me I would be given the death penalty, and it would be carried out. I didn't want to die. After maybe a month in jail, they had a law library and I picked up a Missouri digest of criminal law, randomly. I realized I had the right to represent myself.

"I'd seen an attorney who told me they had a ton of evidence and I just needed to plead guilty, so I made the decision to represent myself. There were two reasons. One was to try and cause as much trouble for the judicial system that wanted to kill me as I could. The other reason is I didn't have anything better to do. I knew that if I let the public defenders handle it I was going to get the death penalty, and I knew that cases very seldom get overturned on review. So if I could represent myself in a manner that caused them trouble, and they didn't know how to deal with it... There were a huge amount of legal mistakes in the case."

Chris Slusher was a defense attorney in Missouri retained as "stand-by counsel" for Billy during the trial, in case he needed legal advice, and he talked to us about this unusual situation for a lawyer to be in.

"Essentially, you're there following things and if he needs you to jump in because he changes his mind. When Billy Armentrout's case began, we were told by him and the court that we would handle certain aspects of the defense, specifically the expert witnesses. So it was a hybrid role," he told us. "There's an old saying that a defendant who chooses to represent himself has a fool for a client. It's usually not considered a smart thing to do. It's very unusual in death penalty cases.

"I think someone like Billy Armentrout, who had been living a life of lying to get drugs and lying to get out of trouble, for him to lie and go to court and say he didn't do something was just a continuation of that behavior. The state did not believe Mr. Armentrout's claim that Mr. Lacey was the primary one that delivered the blows that caused the death of his grandmother.

"Billy Armentrout never shared with me if he had a grand strategy for representing himself. In my contact with him he didn't necessarily come across as cocky and arrogant, but I certainly observed some of that when he was in court. I remember speculating in my mind if he was a sort of mad genius who was hoping it would create issues that would help him legally down the road, or is it simply arrogance, or a combination of the two.

"The judge was in a really difficult position, as he had to balance the right of Mr. Armentrout to represent himself and the prosecution's right to put a case."

Chris Slusher recalled a seminal moment in the trial when a witness, a woman who had been held up at gunpoint by Billy when he was robbing a convenience store, told the court she had been so frightened at the time that she wet herself. When Billy asked her, "So you say this man pointed a gun at you?" she replied, "No, I don't say a man did it, I say *you* did it."

"It was clearly a dramatic point," Chris said. "A point that makes a difference to a jury."

Another dramatic point came when Billy called his mother as a witness. He had to subpoena her to attend: she was not willingly present at his trial to support him. He asked what he was to her.

"You were my son," she told the court.

"You refer to me as your former son?" he asked her. "Yes," she replied.

Billy was found guilty in February 1998, three years after Inez Notter was killed, and he was sentenced to death.

"When he was found guilty, I don't think it was a big surprise in the courtroom," said Chris Slusher. "The state had a lot of evidence based on his prior criminal record. I don't recall Mr. Armentrout expressing any surprise at the verdict of death. It's purely speculation on my part, but I don't believe he necessarily expected to win.

"In my experience representing people in these cases, there is in many of them a fundamental fear of admitting their guilt, because they recognize that what they have done is so terrible. And so it's a conflict within them that makes them not want to admit it. They have to evolve to the point where they can accept their own responsibility. And in my interaction with Mr. Armentrout during the trial phase I didn't see that; he wasn't there yet."

Anna had to give evidence against Billy in court, and being cross-examined by him was a harrowing experience for her. Bridget was also affected by the trial, but ultimately in a good way. She went to prison for two months for tampering with evidence after she got rid of Billy's possessions left at Rick Lacey's house.

"I didn't realize the police wanted them. I wasn't very smart back then. After that I said, man, I'm lucky to be alive, to be out of prison. I need to get away from here, take myself out of this situation."

She moved to Virginia, and although she has since moved back to Missouri, she lives in a different part of the state. Anna also moved away and now lives in Maryland.

"It was a big eye-opener. We made it out of there by the skin of our teeth, and I thank God every day for that," Anna said.

A few months after his sentence, Billy rang his stepmother, Mary, from prison.

"He was trying to reach out to me, we had a nice conversation. But I didn't know which way to bend, I was torn about who to believe and what to think," she said. "I knew his grandmother had been killed, but I didn't know the circumstances."

It was in 2006 that Billy came off Death Row, accepting a sentence of life without parole; his successful appeal was based on the legal problems at his trial created by his decision to defend himself.

Defense attorney Chris Slusher told us, "My reaction was that maybe his strategy had worked. In hindsight, to represent yourself and then insert issues and create legal fights so when you pile up all these issues when you get to appeal, you essentially wear the other side down. And I don't know exactly that's what happened, but I suspect it was part of it. For example, he asked for the state public defender system to pay for depositions, and that became a big legal fight that the judge had to oversee, and it was raising issues."

Wendy and Mary kept in touch with Billy for a few years, and Wendy went to the prison when he married his pen pal, Donna, a relationship that started when he was in prison. We made contact with Donna for our film, but never managed to meet her.

It was in 2010 that Billy's life changed when he took an ICV class. He told us that he took the course because there was a rumor that the prison authorities were going to remove inmates from the premium paid jobs in the jail if they didn't do some of the therapeutic programs on offer, and he didn't want to lose his job. He was very involved with his work and found it fulfilling. He worked in the factory at the prison, where a range of metal objects are made, and quickly discovered new skills. He engineered and built a new desk-building jig for the

factory, increasing capacity by at least 25 percent. He rede-
signed other equipment and products and created a line of
wind chimes, swing chairs, and benches, all with ornamental
metalwork, all for sale. To cope with demand, the jail bought
a computer-controlled cutting machine, which, according to
the factory manager, was necessary to grow "the burgeoning
business that Mr. Armentrout had literally carved out with his
own hands."

He has made model motorcycles, a replica battleship, a
train, and a pirate ship. Perhaps his most imposing achieve-
ment is the large nameplate on the wall outside the prison,
flanked by metal state seals.

"Of course, they didn't let me out to hang it on the wall,"
he said, wryly.

The prospect of losing this work was behind his decision to
take the ICV.

"I didn't take it because I wanted to have counseling or to
listen to the fact that I messed up or I've messed people up."

But the course had a profound, and unexpected, effect
on him.

"I had an awakening. I finally understood that my actions
and my choices were the reason for where I was. I finally took
responsibility. They have a panel of the mothers of murdered
children and other victims of crime, and one told us the story
of her daughter being murdered. They ask each one of us what
we did, who we are, who was our victim."

The facilitators running the course were other inmates.
"They started talking about their crimes and taking responsibility for them. At that point I realized I couldn't keep saying
that I didn't do it. I took ownership of it. We went round the
room. There were about fifteen inmates there and several of

them knew me, and to the absolute astonishment of everybody in the room I finally said I murdered my grandmother. I
said, 'Her name was Inez Notter and I beat her to death with
a baseball bat.'

"You know, I had repressed the memories and feelings and
had even convinced myself that I didn't do it. I took accountability for it for the first time in my life. That was the hardest
thing I have ever done, to sit there and admit what I had done
and the damage that I have caused throughout my life and
how I hurt so many people."

Randy Knese, another inmate at Potosi Correctional
Center, was the facilitator for the course that Billy took. He
lived for twelve years in the same prison wing as Billy, and
he was very surprised when Billy agreed to take the course.
"When I first came to Potosi I didn't really get to know him
because of the stories I heard about him. In prison you have
two different types of inmate. The convict is the tough kind of
guy; he doesn't deal with the staff unless he has to. Then you
get the inmate who works with the staff and does programs,
goes to church, gets involved. Billy was more the convict. So I
kind of kept my distance."

They got to know each other playing sports.

"He had this attitude about him that he was not a happy
person. And after I got to know him, I found he came from a
broken home. He was bitter, angry. For years he told a story
claiming innocence about his crime. He stood on the fact that
he was innocent and that he didn't commit this crime, that he
got a raw deal. When I first knew him, he didn't have no use
of classes. So when one day he said he was going to sign up for
ICV I was like, I want to be part of this class.

"Something got to him. At the end of the class we have

a victims' panel when they tell their stories about how their loved ones were murdered. It left you in a state where you couldn't hide anymore, where you were like, damn, I did that to somebody and this is how the family feels.

"And he said what the truth was about when his grandmother was murdered. Hearing him say it was, like, a wild moment. So after the class I told him I was proud of him. And as time went on he started to grow and change. When a guy comes to the point where he starts telling the truth about things he's done, it's not an easy process to go through. That's a hard transition."

We filmed Randy at Southeastern Correctional Center, where he had transferred from Potosi. He described the transformation in Billy after his confession.

"I saw him laughing freely, he has a very distinctive laugh. He became a more fun-loving, freer kind of guy. He became a person who could laugh things off, walk away, and not want to be in a confrontation over silly things."

After taking the course a second time, Billy himself became a facilitator.

"I've told the inmates my story from start to finish, and I hope that in some small measure that someone took it to heart and it helped them change, so that they realize the pain and damage they caused others.

"Everything I do now, I try to give back. I try to make small changes and be better than I was the day before. I think before I react, and I think whether I'm doing the right thing. I'm not perfect. I still get angry, frustrated at people. But I'm a changed person. That person I was is dead and buried."

As well as his metalwork and acting as a facilitator, Billy also provides sports commentary on the prison radio station

and has his own program, *Trout—No Doubt*. He has qualified as a dog trainer and handler, is actively involved with the
church, and he writes poetry and prose.

"It is easy to see that if he had taken a different path he
could really have made a great success of his life," said Gareth.

When Wendy and Mary listened to the tapes of our interview with Billy, it was the first time they had heard that he
was no longer claiming to be innocent.

"For him to come forward now and admit it and be sorry
for what he has done—he's a better person," said Mary. "I
never gave it a whole lot of thought. The crime was committed and he was serving time for it. But hearing him not fight
anymore, and confess, that's a good thing.

"I'm glad I got to hear his voice. I think he should be given
a chance. After hearing this, it really changes things. I can only
hope for the best for Billy. It's such a sad, sad thing. When I
spoke to Billy I saw how articulate he was and how he had
advanced himself instead of going the other direction; he was
better in himself. And I felt for him. I thought, 'What a waste.'
He could do so much more with his life if he were out, but
that's what happens."

Wendy said, "His letters were lengthy and his descriptions of the things he was doing. He just seemed so caring, he
wanted to know the details of my life, and I genuinely felt he
cared for us. I think he was trying to connect back to a part
of his life that was fondly remembered. There were happier
moments that he could recall, when we were small and I had
a big brother."

Roger Brannan, hearing Billy's own words on the tape,
was deeply affected and found himself unexpectedly shedding
tears.

"He's admitting it. Wow. He knows what he did wrong. After all these years I thought he would still be denying what he did. I hear remorse. You know, I never thought I would hear that from him. It's not going to change anything. It might change something for him but it's not going to bring his grandma back.

"For some odd reason, I believe him. I kind of feel sorry for the guy. But he did wrong and he has to pay for what he did. The reason I'm crying is because of my mom and dad, they taught me right. If it wasn't for my mom and dad I'd either be dead or in jail.

"I wish Billy all the luck in the world, you know, and I hope that someday he could have some kind of happiness in his life. I don't know how happy a person can be in jail, but I do wish him to be happy."

Chris Slusher, the attorney who had been on standby at Billy's trial, also accepted the honesty of Billy's change.

"None of us are defined by a particular thing we have done in our life. For someone like Billy Armentrout, it is one of the most awful things any of us can imagine, but it still does not make up everything that he is. I don't discount the idea that someone like him can be a different person now and finally recognize how awful what they did was."

When we saw Billy for a second interview, ninety days after the first, he talked thoughtfully about why it took him so long to confront the truth of his behavior.

"It has multiple layers. I think the first and foremost layer is denial on my part that I could have done such an act to someone who loved me. I think the second layer is that I didn't want to face that, to accept that. I didn't want to be responsible for it in any meaningful way. The third is that I didn't want to destroy the few people that were in my life. I didn't want to have them leave because of what I had done. I buried the feelings so deep that there were times where I was actually convinced Rick did it. My psychology was such that there were times when reality and fantasy started to blend, to a point where I didn't even acknowledge it to myself in my thoughts."

We played him the tape of Wendy and Mary talking, and his eyes filled with tears at some of the only happy memories he has of his childhood. When he heard Mary giving her account of her marriage and the way his father treated him, he conceded it was true.

"To say that my dad was worse than any other bad dad... OK, maybe he was. Maybe that's the only way he knew. Did I see him be abusive to my stepmother? Yes. Was he abusive to me? Yes."

His contact with his family has been very limited, and he doesn't blame them. One uncle, Bobby, kept in touch, but he has now died. He does not blame his mother for disowning him at the trial.

"It was deserved. I caused too much pain. Sometimes people just can't forgive you. The hurt and the pain and the anguish is too much."

After Wendy's husband and father died, she stopped writing to Billy. He carried on sending her Christmas cards, and she kept them because she intended to get back in touch with him but had never gotten round to it. After being interviewed by us and going over the memories of Billy with her mother, Wendy was determined to reconnect with him. The day of our second interview with Billy was to have been a momentous day for him: Wendy had made the 1,500-mile trip from her home in Las Vegas to St. Louis to visit him later that day.

"It will be the first time I've seen her for a long time. It's absolutely incredible," he told us.

Sadly for both of them, the prison authorities did not allow Wendy into the prison to see him, claiming they had not had enough notice and her name was not on the list of visitors. The distance from her home in Las Vegas means arranging another visit has not been possible. But the two have kept in contact.

Researching the film, we tried to track down Rick Lacey, and with the help of detective Bill McDonough we discovered he died in 2014. Although Billy had owned his crime by then, he never had any contact with the man he had accused of carrying out the murder.

"I owe that man an apology," he said. "I never contacted Rick. He never knew I had stopped blaming him. I thought about it several times but I procrastinated, and I didn't know the channel or the means to do it. I thought it was undoable so I didn't give it much more thought. But learning that he passed is another layer of pain, that I didn't get the chance to tell him I'm sorry. I am sorry for what happened to Roger. I hope me being truthful helps."

Billy has reflected on the fact that he no longer faces execution.

"To be quite honest, I probably should have been killed for what I did, but by God's grace I'm here and I'm going to be an example to others. I'm doing good and I'm being good, and others might look at that and say, 'Well, I knew him when he was a different person and now he's changed and he's better.' And then they may want to better themselves. I get satisfaction from that.

"Maybe I can somehow compensate in a small measure,

because I can never take away what I've done. I got to move on with myself as well as everybody else. If there's one thing you need to understand when you're younger is that you have to think of the harm that you're doing to those who love you. If you say you truly love someone and then you do something that harms them, then you truly don't love them. So stop and think about what is going to harm them. If I hadn't got off the death penalty, I don't think I would have admitted it and taken responsibility, and I would have died a sad and lonely death. If you're truly remorseful and you recognize the devastation that you caused by taking another person's life, I think you can move on from it. I have been dishonorable for most of my existence, I will not be dishonorable anymore."

For Gareth Morrow, there is no doubt that Billy's repentance and redemption are real and deeply felt.

"It was a privilege to talk to him," he said.

IMAGE CREDITS

ABOUT THE AUTHORS

Danny Tipping is CEO of Transistor Films, a Sky Studios company. Ned Parker is an executive producer for Transistor Films and is the host and creator of the *Letters from A Killer* podcast. Together they have over thirty years' experience in the television industry, most recently at Znak & Co, where they oversaw the production and delivery of hundreds of hours of high-quality, award-winning factual and factual-entertainment programs to leading broadcasters around the world, including PBS, Discovery Networks, National Geographic, A+E Networks, Sky, UKTV, Foxtel, and Netflix. *I Am a Killer* is their first book.